DYNASTY
OF FAITH

A Parent's Guide To Passing Your Faith
To The Next Generation

Elizabeth Moore Beasley

Dynasty of Faith: A Parent's Guide To Passing Your Faith To The Next Generation

Jones Media Publishing
10645 N. Tatum Blvd. Ste. 200-166
Phoenix, AZ 85028
www.JonesMediaPublishing.com

Disclaimer:

The author strives to be as accurate and complete as possible in the creation of this book, notwithstanding the fact that the author does not warrant or represent at any time that the contents within are accurate due to the rapidly changing nature of the Internet.

While all attempts have been made to verify information provided in this publication, the Author and the Publisher assume no responsibility and are not liable for errors, omissions, or contrary interpretation of the subject matter herein. The Author and Publisher hereby disclaim any liability, loss or damage incurred as a result of the application and utilization, whether directly or indirectly, of any information, suggestion, advice, or procedure in this book. Any perceived slights of specific persons, peoples, or organizations are unintentional.

In practical advice books, like anything else in life, there are no guarantees of income made. Readers are cautioned to rely on their own judgment about their individual circumstances to act accordingly. Readers are responsible for their own actions, choices, and results. This book is not intended for use as a source of legal, business, accounting or financial advice. All readers are advised to seek the services of competent professionals in legal, business, accounting, and finance field.

Printed in the United States of America

ISBN: 978-1-948382-56-4 paperback

DYNASTY OF FAITH

*A Parent's Guide To Passing Your Faith
To The Next Generation*

Elizabeth Moore Beasley

Jones Media Publishing

DYNASTY OF FAITH

A Parent's Guide To Passing Your Faith To The Next Generation

Elizabeth Moore Beasley

Jones Media Publishing

DEDICATION

It is with Love,
Thankfulness and Joy in my Heart
that I dedicate this book
To the Glory of God, My Father,
and his Son, my Savior and Lord, Jesus Christ

In Loving Memory of my parents, Wanda and Victor Moore

And my grandmothers, Hattie Vissering Moore,
Lillie Nora Vissering and Ruth Higgins

And

In honor of Bill Beasley, my wonderful husband and soulmate: "Your love and support makes my life and work complete." To my grown children, Emily Grace Blais and Andrew Thomas Beasley, "You give me joy, friendship and make me proud that my hard work as your mother was so worth it. Thank you for being my cheerleaders!"

ACKNOWLEDGEMENTS

I love and appreciate my husband, Bill. You have supported me as I spent hours at the computer composing this book since my first inspiration many years ago. Your time to listen to me read these stories and messages aloud are gifts and contributions, and your love and wisdom is beyond valuable!

I am grateful to my Friend, Lynn Sargent and my daughter, Emily Blais, for your expertise in reading and editing for me. To my busy son, Andrew Beasley: thank you for taking time from your work schedule to read my book and give me your wisdom!

A special thank you to my smart and sweet friend, Yanel Zuniga, who spent your lunch breaks and time helping me with the technology. I am grateful also to my cousin, Jonah Martinez, for your technology help, as well.

A special thank you to my longtime Friend, Eleanor Sherfield, for cheering me on to finish! I appreciate you for taking time from your busy schedule to coach me about ZOOM calls–and for your prayers.

To my cheerleaders: Cousins: Kristi Truelove and Sally Jones Smith, and my adult kids, Emily Blais and Andrew Beasley, and to my "Encouraging Coach", Donita Easley, Hearing those words, "I can't wait to read it", is so motivational! Thank you to each of you!

Often, people who pray are the people behind the scenes that maybe only God knows are working too! I'm especially grateful to you who prayed for me and for this book to reach the readers who will benefit from it: Kristi Truelove,not only my cousin, but my Friend; Ashley Sharp and prayer group members at church; and Hettie Lou Brooks, my mentor and teacher.

Thank you to Karen Kennedy, my longtime friend of nearly forty years, for catching my vision and for drawing and painting my Book Cover!

To my Publisher, Jeremy Jones and your Team: You do a great job to guide the author, step by step, to completion. Thank you so much!

Thank you especially to The Trinity: God the Father, God the Son and God the Holy Spirit. This is my story because of you and your goodness to me and six generations of our family. Be glorified through my offering of written stories, testimonies, and scriptures.

DYNASTY

Verse

Deep in the heart of a prayerful youth
The utterances of the words "send me a wife"
One who will cherish my children and fill their life
With love and discipline to begin the line

Chorus

May our children live for you
Let them keep and hold the line
May our blood be a promise
If we're involved, they'll see Divine

Verse

Deep in the soul of a younger man
Was a path forgotten by many men
A conception conceived by a greater hand
One who builds tradition to reach the land

Chorus

Verse

Deep in the halls of my father's mind
There lives a dream of majesty
Where mortal pilgrims live consciously
Connected by one seed eternally

Chorus

Bridge
Give me a generation
Give me a dynasty

Chorus

Words and Music by Andrew T. Beasley (Copyright)

CONTENTS

INTRODUCTION

Someone once said, "A person can rise no higher than her leader." If a child is to grow into the person God intended her to be, she must have adults in her life who truly lead by example. I am blessed to be one of those people who had godly role models. During my formative years, they were seizing the day to teach character building lessons. They worked to instill in me the virtues of love, joy, peace, patience, kindness, goodness, gentleness, and self-control.

My parents and grandparents were truly available to me and because of their strong influence in my formative years, I have been equipped with the tools needed for living a healthy, happy, productive life, though not without difficulty. Through my own personal trials, I have grown. While looking at those same role models, I have drawn strength from them because I have observed their reaction and endurance in their own trials. They looked to Jesus as their source!

I believe that many young people today are struggling and failing because they need godly role models who spend time with them teaching them and making them feel loved and secure. They have few or no adults in their lives who are modeling righteous living before them. My role models were not perfect by any means; as you read this book, I hope you see some of their weaknesses.

Despite those, they did more of the right things than the wrong things, and God made up the difference!

The word "sacrifice" is not a politically correct word in today's vocabulary, but it is a very Biblical word. In Mark 8:34 Jesus said, "Whosoever will come after me, let him deny himself, and take up his cross, and follow me." Many parents want good character in their children, but wrestle with our culture. There is hope. I have walked the parenting journey, and God has helped me succeed in training my children. You can do it too.

It is my prayer that the stories of our families of faith will bring encouragement and hope to you. As I have shared our struggles, and our victories and the ways that God has guided us in the little things as well as the big, I hope you will see how our faith in Christ and doing it His way has made a difference in the generations of our family. God gets involved with our lives as we live in obedience to His Word—The Holy Bible— and we get to enjoy the abundant life He promised through His Son, Jesus Christ.

CHAPTER 1

FOLLOWING DADDY'S FOOTSTEPS

"Pay close attention, my child, to your father's wise words and never forget your mother's instructions. For their insight will bring you success, adorning you with grace-filled thoughts and giving you reins to guide your decisions." (Proverbs 1:8-9).

Our Courtship

(How my parents met and married, as told by my mother, Wanda Ruth Jones Moore)

Once upon a time, just like the fairy stories, my Prince Charming rode up on a horse; but I was too young at that time to be interested. I must have been about eleven, and I was very much the tomboy, playing softball on the Naples (TX) Elementary playground.

"Who is that boy?" I asked one of my teammates.

"Oh, that's Victor Moore," one of the high school students said, ...and I continued playing ball without a single romantic thought until...

2 Dynasty of Faith

My Sunday School teacher at the Methodist Church, Mrs. Hattie Moore, who happened to be Vic's mother, hosted a class party to welcome her son home from Japan, where he had served with the army occupation forces after World War II. Thus, at the age of thirteen, I was formally introduced to Vic, along with my other classmates. The six years difference in our ages appeared to be a real barrier to any relationship other than friendship. He was too old; I was too young. But I admired him from afar, as he escorted Hope Hampton, a very popular high school girl, to church functions.

When I was sixteen, much to my amazement, Vic approached me after church one Sunday morning and invited me to go on a picnic with him. As I recall, we drove to Daingerfield State Park; and, from our very first date, we were totally compatible. He prepared the tuna sandwiches, and I thoroughly enjoyed the outing. Conversation flowed freely, and we really seemed to "hit it off." Other dates followed, and we soon became an "item" as they say today; but that first kiss was a long way off—a whole year away!

When school started that fall (1950), I was living in Dallas with my paternal grandmother. Vic was in the reserves, and in October he was called to active duty in the Korean War. In January 1951, he was severely wounded and shipped back to the States, to Brooke Army Hospital in San Antonio.

Much to my surprise, my grandmother allowed me to ride the train to San Antonio and visit Vic in the hospital one weekend. His mother had a hospitality room there, and she invited me to stay with her.

Vic was in and out of the hospital for fifteen months, but we continued to see each other whenever possible. The letters flowed freely—so freely that my grandmother was afraid we were getting too serious, and that I wouldn't finish college. She also feared that, because of his injury, Vic would be unable to make a living for me, if we married.

You guessed it. Grandma made up her mind to break us up. She informed me that she would cut me out of her will, and that I would have to leave her home if I failed to comply. By that time, I was attending Southern Methodist University on a full scholarship.

The hardest thing I had ever done was to break the news of Grandma's ultimatum to Vic. As fate would have it, we went on another picnic that evening, but it proved to be one of the saddest evenings of my life. Vic had already told me that he loved me. Now I had to tell him that I had seriously analyzed my feelings for him, and that I thought the world of him as my best friend, but I was not in love with him. As a result, I needed to stay with Grandma and finish college. My education, not her will, was the main motivation. Both Vic and I cried at least a million tears and said our goodbyes. Approximately two years passed before I saw him again.

In the interim, both of us dated other people. Vic was in college at East Texas State University (now Texas A & M) and I continued my studies at SMU. As a member of the SMU Choir, I met and started dating a theology student. Our relationship developed fast, and we were soon engaged to be married. But he was a very jealous person and a very haphazard student; and I began to see that the relationship wouldn't work. Besides, Grandma Jones disliked him because of his lackadaisical study habits.

"If you marry him," she warned, "you'll be writing his sermons for him."

One Sunday afternoon the phone rang, and I was shocked to hear Vic's voice. He wanted to drop by and see us since he was in the Dallas area. Much to my amazement, Grandma allowed him to come; in fact, she seemed to welcome him back!

During the afternoon, I told Vic that my fiancé and I were not getting along well, mostly because of his jealousy, and that I wanted to give his ring back and date Vic and him on an equal basis until I could make up my mind. Vic welcomed this decision, and we even planned our first date. Believe it or not, Grandma seemed to like the idea as much as we did; but my fiancé would have nothing to do with this arrangement.

"It's either me or him."

That made my decision easy. I told him goodbye forever and never looked back.

Vic and I went out to eat at the Italian Village restaurant and had a marvelous time together. Our second date was my graduation, and that very night we became engaged. That was May 1955, and in September we were married in a beautiful ceremony at the Methodist Church in Naples, Texas. The rest is history. We spent more than 50 wonderful years together—the happiest years of my life! Both of us had prayed that God would lead us to the right mate, and He truly gave us "the desires of our heart." (Psalms 37:4).

*   *   *

My parents made their first home in Sulphur Springs, Texas, where Daddy worked for a dairy operation. He cooked their first meal, but Mother learned the art quickly. In the spring of 1956, Daddy got a job at Lone Star Steel Company in Lone Star. He and Mother, pregnant with me, moved to Naples to live with Daddy's mother and grandmother on the Vissering Ranch where he grew up.

My parents, Victor and Wanda Moore, were planning before I was born for me to know Jesus! They named me Elizabeth, which means "consecrated to God." Fully intending for me to live up to that meaning, they raised me with that goal in mind. Their lifestyle, decisions, opportunities, and our conversations would create an atmosphere of faith in our home, whereby they could mold me into a disciple of Christ.

When I entered the world in September 1956, people were immediately reminded of my daddy when they looked at me through the hospital nursery window. "That baby looks like Victor Moore," they would say. I loved my Daddy and thought he was handsome. He was the leader I wanted to follow, not only in my heart, but also in his physical steps.

Daddy's parents both lived in Naples, Texas during the 1920's. Cluren Ross Moore was a barber. He married Hattie Vissering Moore on October 5, 1924. They bought their first home in 1927, a large Victorian house on Wheatville Road, about three blocks from town, and Granddaddy Moore walked to work every day.

The next year, June 1928, Daddy was born in the living room of their home after his mother had a very difficult labor. Unfortunately, eighteen months later, April 1930, my Grandfather, Cluren, died in the other front room of the family home, leaving my grandmother a widow with an eighteen month old son to raise during the Depression!

Gran realized that she would need her own father's help to raise her son to maturity. God provided for Daddy's upbringing through his strong, maternal grandfather, H. J. Vissering, and three uncles, who became Daddy's mentors. My grandmother decided she could not stand to go back into the home where her husband had died, so she and her small son moved to the Vissering Ranch to live with her parents. Sometime later, she turned that home into a rental property for income. She raised Daddy and spent the rest of her life in her parents' home working to help run the farmhouse and ranch.

Papa Vissering, Uncle Fred, Uncle Jack and Uncle George instilled in Daddy a love for livestock and land as he grew up riding and raising horses, cows, and hogs. At the H.J. Vissering Ranch in Naples, Daddy received a kind of "agricultural education" before he ever went to college. He learned to love his farm animals, especially horses, and the land and how to take care of them. Papa Vissering died in 1940, when Daddy was twelve years old, but his mother and his uncles continued the task of training him.

As a student at Naples High School in the 40's, Daddy rode a little horse named "Bill" from the Vissering Ranch to school, the distance of a mile and a half. While he was in class, his faithful steed would go over near the current Naples water tower and eat the green grass until Daddy got out of class. Some days he left the horse at home and rode into town with his mother to school, but he kept a hay rope in his pocket! Sometimes "Bill" would get out of the lot at the farm and come to the water tower by himself. Daddy would look out the classroom window and see his horse over there grazing; when school was out in the afternoon, he would put that hay rope around Bill's neck, jump on him and ride him bareback all the way to the farm. I think you could say Daddy was a horse whisperer! He was photographed standing on his head on the top of a horse and then standing on the saddle of a horse.

Daddy loved adventure. There were days that he would get distracted on his way to school when he saw a rabbit run across the road! My grandmother wanted him to get better grades and discussed that with her son's teachers. They said they liked Cluren Victor just the way he was because he was a "well-rounded" person. To earn money, he raised hogs and watermelons.

Graduating from high school in 1945, Daddy enrolled in Tarleton College in Stephenville, Texas. He became the President of the Wesley Foundation, the Christian student organization of the Methodist Church. A Commander in the Wainwright Rifle Corps, he was the man who made the calls to the unit as they marched. He made many friends and had several beautiful girlfriends while in college.

My father joined the army in 1946 and was sent to Japan for a tour of duty. The emperor had a horse that nobody had been able to ride. Daddy was given a chance to ride him and was able to do so! It's an iconic picture I love of Daddy, sitting atop that emperor's beautiful black horse!

When he came home from his tour of duty in Japan, he was satisfied that he had served his time in the military. He joined the Reserves and planned on benefitting from the GI Bill to complete his college education.

Shortly after he entered the Reserves, he was called to fight in the Korean Conflict on the front lines! He was a gunner. God spared Daddy's life when he was wounded by a Chinese sniper there on foreign soil. The bullet went through his hip, barely missing his spine and came out the other side. He lay on five inches of snow for five hours in freezing temperatures, while Chinese soldiers walked all around him with fixed bayonets. Being a person of faith, common sense, and wisdom, Daddy hid his "cold" breath under the collar of his jacket, making the enemy think he was already dead.

During his long stay in Brooke Army Hospital in San Antonio, he was cheered on in his healing process by numerous visits from his mother, aunts and uncles, and cousins. His family and friends sent him an outpouring of love in letters and cards. The Naples postmaster told someone they had never seen as much mail go out to one person as to Daddy!

After he had recovered, he hitchhiked from Naples to Commerce to complete his degree at East Texas State University in May 1955. It was truly a day to celebrate for him and his family.

Daddy was twenty-eight years old when I was born, and his maturity and experiences made him a wise, knowledgeable, and caring father to me. From my earliest memories, I wanted to go with him to town, to work, and to the farm. Daddy did the grocery shopping for our family, and I would follow along to Foster's Grocery Store, just blocks from our house. He taught me not to ask for candy, but I soon learned if I would obey him, he would buy me something because it was his idea!

Working in the Personnel Office at Lone Star Steel Company required Daddy to sometimes go in on Saturdays. When I was about three, he started taking me with him occasionally. While accomplishing his duties, he allowed me to use the typewriters and adding machine. I loved office work and pretending at that young age. As serious as a four-year-old can be, I told him more than once, "Daddy, one day I will come to work, and you won't have to!" He called me "his little secretary."

When I was four years old, our family of three attended the Lone Star Steel Credit Union meeting. They were giving away a red transistor radio that night. Looking for someone to draw the winning ticket from the spinning basket, they called on me. I reached into the bin of tickets and surprise, surprise! I drew my own Daddy's name! We had our picture made together, and it appeared in the plant newspaper, *The Star*.

My favorite and most frequent place to follow Daddy was to the farm, where he grew up. Daddy's mother, Gran, still lived there and took care of my great-grandmother, Mama Vissering. I not only got to follow Daddy around, but I also got to see my grandmothers too. A child could always find something to do "at the farm."

Daddy owned cattle and horses. He would take me with him to put out hay in the winter. When I was small, he would load the truck with hay, drive into the pasture, put it in low gear, and then get in the back of the truck with me and push the hay off. I was his helper, opening and closing gates as I got old enough.

One evening when I was three years old, Daddy needed to go to the Shepherd Place, a large acreage he leased in which to keep his cattle, located next to the Vissering Ranch. For some reason, he did not want me to go along that day, but I was disobedient and followed him anyway. After a short time, my grandmother missed me at the house. Daddy had a hired hand named Earl, whom they sent to look for me. I had already traveled on my little, short legs a good distance from the house, and was near Wheatville Cemetery and the gate to the Shepherd Place when he found me. He picked me up and carried me back to Gran and Mama. I don't remember it all, but I'm sure a spanking followed because my grandmother and parents were always teaching me obedience.

My father instilled in me a healthy respect for the house of God. First, I was expected to go to the restroom after Sunday School and before church so I would not need to get up during the service. Daddy felt that people moving around was a distraction to those trying to hear the sermon! There were several things he did not allow me to do during church. Talking, chewing gum, turning around to look back at someone, and sitting on the back row, were all behaviors of which Daddy did not approve! He preferred that I sit on the same pew with him and Mother. I usually sat right beside Gran on the second row from the front, and he and Mother sat on the other end of the same padded pew. As a little girl, I could draw pictures on a piece of paper, but knew to clean up my area at the end of the service.

Our church was cleaned weekly by the members. Mother took her turn, and I helped her. I learned to love God's house by behaving properly when I attended services regularly and through helping take care of the building. We would vacuum the green carpet, dust the pews, clean the bathrooms, arrange the songbooks, straighten and dust the Sunday School rooms, and sweep the front porch. After carrying out the duty of cleaning the church for a while, I didn't always want to take my time on Saturday to do it, but felt good about it afterward. Daddy did his part to help maintain the grounds by driving his tractor and brush hog over the acreage that was too large for a push mower to cover.

Horses began to interest me at the age of three, and Daddy started teaching me to ride. My grandmother had a big gelding named Stroller that she had raised from a colt. Stroller was perfect for kids of all ages, so he became my horse. As I got older and more experienced, Daddy would ride Prince, his beautiful stallion, and I would ride Stroller; together we would round up the herd of cattle or look for a stray. That was quite a confidence booster for me as I helped my father. He would tell me where to go and what to do to accomplish the task. I hoped to please him and not let the cow get away. Daddy was a brave cowboy. He would do whatever it took, no matter how long, no matter how hot or tired he was, he persevered and endured until he accomplished the task at hand.

He loved being on the farm, and I loved being with him. In fact, those are some of my happiest memories growing up: when Daddy and I rode horses together. I felt loved and free! Sometimes, as we rode along together in the woods, we would sing. He taught me this special song:

"As I was out riding this morning for pleasure
I saw a cowpuncher just riding along.
His hat was thrown back and his spurs were a' jingling
And as he approached me, he sang me this song.
Whoopi tie I-oh get along little dogies
For your misfortune is none of my own.
His hat was thrown back and his spurs were a' jingling
And as he approached me, he sung me this song."

Besides sparing Daddy's life during the Korean War, God protected him from death on numerous other occasions—a ruptured appendix and a burning motorbike. One day as a teenage boy, he was sitting in the big barn hallway eating a watermelon; when he opened his mouth to take a bite a bee flew in and stung the roof of his mouth! His throat started swelling so he could not breathe. He survived that too!

Daddy had a horse accident that could have taken his life. It occurred when I was about ten. I remember being out in the yard one afternoon when I looked up and saw my hard-working Daddy walking toward the back door with his left arm against his side. Someone had driven him home and let him out on the street in front of our house. I knew something was wrong with him. We got him in the house and saw that his arm had been injured; he needed a doctor. As it turned out, they admitted him to the hospital for a one-night stay to treat his arm and observe him.

He told us what happened that afternoon that was a near tragedy. Any cattle owner knows that a cow can get away from the herd and someone has to go get her. As Daddy had ridden Prince into a neighbor's pasture to bring back a stray, she was getting away and he kicked Prince up to a full gallop. I can picture my Daddy, the big man he was, sitting in the saddle on that beautiful stallion, cowboy hat on his blond, but balding hair, reigns in his right hand, his left arm against his side as he moved swiftly across the hilly terrain in fast pursuit of the stray.

The afternoon sun was in his eyes, which blinded him from seeing directly in his path: a guy wire running at an angle to an electrical pole. Galloping across the unfamiliar pasture, the agile quarter horse caught the brunt of the wire, wounding him severely, but protecting Daddy from being decapitated!! The impact knocked Prince and Daddy to the ground. I know that God spared his life again—just maybe so he could continue being the father I needed! The stallion was so wounded that he could hardly drink water and it was a very long time before he seemed normal. Many years later, Prince died with a deep scar and indention in his neck from the day he took the guy wire blow and saved my daddy's life!

As Christmas approached each year, Daddy and I would go to the woods, choose and cut us a fresh cedar Christmas tree, mount it on a piece of wood, and put it in the living room in front of the window. Finally, closer to Christmas, he would get the lights on, and we would decorate with ornaments and silver icicles. As I grew older, it became my job to pick all the needles out of the carpet after the tree was taken down! (Ugh.)

One Christmas tradition that my parents held was waiting until Gran and Mama could get to our house before I could come into the living room to see what Santa Claus had brought me. That was a very difficult wait, so I'm sure that patience was instilled in my young heart every Christmas morning! I remember expecting a bicycle at the age of six or seven and could hardly wait to actually see it. Our grandmothers finally arrived and I was given the "go" to the living room. My anticipation met with excitement when I beheld a shiny blue bicycle, which I enjoyed riding in my yard, on my street, and to the farm.

One of my earliest Christmas presents from Mother and Daddy was a small nativity scene, complete with the barn, the angel, Joseph, Mary, Baby Jesus, three wise men, a shepherd, sheep, and a donkey. One of the highlights of each Christmas thereafter was getting out that box and assembling each figurine on a table in our entry hall. I was taught at an early age that Christmas is Jesus' birthday: "For God so loved the world, that He gave his only begotten son, that whosoever believeth in him should not perish but have everlasting life" (John 3:16).

A Father Protects His Children!

At an early age, I learned that sometimes parents say "No," but can't explain all the reasons why. Today, I realize that is just like God; he does not owe us an explanation, but we can trust him to always have our best interest at heart. His "No's" are to protect us.

When I was a little girl, about eight or nine, Daddy rounded up the cows at his "Dipping Vat" corral. I wanted to go with him and at least sit on the fencepost and watch. He would not let me go that day, and I was very upset. The only explanation he gave me was that I didn't need to be there with all those men helping him. That didn't make any sense to me at the time because I didn't understand. It reminds me of Proverbs 3:5-6. Several years later, I came to understand why I had to stay home that day. Daddy did not believe it was appropriate for me to be present while the men castrated some calves.

Daddy built a relationship with me as we "hung out" together! We would go into the feed store and some adult would say, "Vic, who is that you have with you?" Daddy would say, "Oh, I picked her up on the side of the road; she's my sidekick." We would ride in the truck and talk about many subjects—people, nature, family, the Lord. Proverbs 4:4-7,10 summarizes the life lessons my father wanted me to remember:

"My father told me, "Take my words to heart. Follow my instructions and you will live. Learn to be wise and develop good judgment. Don't forget or turn your back on wisdom, for she will protect you. Love her, and she will guard you. Getting wisdom is the most important thing you can do! And whatever else you do, get good judgment...My child, listen to me and do as I say, and you will have a long, good life."

Gran and Daddy always had a huge garden on the plot of ground next to Mama's house. Daddy in his blue, long-sleeved coveralls prepared the rows for planting with a walking plow and two mules named Kit and Kate. I would take off my shoes, roll up my pants legs and follow right behind him, stepping in the footprints he left in the freshly plowed dirt. That was actually the physical manifestation of a little girl's heart; I wanted to follow my father! I loved to feel the cool, brown soil against my feet. After the many rows were prepared, he would plant sweet corn, tomatoes, potatoes, onions, garlic, and peas. At harvest time, my parents and grandmother would pick the vegetables and then work in the hot, farm kitchen to can them for winter groceries. They loved to have enough to share with others, so the garden was huge.

Learning Patriotism

Daddy taught me to love America! As a veteran, he knew the price of freedom. One of the first things he taught me at the age of three was the Pledge of Allegiance to the American Flag. When we would go to town together, he would have me recite to other people what I had learned, and they always seemed to enjoy what I had memorized at such a young age.

A very compassionate and generous person, Daddy loved to help people. My first memories of helping other people involved giving them a ride to church. We had several single Moms in our fellowship who did not have transportation.

Church friends and farm hands were recipients of Daddy's generosity. Sometimes he had difficulty striking the balance between giving and selling. On several occasions, when he had an old car he wanted to sell, he would finance it for someone; if they did not pay him, he never repossessed it. He believed that love could overcome a lot. His love and compassion for people of all walks of life inspired me.

Daddy especially loved my mother. They enjoyed being together and were best friends. He would say to me, "Did you know you have a wonderful mother?" They always celebrated their anniversaries. I loved that because it meant I got to spend the night or weekend with my Gran at the farm. My parents reminisced about how they met and their dating years. On a family outing, they might just start singing an old love song together!

The summer after second grade my parents showed how much they trusted me and our cousin, Charlotte Tomberlain Tatum, when she invited me and her younger sister, Martha, to visit her at her home in West Texas. We spent two weeks with my sweet cousin and her husband, Richard, a Baptist pastor, and their two little sons, Peter Mark and John David. We helped Charlotte take care of them. Their house was within walking distance of town; one fun thing Martha and I did was to walk by ourselves to the pharmacy where we sat on the bar stool at the fountain and ordered the best cool and refreshing limeade!

Charlotte decided that she, Martha, and I would form a trio to learn a special song for church. She chose one from the hymnal that I did not know, and I was supposed to learn the alto part, which was difficult for a third grader. After days of practicing at home, the three of us stood up at church and harmonized as we sang the hymn entitled "Our Best." "Every work for Jesus will be blessed. But He asks from everyone his best. Our talents may be few, these may be small, but unto him is due our best, our all."

Charlotte was a special cousin, a godly woman who always made me feel loved, and I loved her. She went to be with Jesus at the age of 54, after a long battle with her health.

My father strongly believed that Mother should stay at home with me. He worked two jobs, the steel plant and his cattle ranch, so that she would not have to enter the workplace when I was growing up.

Finding God's will and doing it was of great concern to Daddy and Mother. They taught me to seek God and His will above all things. When I was a young teenager, we had a situation in our church, which required much wisdom and perseverance. Daddy was an elder at the First Assembly of God; and he was a peacemaker. When difficult situations arose, he and Mother sought the mind of Christ about the matter. They did not jump up and do something hasty; their decisions were made with God and the Body of Christ in mind.

"Finding God's will and doing it" is something each of us needs to practice as a lifestyle. Too many people think only of themselves or what feels good for the moment. What will my decision or actions produce in the short run and the long run? Who will be affected by my decision, and how will they be affected? Living in the perfect will of God is the best place to be, and there is peace and God's full provision.

One of the hardest things for me about growing up was legalism. A person can only "perform" so long; freedom comes when one finds grace. For me it would be many years of "trying to get it right." If the adults in my life had mixed a lot more grace with their love and guidance, my childhood would have been much more balanced. Daddy was strict, always watching what I wore, and even my expressions. Because he showed his love and attention in countless ways, I knew he loved me, but I was checking my actions to measure up to his and God's expectations. That was hard! But, I didn't want to disappoint God, or my parents and grandparents. Thankfully, the Christian life is a journey, and down the road, God had a plan for helping me to find grace.

My parents' generation and those before them knew what it meant to go through hard times and keep their faith. They didn't get angry with God when things were difficult because they expected life to be challenging. They were thankful for the good times, and knew God's promises, one of which is "Many are the afflictions of the righteous: but the Lord delivered them out of them all" (Psalm 34:19).

God's Protection Under Fire!

When I was in the sixth grade, our family had a very difficult experience that could have been tragic. We experienced God's protection. Daddy was a Company man, working in the Personnel Office during a strike in the late sixties. He was actually hiring people to replace union employees who would not go back to work. My parents had just bought their first brand-new car, a beautiful, shiny, luxury Ninety-Eight Oldsmobile, which was parked at an angle in our front yard. About three o'clock one cold morning, Daddy heard a noise and smelled gunpowder. He got out of the bed and walked through the entry hall and into our dining room where he felt something under his feet. Flipping on the light, he saw the broken glass on the floor. The China cabinet was shattered. Then he looked across the room to see where a bullet from a 30/30 deer rifle had come from outside, through our dining room wall, through the back of the China cabinet, and into the wall behind it!! On the other side of that wall, my parents and baby sister were sleeping!!!!

As Daddy continued to investigate this horrible deed, he noticed that our brand-new car had also been shot, shattering the windshield, bullet holes penetrating the doors all the way inside the car into the upholstery. It was a very sobering time. After that, Daddy went into the plant and stayed for six weeks because it was too dangerous for him to make the trip back and forth every day. We never knew who shot at us. God knows, and he protected us on that night when our family was in harm's way!

Daddy Was My Cheerleader!

My listening friend and cheerleader was Daddy. I looked forward to telling him my plans because he was usually excited with me. He didn't immediately point out all the reasons my ideas would not work. As a listener, he would hear me out and then give me some food for thought. One of his wise sayings was "You have two ears and one mouth," he said, "which means you should listen twice as much as you talk."

A Father Obeys "The Great Commission"

Daddy was a witness for Jesus. Whether he was on the job or at the feed store, he looked for ways to share his faith with others. At the end of the day, he would come home and tell us about his witnessing experiences. That caused me to want to tell others about Jesus too!

A Father Teaches His Children

One of the best things Daddy did for me was our father-daughter talks. He sat me down one day when I was a young teenager and explained to me the differences in the way men and women think and view the opposite sex. These talks gave me knowledge and wisdom to make godly choices. He taught me how to pick a husband. "Don't marry the person you can live with; marry the person you can't live without," Daddy said.

A Father is a Lifetime Friend

After I left home and went to college, I knew I always had a friend in Daddy. At Southwestern Assemblies of God College, I remember having a phone conversation with him. "God called me by my first name; I heard Him say "Elizabeth;" Daddy loved that. Read Psalms 139 to understand how much God knows and loves you!

Daddy became my friend in the course of everyday living; nobody can ever take that away. Christian psychologists say that a child gets his impression of God from his father. A father must affirm his teenage daughter and teach her that she has what it takes as a young woman. Daddy did that for me and believed in me. He knew that teaching me to obey him must precede my obeying God. We can only follow the path to which God calls us if we trust and obey. Jesus said in John 15, "If you love me, you will obey me." Growing up around Daddy, I learned to trust him, to obey him, and to receive the consequences if I didn't.

My father had a way of making a person feel at home in God's big, beautiful world! He saw land and loved it. He saw the fall foliage and loved it. He saw the animals, especially horses, and loved them. He saw God in His creation. Finally, last but not least, he loved the people God made—old, young, rich, poor— and his family, and I knew it!

CHAPTER 2

MOTHER: SINGER, TEACHER OF GOODNESS, INTERCESSOR

"The aged women, likewise, that they be in behavior as becometh holiness, not false accusers, not given to much wine, teachers of good things; That they may teach the young women to be sober, to love their husbands, to love their children, to be discreet, chaste, keepers at home, good, obedient to their own husbands, that the word of God be not blasphemed"(Titus 2:3-5).

When I think of Mother, she is wearing her red robe early in the morning, and she is sitting in her warm, cozy kitchen. Lying in front of her on the large, round oak table is her open Bible and a cup of hot coffee, sweetened with two teaspoons of her favorite hazelnut creamer. She has read her Bible and had her prayer time with God, and greets me in her normal, jovial morning mood.

My mother, Wanda Ruth Jones Moore, was born March 1934 on the first day of spring, at her maternal grandparents' home in Naples, Texas. Her mother was Bonnie "Ruth" Brown Jones, daughter of William Talmond Brown and Jo Ross Franklin Brown.

Her father was Charles Brackett Jones, Jr., son of Charles B. Jones and Stella Jarnigan Jones, from Dallas, Texas.

Mother's grandparents were strong Christians, especially Jo Ross Brown, who was a great woman of God, and who did everything in her power to train up her children "in the nurture and admonition of the Lord." "Pappy" Brown, a farmer, was a fine man too.

Mother's parents, Bonnie Ruth and Charles, met and married in Dallas, where Ruth was a secretary for W. A. Green Company and Charles delivered milk for Metzger's Dairy. He also was the drummer in the Magnolia Petroleum Orchestra. Times were hard during the Great Depression. Charles lost his job with the dairy, and they moved to Naples, to the farm where Bonnie Ruth's parents and siblings lived.

Ruth had six siblings, most of whom had not yet left home— four brothers and two sisters, Esther and Imogene. The Brown brothers— Oscar, Lawrence, Houston and Leon— were adept at farming, having grown up in that lifestyle; but Charles was a city boy, who, for the life of him, couldn't plow a straight row! The boys laughed at him mercilessly.

Mother's parents welcomed her into the world while they were living at the farm. Her uncles helped her Daddy build a one-room log cabin on the hill across the road from Granny and Pappy Brown's house, and that was home to Charles, Bonnie, and their new baby girl.

When Mother was four months old, tragedy struck. Her daddy became very ill. His kidneys stopped functioning; and Dr. Smith, the local physician, seemed helpless to do anything about his plight. Grandma and Grandpa Jones sent an ambulance to Naples, and they carried their son, Charles, to a Dallas hospital for emergency surgery; but he died, at the age of 27, before the doctors could operate.

Ruth was left with a four-month-old baby in the heart of the Depression! Grandma and Grandpa Jones took them into their home in Dallas. Ruth got another job at the W. A. Green Co., and Grandma Jones took care of my mother. Ruth spent the evenings and weekends with her baby daughter, and Mother treasured the many happy memories they made together.

Charles Jones, Mother's daddy, had been married before—to Elsie Dortch—and they had a son named Robert (Bobby) Lloyd Jones. Their marriage ended in divorce. Elsie developed tuberculosis, from which she died the same year as Charles, in the fall of 1934.

When Mother and her mother, Ruth, moved in with Grandma and Grandpa Jones, six-year-old Bobby was already living with them. Ruth took Bobby under her wing, and she and the two children shared many happy evenings. She would read fairy tales to them or take them to City Park, just a block away. Mother sang her first solo ("Happy Birthday") at the park at the age of 5 and won first prize in her age bracket. On Sundays, Ruth took the children to Pilgrim's Chapel, a small Methodist Church. Ruth must have been very grief-stricken when she first moved with her baby daughter to Dallas, but my mother has no memory of her ever being anything but cheerful.

Grandpa Jones worked in the toy department of Cullum & Boren, a sporting goods store. Mother and her brother, Bob, ran to meet him each afternoon, as he walked home from the bus stop. They raided his pockets, which were usually filled with Hershey's kisses! At Christmas, there were always lots of toys, not from Santa's bag, as they supposed, but from the Cullum & Boren Toy Department.

Grandma Jones had a boarding house. The whole second story of her large white frame house was rented out to single men. It was hard work keeping the rooms clean, changing and laundering the sheets, etc. The boarders were very gentlemanly, and absolutely no women were allowed upstairs. Since they had a separate entrance, the men were seldom seen by the Jones family, except when they paid their rent.

When Mother was five years old, she and her mother moved into an apartment in Oak Cliff, a neighborhood in Dallas, leaving

Bobby with Grandma and Grandpa Jones. The landlady, Mrs. Butler, took care of Mother while her mother worked. They had not been living there long when Ruth became ill, and they had to return to Granny and Pappy Brown's home in Naples.

By the end of that summer, Ruth had recovered enough to move to Shreveport, Louisiana, where she worked as a secretary for Selber Brothers Department Stores. She allowed Mother to stay with Granny and Pappy Brown in Naples where, in September of that year, she started school. Since the Brown home was about a mile and a half from the highway, where the school bus stopped, Mother walked with her mother's youngest sister, Aunt Jean, and the neighbor children three miles a day. Her grandparents had no car at that time.

Mother's first year of school was memorable. Mrs. Gladys Martin, a truly gifted educator, was her dearly loved teacher. School was easy for her, and she really enjoyed learning. Reading became her favorite pastime, but she made A's in every subject. She made some good friends, and had great fun at recess playing jacks or jumping rope, etc.

Mother enjoyed living with Granny and Pappy Brown. She played in the sand with her cousins and washed canning jars for Granny, who spent many hours putting up the produce from her garden. Mother's little hands were small enough to fit inside the jar.

Granny had a deep pit beside the front porch, where she kept her pot plants in the winter. Someone had placed a couple of boards across the pit, so Mother and her cousin, Milton Brown, decided to walk across the boards. Milton lost his balance, and when she tried to catch him, they both fell into the pit. Mother broke her nose on a brick, and Granny called Dr. Smith. After that accident, Mother's nose always had a slight bump in it—a fact which later in seventh grade got her the part of the witch in the play Hansel and Gretel!

Granny Brown was a strong disciplinarian. Once Mother called someone a fool, and Granny told her sternly that the Bible said you were in danger of hell fire if you said that. She made such an impression on Mother that she ran out into the pasture, threw herself down on the ground, and prayed that God would forgive her! She never ever called anyone else a fool!

Granny, Pappy, Aunt Jean, and Mother attended church at Rocky Point Congregational Methodist Church, located about 2 miles from their farm. Many years later, as Mother was praying at the altar of her church in Naples, the Lord impressed on her that she was saved in answer to Granny Brown's prayers!

In the summer which followed Mother's first year of school, Granny Brown died as a result of problems with her gallbladder. After the funeral, Mother went to live with her mother in Shreveport, where in September she entered second grade. She remembered almost nothing about that school, but one memory from that winter stuck with her throughout her life. On December 7, 1941, from their upstairs efficiency apartment, she heard the newsboys on the street shouting "Extra! Extra! Read all about it! Japanese bomb Pearl Harbor!" She pressed her small face against the windowpane and watched them in total awe. Little did she realize at that tender age the dire consequences of that event.

At Christmas vacation, Mother went to visit Grandma and Grandpa Jones, and Grandma Jones asked Ruth if she could keep Mother there for the rest of that school year. Since her mother consented, Mother finished second grade at City Park Grade School in Dallas. Once again, she was back with her older brother, Bobby (later shortened to Bob), and they had some great times together.

Much to Mother's surprise, her mother, Ruth, remarried in February, but she did not meet her stepfather, Henry "Grady" Higgins, until the conclusion of the school term. Ruth and Grady went to get Mother in May and took her with them to Amarillo, Texas, where Grady, a carpenter by trade, worked in construction until the end of the summer.

At the end of the summer, the family of three returned to Naples, where, for the first time, Mother met Grady's parents,

Mabel and Arthur Higgins (Granny and PaPa). By the end of the first evening, Granny had given Mother so much loving attention that Mother begged Ruth and Grady to let her live with Granny and PaPa Higgins and return to school in Naples, where all of her friends were! Wonder of wonders, they allowed her to do just that, and she actually lived with her step-grandparents for six years! Granny said Mother was the daughter they never had. (They raised three sons.)

When the school year opened, and Mother was back at Naples Grade School, she searched for her friends; and when, to her surprise, they were all seated in the fourth-grade classroom, she simply went in and sat down! You guessed it! She skipped the third grade! She learned her multiplication tables in the fourth grade by the light of the kerosene lamp. No electricity at Granny's yet.

Mother's fourth grade teacher was a hard-nosed disciplinarian, but in general, a good teacher. One negative memory surfaces: Her assignment in geography was to draw a canal. She did her best, knowing art was not her strong suit, but she was even more convinced of the fact after her teacher held up her picture and ridiculed it to the entire class! Words are powerful! For the rest of her life, Mother always said that she could not draw anything!

In the fifth grade, Mother was still living with Granny and PaPa Higgins. Her teacher was Mrs. Exie Tolbert, and their classroom was on the second story of the old Naples Grade School. She remembered a lower grade in conduct because she couldn't resist talking in Mrs. Tolbert's class!

Mother loved being with Granny and PaPa! She loved every minute of it — almost. PaPa wouldn't let her stay up past 9:00 p.m., and that bothered her because she wanted to read or study later. By this time, her grandparents had electricity, but she would put something under the door so the light wouldn't show and read it with a small kerosene lamp. She knew that PaPa was very conservative, and if he saw the light on, he would flip off the switch.

Granny taught my mother how to keep house. She had chores every day. One morning, before leaving for school, she would make her bed and sweep the floors on the east side of the big house. The next morning, she would make her bed and sweep the two rooms at the center of the house. On the third day, she would make her bed and sweep the west side of the house, then start all over. Frequently on Saturdays, she mopped the floors and waxed them and dusted the furniture. She loved to listen to "Let's Pretend," a radio program which aired every Saturday at 10:00 a.m. It irritated her that often Granny would call her to do chores right in the middle of the program! But Mother says, "Granny loved me, and so did PaPa!" If she was in his good graces, his nickname for her was "Possum." If she heard him say, "Wanda," she felt sad.

During the summer after fifth grade, Mother traveled with Ruth and Grady to Alameda, California, where Grady worked in the shipyards. They lived in a housing project there, and since the schools were crowded, they went to class only half a day. Mother wanted to be back in Texas with Granny and PaPa Higgins.

World War II ended that summer after she turned eleven, and they were glad to return to Naples, where she prepared to enter seventh grade. Mrs. Veneta Bryan was her teacher, and what a teacher she was!

When Mother was thirteen, Ruth and Grady had a baby girl named Linda Gail. Seventeen months later, Donald Wayne was born. Although Mother never lived with her younger siblings, she loved them and was very much part of their lives as they grew up in Hooks, Texas and visited our home many times through the years.

Mother spent her high school years in Dallas living with her Grandmother Jones. She attended Forrest Avenue High School and graduated with honors there in May 1951. A store in Dallas presented the "A-Harris Scholarship" to one girl and one boy in the city of Dallas every year. Mother won that four-year scholarship to Southern Methodist University and began classes there in the Fall of 1951.

At SMU, Mother met some new friends who invited her to a campus organization called InterVarsity Christian Fellowship. Although my mother had attended church and been active in church her whole life, she noticed those Christian students had something she did not have.

The following is her testimony she wrote years later in 1977 for the Jacket of the vocal recording she made called "To God Be the Glory":

> As a child, I longed to know the God that my mother had told me about. During many revivals, I walked the church aisles and tried to commit myself to Him. But it was not until 1951, as a lonely, disillusioned college student, that I really met Him personally, as Savior and Lord. At the point of desperation, I threw myself upon Him and asked Him to enter my life and take full control. And He did! Peace and joy flooded my heart as I felt His very presence lift the burden of sin and misery. My life has been different ever since. Although new problems and burdens arise daily in my role as wife and mother, I now have a Problem-solver and a Burden-bearer who assures me that I can do all things through Him. (Philippians 4:13)

*   *   *

You have read about my parent's courtship and marriage—When Daddy's new job began in the Spring of 1956, my parents needed to move back to Naples. Because they had no furniture for a house and rentals were in short supply, they lived with Daddy's mother and grandmother on the farm. My mother had only been married for a few months and was expecting me. She shared the household chores with her mother-in-law and grandmother-in-law in a big farmhouse with few modern conveniences.

Gran and Mama had no indoor plumbing, no running water, and no heat, except the fireplace and the wood cook stove, and the old farmhouse would get very cold. The summers were very hot, with absolutely no air conditioning, just some oscillating fans. They cooked their food on a wood stove and a hotplate. Water had to be drawn from a well on the back porch; to get hot dishwater, it had to be heated in a large pan on the wood stove.

When Mother delivered me with the help of Dr. James S. Leeves, in September 1956, at the David Granbury Memorial Hospital, she carried me home to Gran and Mama's house, which would be home to us for the next year and a half. They say that the things we do and the things that happen to us are in preparation for our future. Those canning jars she washed for Granny Brown when she was just six years old were just a foretaste of life on the Vissering Farm in the 50's.

Mother said that one winter she mopped the kitchen floor, and it froze over so she could skate on it! That same winter all the water in the fishbowl froze except the part where the castle sat, and the fish could swim in and out.

In the summertime, when the garden came in, Gran and Daddy had mother helping them pick and can tomatoes. The temperature soared in the kitchen on a summer day when the wood stove would be fired up to cook and steam the tomatoes and prepare the jars for canning. My mother got right in there, even though she was really a city girl, and did her part. She was not opposed to hard work or the lack of convenience. Most people today would have decided that those living arrangements were a bad idea right then and there!

With two great parents and two loving grandmothers under one roof to watch over me, I was blessed from day one with plenty of attention and love. My cousins tell me that Gran and Mama doted on me and called me "The Baby."

One day in 1957, a stranger named Paul Elrod came to talk with my grandmother. He told Gran that God had told him to move to Naples to start a new church. In obedience to God's word to him, he was quitting a great job in Dallas, and he wanted to rent the house Gran and her husband had bought together in 1927. He wanted the house for his family's residence and for starting the new church God had called him to. Being a carpenter, Brother Elrod was willing to work on the house to improve it. Mama Vissering encouraged Gran to rent the house to the new minister that day.

First Assembly of God Church, Naples began in the front room of the house on Wheatville Road, in May 1957 with Brother Elrod, his wife, Mary Dean, and their two children, Paula Dean and Robert Sherrill. Their third child, Victor, was born a few months later in September. Brother Elrod followed through with his promise to Gran and improved the large, old house by adding closets, enclosing the porch to make a bedroom, and getting the house in better shape for living and preservation.

My Childhood Memories in the Little White Frame House

In addition to her house she rented to the Elrod family, Gran owned the small two-bedroom frame house across the street from them. The three of us moved into the little white house in 1958, where we became neighbors to the Elrod Family. Paula, Robert, and Victor Elrod became my first friends and playmates, along with my Vissering cousins, Martha, Ben, and Glenda.

It was in that little white frame house that I remember Mother reading nursery rhymes and fairy tales to me before I took a nap every afternoon. She says that I could quote nursery rhymes from memory by the time we moved there at age eighteen months. I had the story so memorized that when she would doze off to sleep while reading to me, I would correct her by filling in the gap with the right line from memory.

A Bible Story before bedtime was a nightly routine for Mother and me. My favorite one was about the little boy who gave his lunch to Jesus to help him feed the five thousand hungry people. The story was very personal because the author always asked the question at the end, "Don't you wish you could have been the little boy (child) who gave your lunch to Jesus?" "Yes!" In my heart, I was there, and I was the little child who shared my fish with Him! A love for books was imparted to me at an early age by Mother.

She miscarried when I was three years old. As she lay in her hospital bed recovering, she listed things to do when she got home. One item on the list read, "Get Elizabeth Ruth under better control." Both of my parents believed Proverbs 13:24 that says, "If you withhold correction and punishment from your children, you demonstrate a lack of true love. So prove your love and be prompt to punish them." They were determined on a daily basis to train me up by that.

My long, thick hair was washed and brushed by Mother. I would sit on the stool in front of her dresser mirror, while she brushed and combed the painful tangles from long hair that had never seen a pair of scissors. "No More Tangles" had not been invented in the 50's-60's. When she would pull my hair, I would groan; she must have felt bad about it, but in her own way would laugh at me as she tried to complete the difficult job of styling it. One day at the age of three or four, exasperated with Mother for pulling my hair, I said to her, "I try so hard to be nice to you that I can't hardly stand it, and you still spank me sometimes."

The narrow street that ran in front of our house was busy, and people drove too fast. Mother told me not to go into the street, but I would walk to the very edge of our driveway to talk to young Victor Elrod, who was standing at the edge of his. Before I knew it, we would be playing in the Elrod's yard! In my eyes, "the grass looked greener on the other side of the road." Mother spanked me again and again for crossing that street without her permission. Finally, after much consistency on her part, I started obeying her. I was still tempted, but the memory of the pain inflicted by Daddy's belt made my memory sharp! "To discipline and reprimand a child produces wisdom, but a mother is disgraced by an undisciplined child" (Proverbs 29:15).

In his book, *The Strong-Willed Child*, Dr. James Dobson addresses this important character trait found in many children. Some children are more compliant, but others, like me, are very determined to do things their way. It is critical to a child's character development to begin to shape the will of a child in those toddler/ preschool years. If that disobedience goes unpunished or ignored, it will likely result in undisciplined, disobedient, disrespectful, and rebellious behavior in the teenager and adult. If a child's strong will is brought into submission and obedience during those formative years, he/she will likely be a more productive adult who can do great things because of discipline and self-control.

However, if that strong willed child at three is allowed to do as she pleases, without restraint, there will be problems ahead. Proverbs 19:18 states: "Discipline your children while there is hope. If you don't, you will ruin their lives." Proverbs 22:15 says: "Foolishness is bound in the heart of a child; but the rod of correction shall drive it far from him." Proverbs 23:13 reads: "Don't fail to correct your children. They won't die if you spank them. Physical discipline may well save them from death." Proverbs 29:17 says: "Discipline your children, and they will give you happiness and peace of mind."

Many parents today want their children to be "free" to express themselves. That philosophy doesn't work. Didn't the serpent in the garden of Eden try to disprove what God had already told Adam and Eve, "If you eat of the fruit of that tree, you shall not surely die." Satan appealed to Eve through human reasoning. The devil is the author of lies, and often his messages contain half the truth in order to entice. Even in the Garden of Eden, the only perfect place on earth, Adam and Eve were not free to do anything they wanted; because God loved them, he put boundaries there to protect them. We must also establish boundaries for our children, and when they cross those lines, we must do what is uncomfortable and correct them. We are created and made free to do the right thing! When we overstep those boundaries and try to do it our way, pain will come to us and those we love!

Our guide in Christian parenting must be the Bible or we will not have happy homes with godly sons and daughters. Our opinions or the philosophies of some college professor or modern book will not give us the result we are looking for. Don't be deceived by what feels or looks right or what others do or say. Proverbs 29:18 says clearly, "When people do not accept divine guidance, they run wild. But whoever obeys the law is happy." Parenting according to God's word is hard, but certainly gives us the best result. God gives us this promise: "For our earthly fathers disciplined us for a few years, doing the best they knew how. But God's discipline is always right and good for us because it means we will share in his holiness. No discipline is enjoyable while it is happening —it is painful! But afterward there will be a quiet harvest of right living for those who are trained in this way" (Hebrews 12:10-11).

Mother Taught Me to Pray

Mother had a nightly routine with me; she always came and knelt beside my bed, and listened to my prayers and then prayed for me. At first, I learned "Now I lay me down to sleep, I pray the Lord my soul to keep. If I should die before I wake, I pray the Lord my soul to take." At an early age, I was very aware that heaven was a real place, and I wanted to go there when I died. As I matured, Mother told me that I was getting old enough to talk to God by using my own words, much like I talked with her.

As a preschooler, I was very attracted to babies. I can remember sitting with Gran in the church on a Sunday morning as a three-year-old. As soon as the "Amen" was said, I would go to see the new baby in his mother's arms or make a beeline for the nursery. From playing with the Elrod children and my Vissering cousins, I had observed that they had brothers and sisters, and I wanted one. I began praying every night that God would send me a baby brother or sister. Mother remembered that finally I got tired of waiting on God to answer and one night I just said, "God, send us a baby!" Then I took a long break from my baby prayer petition.

Mother was a singer and a soloist in our community. When people got married or had a family member to die, they asked her to sing. She did so beautifully and looked at the opportunity as a ministry because she had a servant's heart.

A New Church Home_

When I was about four, my parents were both Sunday School teachers. They were very concerned when they began to notice that their lesson books were more a social lesson, not much Bible. They also noticed that their church did not really teach salvation as a personal decision to follow Jesus. Mother wrote a letter to the leaders on a higher level, who make decisions for the literature, etc. for the local church. They wrote her back agreeing with the truth she stated in her letter, but they did not change anything.

My parents and grandmother decided to visit the First Assembly of God Church. By that time, the small congregation had purchased some property about two blocks from Main Street. Brother Elrod, the carpenter, had built a small, white frame building and moved his growing flock from his house to the church on the hill.

Mrs. Elrod and Mother visited together at the Elrod's kitchen table very frequently. Mother observed that Mary Dean was such a joyful and peaceful Christian. Although Brother Elrod had done work on the rent house, there were still kitchen cabinets with no doors on them. Mother couldn't figure out why her neighbor could be so joyful in her surroundings. As the two homemakers had numerous discussions over many cups of coffee, Mother learned that her neighbor had received the Baptism of the Holy Spirit with evidence of speaking in tongues. That was the explanation for that joy and "inner glow" that Mother observed in her special friend!

It was a hard decision for my parents and grandmother to change churches. They loved the people at their church. After giving the big decision some time, discussion, and prayer, Mother, Daddy, and Gran joined the First Assembly of God Church.

Sometime later, Mother received her prayer language too. That experience strengthened her prayer life and equipped her for living the spirit-controlled life, as commanded by Jesus to his followers in the New Testament (Acts 1:4) (Acts 2:4).

Through Bible stories, attending Sunday School and Church, prayer in our home and by living the life before me, my parents created that atmosphere of faith whereby I realized my need for a Savior. I made the decision when I was five years old to ask Jesus to forgive all my sins and to come into my heart to live, to be my Savior and to make me like Him. Mother led me in the sinner's prayer one night at home. Our church did not have a baptistry, so the custom was to baptize at the pond of one of our members, Mr. Bill Fannin. Mrs. Elrod took her accordion for some worship music as we stood on the bank of the pond, and Brother Elrod baptized me. I was watching Mrs. Elrod play her accordion and hoping I would do that one day too!

About a year later, having learned about the Baptism of the Holy Spirit through my mother and my church, I wanted to receive my prayer language as well. I received my prayer language one night at church, and was very happy about it. This "heavenly language", my own personal communication with God, is a gift from The Holy Spirit to help and empower me to live the victorious Christian life.

Starting School

Kindergarten was not required in the 60's. Some parents sent their children to private kindergarten, but Mother felt that I did not need it because she had worked with me and taught me at home. Having a September birthday caused me to be nearly seven when I began first grade. I had a wonderful teacher named Mrs.

Brown. She was very patient and kind, and I loved learning to read and write. My parents' positive attitude about school, the peaceful environment in the classroom, and my new classmates contributed to making my first year of school a great experience.

Teachers do set the tone in the classroom and impact lives for a lifetime. In that small, public school, each of my teachers knew my parents, and one or two had taught my mother when she was a young girl.

In addition to the three R's, my second-grade teachers, Mrs. Hummel and Mrs. Maxine Davis, taught me and my classmates cursive writing and phonics. I especially loved the bird book Mrs. Hummel helped us make. Each day she would give us a handout with a picture of a different kind of bird. We had to color it correctly and write something informative about it in the lines below the picture. During the second semester, I anticipated every day what new letter we would learn to write in cursive!

It was in second grade that I became a Brownie Girl Scout in Troop 108. Our leaders were Mrs. Skelton, Mrs. Higgins and Mrs. Lancaster, mothers of my friends, Bobbie Skelton, Debra Higgins and Andrea Lancaster. We met once a week after school at the Naples Community Center. The fun with friends, refreshments, crafts, and earning badges were the highlights of Brownies. We met together as a troop through second and third grade, selling Girl Scout Cookies. One of my favorite things was a bike trip we made into Cass County to Bobbie's grandparents' house and farm in Bryans Mill.

Mother modeled humility and a good attitude for me! One day when I was about seven or eight, she got a phone call early one morning to substitute at school, so off we went together. Brother Elrod was decking our house for a new roof, and there was no rain in the forecast. However, with the roof off, the rain came down! We came home that afternoon to a soaked house! Mother mopped puddles of water from the mahogany furniture she had inherited from Grandma Jones. She would put an ice pick into the wallpaper and water would run out. The inside of the house was ruined, and we had to move out where it could be remodeled. I thought we would get to move in with the Elrod family, and I could live with my friend Paula! However, I quickly learned that was not my parents' plan for our interim housing. We moved to the farm and lived with my grandmothers again for three months. Mother didn't tell Brother Elrod off or threaten to sue him. I'm sure we had insurance, and it was one of those unfortunate things that happen in the course of living in this imperfect world.

Mother was there when I came home from school every afternoon. I would talk with her over a snack and tell her the positives and negatives about the day. She did her best to encourage me when I felt lonely or overwhelmed. I knew I could trust her to keep my confidence.

A New House and Answered Prayer!

The summer after I finished second grade, the Elrod family bought their own home on Daingerfield Street in Naples. We then moved into the large house across the street that they had rented from my grandmother. It was an exciting time to have so much more room inside and outside too, even though I missed having the Elrod kids as my neighbors.

Mrs. Dorothy Huddleston was my third-grade teacher, and I really liked her because she was so kind and took a personal interest in me. That year our school integrated, just as our second-grade teachers had informed us.

In the spring of my third-grade year, Mother and Daddy told me that Mother was going to have a baby in November! Gran was there, and we danced a jig around the room! After I thought about the news for a time, I told Mother, "I know why God is just now sending us a baby; we didn't have room for one before!" That was definitely a faith-building experience. After all the times I had prayed, God had finally answered! That was probably one of my first lessons that persistence in prayer does pay off.

In 1966-67, I was a fourth grader at Pewitt Elementary School. Our Brownie Troop had moved up to become Junior Girl Scouts. We had new handbooks, new badges to earn, new uniforms, and new leaders. Mrs. Dorothy Jordan and Mrs. Margaret Griffin became our new leaders, with several of the other mothers assisting them when needed.

Mrs. Louise Davis was my fourth-grade homeroom teacher. She taught me every subject that year except math. She had a reputation for being a strict disciplinarian, and she truly lived up to it. She had some rules that students were expected to follow; if they didn't, there was punishment.

One of her rules was related to our weekly spelling test. She would say the word three times. First, by itself; second, in a sentence; and third by itself. The rule was that if she caught a student writing the word before she said it the third time, they would get an "F" by that word! Her other rule was that if a classmate was spanked at school, we were not to tell anybody about it.

In fourth grade, I learned that October was "National Cat Month." My teacher had an art contest to see which of her students could draw the best cat. I surprised myself! I won third place, and the award was a free kitten !

By November 9, our new baby was due any time. That afternoon, I rode with Mrs. Davis after school to Daingerfield to choose my free kitten from a family who was donating them. I chose the solid white one and named it "Snowball." When we got back to Naples, we learned that Mother had gone to the hospital. I was so excited when Mrs. Davis invited me to stay with her. Mamma was coming to cook and take care of Daddy and me at our house while Mother was in the hospital and recovering.

My Baby Sister Was Born

Another November day in fourth grade, I was having my regular school day schedule until we heard someone knocking on the door. It was Daddy and the office secretary coming to tell me that I had a new little sister named Mary Evelyn. She was very tiny and barely missed the incubator.

We were so proud of her. When we brought her home, we had to quarantine her from anyone who was sick because her immune system needed time to develop. I was the ten-year-old watchdog over her, screening the visitors at the door. Adults loved having a little girl asking them if they had a cold or anything contagious before they entered our home to see our new baby!

Mrs. Lee Davis became one of my favorite teachers. She gave the opportunity for her students to participate in the Interscholastic League Picture Memory Contest. We studied and practiced for weeks to memorize the names of all those famous paintings, the artist's name and nationality. When the big competition day arrived, we rode the school bus to Ore City High School where we won first place! Our teacher kept her word to us and had all of us Interscholastic League winners to spend the night at her lovely home as our reward!

Fun Times with Our Jones' Family Relatives

The summer after fourth grade, my parents, baby sister, Gran, and I traveled to Montgomery, Alabama to Visit Uncle Bob Jones, Aunt Liz, Janet, and Sally. Uncle Bob made a career of the Air Force, and he was stationed at Maxwell Air Force Base at the time. Our trip to Alabama took us through Vicksburg where Daddy found a dairy that made the best ice cream. Our favorite was the black walnut, which we would get in a large cup and enjoy for miles down the road. That was a routine stop each time we traveled through Mississippi.

Once in Alabama, we spent a night or two at Uncle Bob's lovely home and then traveled to Lake Martin, about an hour away, where our two families rented a lake house for the week. My uncle had purchased a deck boat, and we all enjoyed riding around on the lake and picnicking on a special little private island we found. All of us were refreshed by swimming while Uncle Bob grilled his delicious hamburgers for us. Janet, the "fish" in the family, even got Gran, who could not swim, out in the water on a raft.

Mary Evelyn was only six months old, so the playpen was brought aboard the boat and she rode in it on her tummy. Of course, my grandmother had to make sure she didn't get sunburned, so she tied a handkerchief around the baby's head as a scarf, and off we sailed for a great time together. Instead of the tan I really wanted, I suffered several days with one of the worst sunburns of my life. At the end of the week, my family went home, and I got to stay with my cousins!

Aunt Liz and Uncle Bob wanted me to learn how to swim, so the following week it was time for swimming lessons at the base pool. Janet and Sally, who already knew how to swim, took lessons as well. Aunt Liz took her beach bag with some snacks and sat at the shallow end of the pool. She was ready to come rescue me when she looked up on the first day, and my instructor had us lined up ready to go off the high diving board! Those swimming skills were a gift so that I can always be safe and maneuver myself in the water.

Mother also had the gift of hospitality. After we moved from the small house, Daddy and Gran took it as a rental house. Nearly every woman who lived in that house loved to come over to drink coffee at Mother's kitchen table. I guess that God anointed that kitchen years before when she and Mrs. Elrod had visited there together! She always welcomed the neighbor lady and her children. Years later, after I became an adult, Sandra, one of those former neighbors, told Mother, "My family will be in heaven because of you."

Although Mother was a full-time homemaker, she used her teaching skills and found it very rewarding. There were years when she was the youth leader at the First Assembly of God. Then there were a number of students she tutored at our home. Debbie was a little girl from our church who could not speak or hear. When Mother taught her how to read lips, her whole face would light up when she would talk using her new skills. Mother also taught several talented singers some voice lessons. She had the ability to love and equip each student to improve their skills and help them enjoy their life more!

Fun Times in Junior Girl Scouts

When we were in the sixth grade, Mrs. Jordan suggested that our Girl Scout Troop begin working together to make enough money for us to travel to Washington D.C. the summer after 8th grade. We had car washes, spaghetti dinners, rummage sales, and the annual cookie sale, as we planned for the big trip over a two-year period. During that time, we were also having meetings, earning badges, and making contributions through service projects in our community.

Some of my favorite activities we did were hikes and picnics. We would meet at *Netco Store,* downtown on Saturday morning with our picnic lunch. A routine purchase in the right season was a pomegranate from inside the store, and we would walk down the road eating those little fruits. As we walked along, we sang, "I'm happy when I'm hiking, pack upon my back, With a right-good friend, till the journey's end, Ten, twenty, thirty, forty, fifty miles a day," or "The ants go marching one by one hurrah, hurrah..." We would hike until we arrived at Mrs. Jordan's farm, and then we would have our picnic and a meeting.

Entering junior high was a big deal for several reasons. We would have lockers and change classes. The girls could be cheerleaders or in the pep squad and the boys could play football and basketball. We continued to be departmentalized, but that year, we, the students, would go to the teacher instead of the teacher coming to us. I was crushed when I made my first C in Math on my report card in seventh grade!

In junior high, we could run for an office on the student council. As a seventh grader, I ran for President; my friends Suzy and Debi ran for Vice President and Secretary. Our "ticket" did not win, but we did our best and learned a little about the election process.

In the fall of 1970, I entered the 8th grade at Paul H. Pewitt Jr. High. That was the first year that Pewitt School included the campus on Highway 67 as well as the campus that was formerly Carver High School, the all-black school before integration. Fifth through eighth grade was relocated to the former Carver School building, and the eighth-grade class was like the "seniors" there.

Mr. W. C. Beasley was my homeroom and math teacher. He was willing to help me understand the new math concepts. One of the highlights of my eighth-grade year was working in the Principal's Office for Mr. Giles and his secretary, Mrs. Robertson.

In the fall of eighth grade, Mother and Daddy announced to us that they were going to have another baby. When God answers prayer, he is extravagant! I prayed and received a baby sister; now, maybe God would send a brother!

In April of my eighth-grade year, Daddy woke me about 3:00 a.m. to tell me that he was taking Mother to the hospital, leaving me to stay with Mary Evelyn, who was four years, six months. Gran went to the hospital to be with my parents. Sometime later that day, a phone call came. Mother had given birth to a healthy baby boy who they named David Victor Moore. Because my Daddy was an only child, David was the only one who could carry on the Moore name, and that was very important to my parents. When I told Mama Vissering, who stayed with me and Mary Evelyn while we waited, she replied, "The Lord did that!"

I recall that David was born on Easter weekend. Mother had made blue Easter dresses for Mary Evelyn and me. We wore them to our Church on Easter Sunday, and then Daddy carried us to the hospital to see David and Mother and to model our dresses for her.

The following month, May 1971, we had our eighth grade graduation, which was a very special time for me and my class. High school was in full view, and we were very excited.

After two years of working, saving, and planning, June 1971 arrived and Girl Scout Troop 108 was ready for our long-awaited trip to Washington, D.C.. Dorothy and J.W. Jordan, Margaret, H.C. Griffin, and their young son, Buddy, and six excited Girl Scouts, Jan Jordan, Martha Griffin, Rhoda Ranes, Debra Higgins, Brenda Parker, and I were about to get to know each other a lot better! We traveled in two cars and rotated where we sat each time we stopped. The trip through Tennessee and the Smokey Mountains and the Carolinas was some of my favorites. We finally arrived in Alexandria, Virginia at our hotel. By this time, the U.S. Air Force had transferred Uncle Bob and Aunt Liz and their family to Alexandria, Virginia where Uncle Bob was stationed at the Pentagon.

When we arrived at our hotel, there was an ice chest full of Cokes with a welcome sign! Then we were invited to their home for dinner one evening, which was a special time for us all. Mrs. Jordan wanted us to see everything in Washington, and we nearly did! Special places we visited were The Smithsonian Institution, The Washington Monument, The Lincoln Memorial, The Jefferson Monument, Mt. Vernon, Arlington Cemetery, where we watched the changing of the guard, and The White House. It was an awesome, educational trip, and we still spoke to each other and functioned as a troop after riding together 1500 miles there and back!

I returned to my small hometown and wonderful family with a new love and appreciation for our Founding Fathers and our American history. I continued to enjoy my summer vacation from school, and to help my mother with a new baby brother and a little sister. Mother, who worked hard to take care of her family, continued to model a life of dedication and faithfulness to God and to us.

CHAPTER 3

MY GRANDMOTHERS

"The boundary lines have fallen for me in pleasant places, I have a godly heritage."
(Psalms 16.6).

"What a Friend we have in Jesus, all our sins and griefs to bear, what a privilege to carry everything to God in prayer." Gran's favorite hymn, written by Joseph M. Scriven and Charles C. Converse, echoes in my spirit as I remember my wonderful grandmother. Her baby grand piano occupied her front bedroom in that special old farmhouse. Many nights she bathed me from head to toe, as I stood in a cane-bottomed chair in her kitchen; then she carried me "piggyback" to her featherbed, where she tucked me in. Then she sat down on the piano bench and played me old hymns and old love songs like "My Blue Heaven '' before I went to sleep. Gran was a woman of great love, faith, and endurance.

Gran, Hattie Bell Vissering Moore, was born in January 1898 and was the first daughter of twelve children born to Lillie Nora (Mama) and H. J. Vissering (Papa). Papa and Mama made Gran their babysitter because after her they had ten more children. Mama couldn't do all the work by herself. Gran once said, "I started rocking babies when I was so short I had to put my feet up against the wall to move the rocking chair back and forth."

My Grandmother grew up with farmer-rancher parents, and she learned a strong work ethic. Cooking for a large family without the modern conveniences of indoor plumbing and running water, milking and feeding cows, raising livestock, flower gardening, feeding chickens, planting, maintaining and harvesting a vegetable garden made for a lot of work.

It was April 6, 1917, and Gran was nineteen when the United States declared war on Germany, entering WWI. She had a boyfriend named Artice Jackson, who joined the war effort. At some point, Gran left home for North Texas State Teachers College with only three dresses; she was the only child of her family who went to college. However, after she had been at school for only a short time, her sister, Alvena, got very sick, even near death; Gran left college with a 98 GPA and went back to her family home in Bagwell, Texas to take care of her beloved sister.

The greatest part of our nation was involved in the war effort; men went off to war and lots of women filled their former positions. Times were hard. The Spanish Flu was a pandemic that swept across the world and infected 500 million people, resulting in 50,000,000 deaths! If that wasn't enough, Gran got word that her boyfriend, Artice Jackson, was killed in the war. With all the death and disease going on in the world, my grandmother endured a difficult emotional struggle.

On November 11, 1918, World War I ended; it had lasted four years. People celebrated in the streets in New York, Washington, D.C., and Paris.

Papa Vissering moved his family to Naples, Texas

The Vissering Family left Bagwell in January 1919 and moved by train to Naples, Texas to their new home and 500-acre ranch. Gran was only 21, and still single, when she came to her new hometown.

Sometime after that, she met the tall, handsome barber, Cluren Ross Moore. He was much older than her — by eleven years — and was born July 1887. His parents, Kibbell and Annie Moore, were both residents of Naples. Mr. Moore had also served his country in the 34th Infantry, 7th Division, WWI. He was in the Argonne Forest of France when the war ended.

Gran was twenty-six when she married my grandfather, Cluren Ross Moore, in October 1924. She gave birth to my dad at home in June 1928.

Unfortunately, Granddaddy Moore died suddenly on April 28, 1930. Since I never knew my grandfather, it was special to me to find an old newspaper clipping about him. His sister-in-law, Amelia Vissering, described Cluren Moore in an obituary/tribute she submitted to my hometown paper, *The Monitor*,

On Monday night, April 28 the Grim Reaper stole on us unawares and snatched from us a dear husband, father, son and brother, Cluren. He was ever tender, loving, thoughtful and kind to everyone and made of his home and family a shrine. We do not yet understand the Lord's motive in taking him from the family to whom he meant so much, but we do know he is now with the heavenly hosts, beckoning to us from the other shore...

Gran loved her little son, who was only twenty-two months, and preferred his welfare in growing up to her own comforts. For that reason, she never married again, although, according to her sister, Rose, Gran did have the opportunity to do so!

My grandmother, a single mother during the depression, did whatever it took to provide all that was needed to grow a boy into a mature, godly man. She read him Bible stories from Hurlburt's Stories from the Bible, took him to The Methodist Church where she was a Sunday School teacher. She developed his character by teaching him scriptures to live by and with a spanking when he disobeyed her.

To earn money, she did a variety of jobs through the years, which included raising and milking cows, making and selling butter, even "mailing" it as far away as Dallas! Gran knew how to stretch a dollar. She worked at various jobs, including the OPA office during the war and was determined that her son would have a college education!

I was the little "daughter" that Gran never had, and she was my second mother! When I was very young, Gran started talking to me about being an "individualist." She challenged me to be different. "The people who don't like you don't matter anyway," she would say. On the wall of one of her bedrooms hung a wooden plaque with a Bible scripture, "If God be for us, who can be against us" (Romans 8:31). My parents taught me a lot, but it was my grandmother who really instilled in me, "Stand if you stand alone." She would also say, "You and God make a majority." Those truths have been necessary and helpful foundation stones in my life.

The Missing Dentures

My parents always invited Gran to go with us to visit Uncle Bob and Aunt Liz. When I was six years old, she traveled with us in our blue and white 58 Chevrolet (with no air conditioning), from Texas to Sacramento, California to visit the Jones Family. She had very fair complexion; anytime she was going near the sun, she would wear a long-sleeve white shirt. Somewhere between Arizona and California, Gran realized her dentures were missing! To get the teeth, we had to drive all the way back to the hotel where we had spent the night.

Several years later, Uncle Bob was stationed in Montgomery, Alabama. We were enjoying our visit with them when Gran could not find her partial plates! After eating, she would always discreetly remove them from her mouth, and put them into a napkin on the table. When someone would clean off the table, they would pick up the used napkins and put them in the trash. Gran offered a reward to us three girls, Janet, Sally, and I, if we could find her teeth. We really wanted to earn the money, but we were unable to uncover them. Finally, one morning, just before the garbage truck arrived, Daddy went through the trash barrel outside, and there, about halfway down, was a napkin with Gran's teeth wrapped inside!

It wasn't only on trips that Gran's teeth had a way of disappearing! Mother was a fast worker, especially at cleaning off the table. One evening after dinner, she gathered up all the napkins and put them in the wood cook stove to burn. Guess what? Gran's teeth were in one of those napkins!

She put her teeth in a glass of water on the mantle at home at night. Just before going to bed, she wanted to put out the fire. She grabbed that glass of water and into the flames went her teeth! I know her dentist loved to see her coming! Finally, several dollars later, someone decided to buy her a plastic box to keep her newest partial plates in!

Gran watched over my diet very carefully because she didn't want me to ever own "teeth that could be lost!" She carried me to the dentist and tried to help me avoid foods with a high sugar content. She loved pecans so she used them to make everything taste better. If we did eat a piece of candy, she would put a pecan with it. For some reason she kept her black walnuts in the henhouse with a hammer nearby; when she was ready for a snack, she had everything she needed at her fingertips.

Fresh vegetables and fruit were a daily part of our diet. My favorite food from the garden was corn on the cob, and I could eat three or four long ears at one sitting. When my sister was born, my Aunt Lois Brown said, "Now you are going to have somebody to fight with over the wishbone!" I promptly replied, "No, I will have to fight with her over the corn on the cob!"

Gran's Testimony

Our church offered an opportunity for people to stand up and give a brief testimony on Sunday or Wednesday nights. Gran got emotional easily, but she often stood, said a few words, and recited a favorite scripture. Two of those verses that I will always remember are: Psalms 19:14, "Let the words of my mouth, and the meditation of my heart, be acceptable in thy sight, Oh Lord, my strength, and my redeemer." Psalms 103:1-2 is "Bless the Lord, O my soul: and all that is within me, bless his holy name. Bless the Lord, O my soul, and forget not all his benefits..." I am reminded of the many "benefits" and blessings that come to us from having a godly heritage, and especially the many benefits that come to us from living by God's guidelines for abundant life! Many have never heard the good news at all; I have been blessed to come from generations who have shared God's love with me. Their lives are truly a legacy of faith!

Gran had a strong love for her whole family. She passed that on to me with her stories of days gone by and through her actions. She shared a lot of family history, how her father, H.J. Vissering, and his family immigrated from Germany to the St. Louis area. He then ran away from home to make a life in Texas! He wanted to live in cattle country! As we would lay down to go to sleep at night, she would tell me stories of life on the farm. My favorite were the adventures about our collie dog, Corky, and all the predators he helped to capture — possums, armadillos, and even a skunk that got under a chicken nest in the barn! I wanted to hear those same stories over and over again.

During my childhood, Mama was elderly, so it was Gran who literally kept the home fires burning in that cold farmhouse. Although there were three fireplaces, they used only one on a daily basis, and the other two only at Christmas. Most mornings, Gran would be up very early to milk the cows and do her outside chores. Then she would come in to build a big fire so Mama could sit near it and stay warm while she dressed. When needed, Gran would carry a new heavy back stick from the front porch to the fireplace in the morning. With the room warming up for Mama, she would go to the kitchen to cook breakfast on the wood stove or hotplate.

One day when I was a girl, Uncle George, Gran's brother, brought a new electric stove to her and Mama. When he backed his truck up to the front porch to unload it, Mama saw it and said, "Don't you bring that thing in here!"

Gran modeled the commandment, "Honor your father and mother" —which is the first commandment with a promise —"that it may go well with you and that you may enjoy long life on the earth" (Ephesians 6:2-3). Mama Vissering didn't always hear well and would need things repeated; sometimes she would get her feelings hurt easily if she felt someone was not filling her in or were in too big of a hurry to communicate with her. It was common for Gran to get a phone call while she was cooking. Because there were no cordless phones back then, she would come to Mama's room to answer it. When Gran's phone visit was over, Mama would want to know who that was and what they wanted. Gran would tell her a quick sentence and hurry off to the kitchen to check what was on the stove to make sure it wasn't burning; Mama wanted Gran to take time right then to tell her the details of the conversation. I was just a young girl, but I asked Gran why she didn't say something back to Mama. She said to me, "When I look at her in that casket, I don't want to have any regrets."

It was Gran who predicted that I would play the piano. Even at the hospital, she looked at me and said, "That baby has piano playing fingers."

Gran was a pianist on Sunday morning for church. She would allow me to sit in the metal folding chair near her piano, where I felt very important.

When we began attending First Assembly, I would watch Mrs. Elrod at the piano, and she strongly influenced my desire to become a pianist. I would sit on the second pew from the front, beside Gran. With an open hymnal on my lap, I would pretend to "tickle the ivories" like Mrs. Elrod. She could play by ear and used the entire keyboard; that became the desire of my heart.

I would go to Gran's house, sit at her baby grand piano and pretend to play. My cousin, Martha, and I would "play church" together there. I would be the pianist and she was the minister of music!

At the age of eight, when I was beginning second grade, I started taking piano lessons from my cousin, Barbara Manna, who lived in Daingerfield, Texas. With a degree in music from Texas Woman's University, she was very qualified to help me become a musician. Three of my cousins, Martha, Kim, and Kristi, also took their individual lessons the same day that I did. We had a carpool. Every Monday after school, we had a regular routine. The weekly music lesson trips were managed by Mother, Aunt Rose, and Carolyn — our mothers. As it was their turn, each of them would bring us an after-school snack to eat as we left from the front door of Pewitt High School for our evening of piano lessons at Barbara's house.

Barbara and Frankie had a nice home in a peaceful neighborhood. While we waited for our forty-five minute lesson, we sat on their patio or in their den and did homework, talked, "raided" their crackers (we got hungry), and took walks around the block! Ever so often, Barbara, who was also a very good cook, would bake her homemade bread and give us all a hot, buttered piece to eat on our way back home! Yum! Yum! During the Christmas season, Kim, Kristi, and Martha would sing Christmas songs like "Jingle Bell Rock" and "Chestnuts" as we rode back home and enjoyed looking out the car windows at the beautiful Christmas trees glistening in the windows of homes along the route.

Barbara required us to practice the piano five hours a week. The problem was that we did not have a piano at our house. Gran had the baby grand, and Mama had an old upright, the one Gran practiced on when she was a girl.

Every day after school, I would ride the bus to the farm where I would do my hour of piano practice. Mama's room was the warm room, so I practiced on the upright, but many evenings I still felt that my fingers would freeze before I finished.

With her knowledge of music, Gran was able to help me if I had trouble learning a song. By the beginning of fourth grade, there had been two years of going to the farm for the piano practice routine. Homework was heavy and evenings were long. Mother and I were very weary of the schedule and were ready to buy our own instrument.

So, as fourth grade approached, Daddy, Mother, Gran, and I went shopping for the perfect piano. As you may imagine, it was a big day! Finally, after much looking and comparative shopping, we found just the piano at Manor Music Company in Texarkana. From a child's perspective, pianos can be a lot like perfume—after you've tried several, they all start to run together! Daddy and Gran finally decided, and I agreed, that the "Sohmer" piano was the best for me.

Daddy even called the company in New York to talk with them about the "investment" he was making for his daughter! Delivered to our front porch in a large wooden crate, the beautiful cherry stringed instrument with its wonderful tone quality and easy touch was quite a treasured piece of furniture in our home. I loved being able to go home after school and into my own living room to learn my piano pieces.

I took ten years of piano from Barbara, and advanced to play hymns and advanced classical pieces.

Is There a Pianist in the House?

Brother Elrod resigned as our pastor the summer before I was beginning seventh grade. Mrs. Elrod and Paula had been our pianist and organist for years. Who would play the piano? Daddy was already the song leader, and by that time, I could play well in the key of C and G. So, Daddy and I sat down and picked out all the songs in the hymnal in those two keys, and the music continued on. The first song we sang was "There is a fountain filled with blood, drawn from Immanuel's veins, and sinners plunged beneath that flood, lose all their guilty stains." The second song was "Bringing in the sheaves, bringing in the sheaves, we shall come rejoicing, bringing in the sheaves." I continued as the pianist of First Assembly of God Church until 1975 when I left home for college.

Barbara continued to give me lessons through my senior year in high school. During those years, I played for two recitals a year: one at Christmas and then a formal one in the spring. I really dreaded recitals, except for the formal dresses we could wear and the corsages I would sometimes get. My desire was to play so perfectly but learning something from memory to play on a stage before all those people made me very nervous. Barbara would stand behind the curtain listening intently as each student performed their memorized piece. I could tell when someone hit a wrong note; whether she was nervous or pleased at a student's performance showed on her face! I always hoped she would have good expressions when she heard my recital piece through the stage curtain. In the spring of my senior year, Teresa, another senior student, and I played a senior recital for closest friends and family members in Barbara's living room.

Being a pianist has been a lifelong joy for me. When I was growing up, nearly every little girl, and some boys, took piano lessons. Since that time, so many things have changed. Parents have their children involved in so many other activities that will basically end for them when they finish going to high school. Piano lessons were truly a lifetime gift from my parents, grandmother, and teacher, and a skill that is useful in many settings and just for pleasure. Its enjoyment does not end when school is out!

In our family, becoming a musician is part of the legacy of the good life we want to pass on to our children who have an ability for it. My grandmother was a musician, my maternal grandfather was a drummer, both my daddy and mother were singers, and I became a musician. As a little girl, I always migrated to any sort of keyboard. Proverbs says, "Train up a child in the way he should go, and when he is older, he will not depart from it."(Proverbs 22:6). God wants us to look at our child's interests and abilities and assist them in developing those. Our Creator has given each of us different gifts to fulfill us, to equip The Body of Christ, and to make a difference in the world!

The Kitchen

Gran spent a lot of time in her kitchen working and preparing delicious food. It's amazing how those flavors and aromas can take us back in time to a special food enjoyed or a fragrance that evokes a significant memory. One Saturday morning as we were enjoying our leisure, I cooked some bacon in the black skillet, made Bill an egg, and broiled some English muffins. Some apricot preserves left over from a previous recipe looked like just the thing to spread on my muffin. As the breakfast hit my tastebuds, I was taken back to my Gran's kitchen! She would buy dried apricots, steam them, and serve them as spread for our toast. Apricots have a wonderful flavor, are very good for us, and are a great change from the more common jellies of grape or strawberry. Another regular staple on her table for breakfast was her canned fig preserves. It was delicious on toast made in the wood cookstove oven! Her chicken and dressing was wonderful, and my mother always made Gran's recipe.

My grandmother milked a cow every day and made her own butter by churning the milk and molding it with a wooden mold. She frequently had ice cream to eat in the summer by mixing up her banana ice cream and then keeping it in metal ice trays in the freezer. It was the perfect treat on a hot day in July! Cooking was one way my grandmother used her gift of hospitality.

She raised the chicken, killed it, cooked it, and then prepared a big chicken stew, serving it with crackers, pickles, cheese, dessert, and iced tea. Then she invited the Paul Elrod and Robert Elrod families and our family for an evening of food and fellowship. It was great fun on a cold and crisp winter night.

Some of Gran's recipes I remember were her "Butter Roll" dessert and her banana pudding. No box of instant pudding can take the place of that "cooked from scratch" by my grandmother. I just wanted to eat the warm pudding by itself and forget the vanilla wafers and meringue!

Gran and I bonded because she loved me and took time for me. She took time to listen and then to do the things with me that I enjoyed. She took me to Texarkana shopping and out to eat at Bryce's Cafeteria. Since we both loved jewelry, we would window shop at the jewelry stores there. She told me when I got old enough, she would buy me a watch. When I was in the seventh grade, Gran kept her promise and gave me a beautiful gold Timex watch with a square mother-of-pearl face. I cherished the gift and wore it for years.

The last tangible thing my grandmother did for me before she died was to send me to a Billy Graham Crusade. In September 1971, I had just entered the ninth grade when First Baptist Church chartered a bus to take a group to hear the famous evangelist in person. Although Gran did not go, she paid for me to travel with the church to the new Texas Stadium. Billy Graham boldly proclaimed the Gospel of Jesus Christ each time he stood behind the pulpit and thousands of people accepted his invitation to receive Jesus as their Savior and Lord!

Gran was a very influential woman in my life. She modeled discipline, hard work, a strong love of family, perseverance, endurance, and a friendship with Jesus. Although she went to heaven when I was only fifteen, I have continued to draw from the well of knowledge, love, and experiences that she imparted to me.

It is my desire to share with each of my grandchildren the same kind of loving, interactive relationship that my grandmother and I enjoyed, and to teach them about Jesus and the many life lessons they need to be strong, faith-filled Christians. One thing I knew about Gran —she drew her strength from God because she knew Him personally!

MAMA VISSERING, GRAN'S MOTHER AND MY GREAT-GRANDMOTHER

"...You have given me an inheritance reserved for those who fear your name." (Psalm 61:5).

As the short, small-framed family matriarch entered the evening hours of her 91st birthday, she found herself in her favorite game of dominoes with one of her grandsons, Cluren Victor Moore. My great-grandmother, Lillie Nora Brem Vissering, whose name was "Mama" to her large family, was born November 22, 1877. As she played dominoes that evening, she did not know that in the background was a tape recorder set to capture her life's story as Daddy "interviewed" her. The clock on the mantle above the fireplace of Mama's room struck midnight, the domino players continued, and so did the family story.

Family History as Told by Mama in the Taped Interview

"Mama was born to (Paw) Thomas Jefferson Brem and (Maw) Isabella Martha (McGraw) Brem. Paw was named after the president, and Brem is a German name. He was a painter; he made his own paint. Whenever he put it on the walls it stayed there for fifty years! He lived in Clarksville (Texas).

When asked what happened to his paint recipe, Mama shared this little explanation: Paw gave his recipe to his daughter, Kitty, and she put it in the bottom of her trunk. John (last name left out), her husband's nephew, went to Kitty's house one day while she was gone and poured everything in her trunk out on the floor and found that recipe and got it. It wasn't very long...until he had his house painted and everything done! Sold it, I guess, and bought a beautiful home. He treated Kitty mean. Paw made his own paint out of linseed oil, and I don't know what else... John just set himself up!

Mama had four sisters, Kitty, Dora, Belle, and Annie: one brother, Jake. Maw had been married before and had one son, Buck. Paw's three sons from his previous marriage were Lee, Carrie, and Bill. Bill was a good man. Lee said if anybody would live by a certain chapter in the Bible, they would go to heaven. Lee read the Bible, he did. Bill never did get married.

Paw (Thomas Jefferson Brem) came from Bremen, Germany, and it was named for him.

Mama married Harry James Vissering (Papa), (born May 11, 1875) a native of Germany. Papa lacked only two weeks graduating from German school. When his father came to the United States, they wanted him to let Harry James stay two weeks longer, but he would not allow him to do so.

The Vissering family settled in Alton, Illinois, just across the river from St. Louis, Missouri (when Papa was about fourteen). Papa had an uncle that lived in Alton, Illinois. He had several siblings: Annie, Rose, Bertha, Josephine, Minnie, Fred, and George (who died when he was three years old).

Papa wanted to come to Texas. He came to Texas two or three times and his daddy would come down here and get him and take him back! He wanted to come to Texas; he wanted to go where they had cattle ranches. He wanted to come where there were cows!

He came to Old Man George Tuckers, and Mama and her family lived a half a mile from George Tucker. He met Mr. Tucker in Clarksville and got to talking to him, and Papa wanted to go home with him. He said he was looking for a hand, and Papa wanted to go home with him and work. He gave Papa eight dollars a month and his board and rations.

Old Man George Tucker went to the Methodist church, and we did too; that's where I met him (Papa), at the Union Church. Any denomination could preach there. Papa asked Mrs. Tucker, "Which one must he go with: me, Kitty or Dora?" She told him to go with me; he called her "Ma" all the time. The Tucker's had several children, but she told him to go with Mama, and they were older than him.

Mama and Papa got in the buggy and went to Clarksville and got married and nobody didn't know it and even Dora didn't know it. Dora just cried and cried and cried. They had a livery stable at Clarksville where they had horses to let out. They got a big bay horse and went to Clarksville and were married by a justice of the peace. Nobody saw them get married but John Tucker, Mrs. Tucker's oldest boy.

Papa never kissed Mama before they married. No siree. People didn't do that! There were three girls on Peter's Prairie that did that. There were three girls who weren't very nice (And she gave their names after all those years!).

The happy couple set up housekeeping on Peter's Prairie, seven miles north of Clarksville in a little house on Maw's place. They had eight quilts. Their furniture consisted of a bought cook stove, a homemade table, and a bed. Livestock they owned consisted of a cow and a calf that Maw gave them. Papa didn't have any stock at that time. He rode Mr. Tucker's little bay mule a half a mile, crossing a little creek named Bertha.

Mama went to a little schoolhouse with wooden shutters. She studied a pretty good-size geography and a blue-back speller. It had a lot of big, old, long words in it. She wished she still had her blue-back speller. "Incompatibility" was the longest word in there! She was a good speller. She didn't like grammar.

Mama and Papa had twelve children together, three boys and nine girls: Fred, Hattie, Jack, Irene, Lillie Josephine, George, Mary Mildred (after a president's wife), Alvena, Tom (Vera Virginia), Rose Evelyn, Baby Ruth (Martha Ruth). (one baby born to them lived only three hours).

Mama and Papa moved to Naples in 1919."

Naples was originally a community called Belton or Wheatville, Texas. It was there that Papa and Mama worked together on their farm/ranch and parented their large family. One of the reasons for Papa's success is Mama was a good wife and mother for his children! According to our family historian and cousin, Pat Tomberlain, "Mama Vissering did the bookkeeping and banking, and handled milk and butter sales. She ran a large household, doing the cooking, gardening and canning without running water or electricity. She also nursed sick tenants and their children, repaired harnesses and made her family's clothes. Even in the heat of summer, she cooked three meals a day on a wood stove for up to 25 people."

Papa and his three sons worked together raising cattle and mules. Family members who knew Papa said he was a man of integrity and strength. The Visserings attended The Methodist Church.

Eight of Mama and Papa's children lived to be adults, marry and have families of their own in Morris County, TX.

Papa Vissering was able to live his dream as a Texas rancher! He brought the first registered Angus bulls to Morris County. When he died in 1940 at nearly 65 years old, he was running over 500 head of cattle and 105 head of horses and mules. Because he said, "I want to be buried where I can see the cows come up," Mama traded a piece of her land with someone to get the Vissering Family cemetery plot near Wheatville Cemetery.

One of Papa's best friends and business associates was Senator Morris Sheppard. A few weeks after Papa's passing and typed on his "United States Senate" Letterhead, Senator Sheppard wrote the following letter to Mama Vissering:

Washington, D.C.

April 10, 1940

Dear Mrs. Vissering:

The passing of Mr. Vissering was a source of deepest sorrow to me, and I send you and his loved ones my profoundest sympathy.

No man I have ever known had finer and more lovable characteristics. I shall miss the trips I have taken with him in the fields and the woods from time to time. His conversations with me revealed his love of the good and the true in human life. He had those fundamental attributes of true manhood which compose the foundations of what is best in civilization. He had a true reverence for his Maker and is with Him now.

May that same Creator guard and guide you through the years.

With all good wishes, I am

Truly your friend,

Morris Sheppard (his name signed in his handwriting)

A Few of My Favorite Memories About Mama and Papa's Children, My Great Aunts and Uncles and my Grandmother

Uncle Fred and Aunt Amelia Vissering

Uncle Fred was Mama and Papa's oldest son. I was not privileged to know him because he died before I was born. I understood that he very much followed in his father's footsteps as he raised livestock and lived close to the land. From listening to Gran, I picture Uncle Fred sitting tall in a saddle on a good horse, riding into the bottom pasture to look after his livestock, whether to feed them, protect them from rising water, or to bring them to a corral to be doctored in some way. He was a very hard worker.

I remember his wife, Aunt Amelia. She and Uncle Fred had four children: Geraldine, Betty, Fred, Jr. (Son), and Anne. When I was a girl, Aunt Amelia lived with her children, Son and Sue, and was a quilter. Aunt Amelia was a very smart lady, and she is the one who wrote the treasured obituary about my Grandaddy Moore that I shared in an earlier chapter.

Hattie Vissering Married Cluren Ross Moore

Hattie was the second child and oldest daughter of Mama and Papa. You know now that she married Cluren Ross Moore and they had my Daddy. Because my grandfather died early in their marriage, my grandmother had moved in with Mama and Papa when she was a young woman and worked on the ranch and in the house for the rest of her life. Gran was a very hard worker. She was there to take care of Mama Vissering in her elderly years. She considered it an honor and a privilege to do so. She loved her parents, brothers and sisters and all her family.

Uncle George and Aunt Dell Vissering

Uncle George was a pleasant, fun-loving man and definitely a horse trader. He had some livestock and a vending machine business. One evening, Daddy and I dropped by to see him and Aunt Dell, and I can vividly remember Uncle George was sitting at his kitchen table counting all the money he had taken in that day, and I was fascinated by it! Uncle George and Aunt Dell had two children: Patsy and Harry George. They also owned The Dairy Ette in Naples. Everyone loved to go there to get ice cream and a hamburger! Aunt Dell was a sweet and loving, nurturing lady, very much a keeper at home, a great mother and grandmother, a good cook, and seamstress. When I saw Aunt Dell and heard her Southern accent, I always felt she loved me and genuinely cared about me.

Uncle Jack and Aunt Jessie Vissering

Uncle Jack was a very tall, slim, reserved man who smoked a cigar. Like his father, he had land and livestock. When Daddy needed cattle to go to the sale barn, Uncle Jack was the one who brought the big truck and carried them to the sale. Aunt Jessie was a sweet lady, very much the homemaker who worked hard cooking, canning their garden vegetables, sewing beautiful items, growing pretty flowers, and always made me feel loved when we went to their home. Daddy annually took me to Uncle Jack and Aunt Jessie's house on Halloween to trick-or-treat! They always gave those fun orange marshmallow candies. They had three children: Marie, Wesley, and John Paul.

Aunt Irene (Sis) Married Jonah Harte

Aunt Sis married Jonah Harte, and they had four children: Clayton, Forrest, Ikey, and Carolyn. Aunt Sis was a very sweet, pretty lady, with a very pleasant disposition and the most beautiful snow-white hair. She lived on Wheatville Road between us and Mama Vissering in the cutest two-story log house. Her husband and three sons built it themselves.

Like Gran, Aunt Sis played the piano. I spent time with her when she came to spend the night with Mama and I with Gran.

Mama had a storm cellar in her backyard. When a storm came up, we would go in there and stay until it passed over. The roof was made of dirt, and it finally collapsed. Then we got to share Aunt Sis's storm cellar. Her grandchildren, Kim, Kristi, and Ben, were there too waiting! I sure loved the adventure—but not the storm!

Aunt Rose and Uncle Marvin Tomberlain

Aunt Rose and Uncle Marvin married in the 30's and had five children: Barbara, Charlotte, Lillian, Pat, and Martha.

I was privileged to spend a lot of time at Aunt Rose's house. I would go with Gran and Mama when they dropped by to visit. Aunt Rose's youngest daughter, Martha, was only three years older than me, and we were very close playmates. I spent many fun and happy nights and days there with Martha as we played dress up and office. Our favorite thing was to take over Aunt Rose's beautifully decorated Victorian living room for our Tammy dolls and their "elaborate" homes! We would spend hours setting them all up.

About 2:00 a.m., we enjoyed snacks in the kitchen and laughed a lot as the night progressed. After sleeping very late the next day, we got up and told Aunt Rose all about our fun.

Uncle Marvin worked shift work at Lone Star Steel Company, as did so many in the Vissering family. It was steady work and good pay and put the bacon on most tables in Morris County in those days

Aunt Rose was a great mother, cook, seamstress, and a Sunday School teacher at First Baptist Church for 62 years. As each one of her siblings passed away, she took their adult children under her wing and gave them a mother's love!

Aunt Tom and Uncle Vernon Camp

Aunt Tom and Uncle Vernon made their home in Daingerfield. They had two children, Virginia Ann and Phil. Uncle Vernon worked at Lone Star Steel too, and Aunt Tom was a loving mother, homemaker, and an excellent seamstress. When I was engaged to be married, Aunt Tom made my beautiful going-away dress! Aunt Tom and Aunt Vena were very close sisters, loved to play Bridge and 42 with their friends, and during their last years even were able to be neighbors with adjoining backyards! How neat is that!

Aunt Vena and Uncle Murray Nelson

Aunt Vena and Uncle Murray were a sweet couple who worked as beautician and barber in the late 50's and early 60's, in the same building in downtown Daingerfield. Uncle Murray had one of several chairs with some other barbers in the front, and Aunt Vena had her beauty shop in the back part. They kept our family looking well-groomed, and we had fun visiting at the same time.

My aunt gave me my first haircut when I was seven years old and at the very end of first grade. It took her about two hours to cut it. When I went back to school the next day, my classmates thought I was a new student! About eight years later, my little brother, David, sat in Uncle Murray's barber chair for his first haircut. David was Uncle Murray's last customer before retirement!

Aunt Vena was a very sweet, easy-going lady, and I loved to hear her laugh. Uncle Murray loved to tease and was easy going as well, so they were well matched. Their daughter, Gail, had a little girl named Melinda, who was only three years younger than me. Aunt Vena would invite Melinda and me to spend the night with her, and we had fun playing together.

Melinda and I both wanted a baby sister or brother. In March 1966, I remember going to see Gail in the Lake of the Pines Hospital. She had just given birth to Melinda's little sister, Marcia. Melinda was nearly seven years old. I was nearly ten, and I remember saying to Gail, "I'm going to get me a little sister or brother." Little did I realize that my mother was pregnant then and that I truly would have a little sister by Christmas!

*   *   *

I was one of Mama's great-grandchildren. Because Gran lived with her and took care of her, I was with her on a weekly basis doing my piano practice, helping Daddy with his cows there on the farm, and spending the nights. Mama was a very sweet person to me, and I loved her. I enjoyed hearing her talk when she was playing someone a game of dominoes, and she was very competitive! She played to win! I remember that she had a cute sense of humor!

It is hard for me to imagine Mama as a young woman because when I was born, she was 78. However, she was still very much a voice for the truth. She had a strong faith in God and really believed that she would live until The Second Coming of Jesus!

Mama's Wise Words:

The Bible says, "But I say unto you, that every idle word that men shall speak, they shall give account thereof in the day of judgment" (Matthew 12:36).

"Keep your nakedness hidden." Spoken if a female member of her family came in with shorts or a skirt she thought was revealing too much!

"A whistling girl and a crowing hen always come to some bad end."

"A woman's hair is her glory. Then why do women want to cut their glory off?"

My cousin, Kim, reminded us that Mama would softly say to her great-grandchildren as she "felt prompted": "Do you know the Lord?"

Recently, I was literally climbing out of bed, and a little song that Mama would sing came to me. I had been going through a struggle, and those words from so long ago started going over and over in my mind, "Pray and pray and pray, Night will turn to day. If you pray and pray and pray, night will turn to day."

The Chiropractor, Shopping, and Treats

Gran and Mama Vissering went every two weeks to a chiropractor in Mt. Pleasant named Dr. Matkin. They claimed he kept them going strong. A highlight for me was riding with them for their appointment and shopping day. After their "adjustment" from the good Doc, Gran would do her errands, which included shopping for fabric, bakery items, and groceries.

One of our favorite stops in the spring and summertime was at the A&W Drive-In to get a root beer in those frosted glass mugs! They would bring it out to our car and put it on a little tray they clipped to our window. Nothing tastes better on a hot summer day than sipping an ice-cold A&W root beer while we sat parked in their covered parking area. Even Mama would have a little root beer. Mama had a thing about drinking Cokes. She would not do it. She claimed that one time Papa filled a glass with Coke and put a piece of meat in it. When he came back the next morning, the meat was gone. Her conclusion was that if it would do that to a piece of meat, then it would eat your stomach too!

Before going back home to Naples, we always went to Safeway to buy their groceries. My favorite snack was Cheetos. (Yes, they've been making those that long!) Gran would buy me a big bag, but I acted very selfish and didn't want to share. When she gently rebuked me for not wanting to share with her after she bought them for me, I felt very convicted. I would extend the bag her way so she could get a handful, but I still didn't "feel" generous!

It is true that Gran and Mama were seldom sick. They were at church at First Assembly of God in Naples nearly every Sunday morning. Gran would drive Mama over to visit Aunt Vena, Aunt Tom, and families. They often invited them to spend the night and go home the next day. Mama was very much a creature of habit and wanted to sleep in her own bed!

A Big Disguise Surprise

One Halloween, Daddy decided he was going to pull a prank on all of Mama's children. He dressed her up in his coveralls! He stuffed them with pillows to disguise her, and then put a witch mask on her face! He took her to her children's houses trick-or-treating! When they went to (Irene's) Aunt Sis's door, she became so scared when she saw Mama that she picked up a throw rug off the floor, put it in front of her, and started walking backward to get away! In his endeavor to have fun, Daddy didn't realize that Mama's disguise was so good that she could really scare her own kids. He had to reveal her to Aunt Sis and make sure she was OK before he left.

A Game-Playing Family

Mama loved to play games. When I would spend the night with her and Gran, we would play a card game called Flinch and a domino game called Freeze Out. On a cold winter night, Gran would have a fire in the fireplace. We would sit close to the hearth and eat a peeled grapefruit piece by piece while we watched "Johnny Carson," one of Gran's favorite TV shows. Then we would go on to bed and Mama would still be sitting up playing Solitaire. All of her children were big Domino, 42, and Bridge players. The Vissering Family seldom gathered without one of those good games going on somewhere in the house or on the front porch.

Mama's house had a big front porch all the way across. It was a family tradition that every Sunday afternoon her children, grandchildren, and great-grandchildren would come out after church and lunch for a visit together. The porch would accommodate more people with chairs and benches, and the adults could watch us kids playing around in the yard.

We entertained ourselves with games of Red Rover, Mother May I, Hide-and-Seek and Croquet. Sometimes we picked little black seeds that grew in the four o'clock bushes around Mama's porch. Then we would see who had the most in their hand. We hunted for eggs that Mama's chickens had laid. I would frequently have my horse, Stroller, there, and we would take turns riding him. Mama had a fear about us kids playing in the big barn. She was afraid we would get hurt there, so if she missed us, she would start asking about us kids or calling us.

Another fun thing we kids enjoyed in Mama's front yard on Sunday afternoon was a game somebody made up. There was a large horse apple tree just across the road from Mama's house. We would pick up those green, milky things and put them under the back tires of the cars in the driveway and yard. When someone got ready to leave, we would run to watch them "squish" the horse apples as they backed away from Mama's house! Back then, before electronic games and cell phones, kids had to play together and be creative to entertain themselves.

Uncle Murray liked to tease us; he would call us girls "boys" instead. One of my favorite memories is one Sunday afternoon when Uncle Murray took all of us kids to get an ice cream cone at Uncle George's Dairyette, which was located on Highway 67 between Naples and Omaha. It was just a simple pleasure on a Sunday afternoon that really meant a lot to a little girl growing up!

A Vissering Merry Christmas

The story about visiting Mama's house could not be complete without describing our Vissering Christmas celebrations. Several months before December, we would find out who wanted to draw names. Forty to fifty family members would participate.

Just a few days before Christmas, Daddy would go to the woods and get the biggest Christmas tree I have ever seen in a home. A five- to ten-gallon bucket was needed to contain it. The tree would be set up in my Gran's room near her baby grand piano. Mama had some very old German ornaments that we put on the tree. About two days before Christmas, several family members would come to Mama's to help us decorate the tree after Daddy put the lights on.

On Christmas night, many of the Vissering Family members would gather, bringing their gifts, conversation, snacks, laughter, and love. It was the one time of the year when Daddy and Gran would have a fire in all three fireplaces — in Mama's room, Gran's room (the living room), and the big room. I anticipated handing out all the gifts, and there were many!

Barbara would sit down at the baby grand piano, play Christmas carols, and a group of us would sing. My memories of Christmas night with The Visserings out at Mama's are some of my favorites!

*   *   *

Mama and Papa left those who come behind them a "Dynasty of Faith." They lived their lives by God's principles and reaped the rewards. They did the right thing. They stayed together, for better or worse, and their children stayed together too. Dr. Charles Stanley says, "LOVE is spelled G-I-V-E." They attended church and taught their children about our Creator, The God of the Bible, and His Son, Jesus... And that has made all the difference!

MY MATERNAL GRANDMOTHER

"...and in her tongue is the law of kindness."
(Proverbs 31:26).

My maternal grandmother was born Bonnie Ruth Brown, and she was a very kind lady. Her family and friends called her Ruth. Her name was taken from the Biblical character in the Old Testament and means "beautiful friend." I was named after my mother and grandmother—Wanda Ruth and Bonnie Ruth. My middle name took on a whole new meaning after reading the Bible story for myself.

In the Bible story, Ruth was from the pagan culture of Moab. There was a famine in Bethlehem, so a man named Elimelech and his wife, Naomi, and their two sons, Mahlon and Kilion, moved to Moab. There, the sons took wives named Orpah and Ruth. But, Elimelech died, leaving Naomi a widow. Then, both of Naomi's sons died, leaving Orpah and Ruth as widows. Naomi decided to return to her homeland because the famine had ended. Naomi told her daughters-in-law they should go back to their mothers and hopefully find another husband. Orpah did so, but Ruth said, "'Don't ask me to leave you and turn back. Wherever you go, I will go; wherever you live, I will live. Your people will be my people, and your God will be my God. Wherever you die, I will die, and there I will be buried. May the Lord punish me severely if I allow anything but death to separate us!' When Naomi saw that Ruth was determined to go with her, she said nothing more" (Ruth 1:16-18).

Because of her faithfulness to follow Naomi and to honor and take care of her, Ruth found a new husband in Bethlehem named Boaz. Ruth's heart to be humble, loyal, submitted, teachable, and a friend earned her a place of honor! Ruth and Boaz became the parents of Obed, the grandparents of Jesse, King David's Father, and the great-grandparents of King David, placing Ruth as one of the women in the lineage of Jesus! I really love this true story from my Bible and am honored that three generations of us share Ruth's name!

*   *   *

When she was in her twenties, my maternal grandmother, Ruth, married Charles Brackett Jones of Dallas, Texas. Ruth and Charles Jones became the parents of my mother, Wanda Ruth Jones. Unfortunately, my grandfather died when Mother was four months old, leaving Mamma, Ruth Brown Jones, a widow with an infant during the heart of the depression. She remarried when Mother was about seven. Her second husband was Grady Higgins, a native of Naples and a carpenter by trade.

Besides being her namesake, my earliest memories of my maternal grandmother, Ruth, whom I called Mamma, were probably when we visited her home in Hooks, Texas. She and her second husband, whom I called Papaw, worked full-time jobs and parented my young aunt and uncle, Linda and Don, who were nine and eight years older than me.

Every three or four months on Sunday, right after church, Mother, Daddy, and I would make the 45-minute drive to eat lunch with Mamma and her family. Mother would take a dish or two, Mamma cooked everything else, and it was always delicious. One of my favorite recipes that she prepared were her candied carrots.

After lunch, Daddy and Papaw would play dominoes. Mother and Mamma would wash the dishes and talk together as they worked; there was no automatic dishwasher. Then they would sit down on the couch to rest and sometimes grab a much-needed catnap.

I would explore around outside, climbing trees and playing with any kittens because they always had one or more of those felines around. Sometimes, my aunt or uncle would take me to the school playground, which was within walking distance. Swinging high in the air on an old-fashioned swing was enjoyable to me. After that, I would give the old monkey bars a try, which took a lot of strength.

Something I looked forward to every Easter was the milk chocolate bunny that Mamma always had for me. We would eat lunch together. Then, Linda or Don would hide the dyed Easter eggs I had brought from home. I had fun hunting them by myself. I was the only grandchild until my sister, Mary Evelyn, was born in 1966 and then my brother, David, in 1971.

At Mamma and Papaw's house, cherry vanilla ice cream was a special afternoon treat. To pass the time indoors on Sunday afternoons, I would get my aunt's watercolors and make pictures at the kitchen table. I was never able to figure out how to keep those colors and the water from running together!

My Aunt Linda was very artistic, and she painted some very beautiful pictures. After graduating from Hooks High School in the 60's, she went on to North Texas State University, where she received her degree in education and became an elementary teacher.

When Donnie was growing up, he would come every summer and spend a week with us, which was a lot of fun. We introduced him to guys his age in our church, and he went to church camp with them one summer. Donnie also graduated from Hooks High and attended the University of Texas at Arlington. When he brought home the detailed projects he built for class, we always thought he deserved an A. Don became an architect.

I didn't see Mamma daily, weekly, or even monthly when I was growing up because she worked as a clerk typist five days a week at Red River Army Depot. I remember spending two nights with her—one in Hooks and one in Naples. She was very sweet to me. She always got me a birthday present; in the early years, it was usually something that I could wear and was wrapped. When I became an adult, she faithfully sent me a birthday card, a note, and a little money.

Family Reunions

Mamma's family, The Browns, had numerous reunions when I was growing up. Mamma and her siblings— Aunt Esther, Aunt Jean, Uncle Houston, Uncle Leon, Uncle Lawrence, and Uncle Oscar —and their families enjoyed meeting where they grew up; at their parents' home on the Cornett Highway, a few miles from Naples city limits. This is the same home where my mother was born in 1934 and lived with Granny and Pappy Brown.

I also have memories of reunions when The Brown Family rented a couple of lake houses near Lake of the Pines. Some would swim, some would fish, and all would enjoy visiting and eating and playing games. A highlight of those reunions for me was visiting with special cousins, Shirley and Vance Wright from California, and Cathy and Steve Brown from Dallas.

When Daddy made homemade ice cream, some of us kids took turns sitting on the top of the hand-cranked ice cream freezer to keep it steady when it started freezing and turning the crank became hard to do. There is nothing better than homemade peach ice cream on a hot summer day!

As I grew older, so did those around me. Time and age brought new seasons of life for each of us, and distance took us down unique paths that separated us. Love and loss reunites us!

Sometime in the late 60's, Grady Higgins inherited his parents' home in Naples, where Mother had lived for six years with Granny and Pawpaw Higgins. Grady and Donnie would go to

Naples frequently on weekends to work on remodeling the house, making it modern. My mother would invite them to our house on a Saturday for a nice lunch and a visit.

Their project finally completed, both Mamma and Papaw retired. Mamma had worked as a clerk typist for forty-two years! Papaw and Mamma made their move to Naples in early 1972. I was able to see my sweet grandmother more frequently and enjoy that cherry vanilla ice cream! There was a special old swing that hung from an old tree right near their back door. This was a generational joy because my Mother had done some swinging when she lived there many decades before with Granny and Pawpaw Higgins. I had the pleasure of holding the old chain in my hands while sitting on the board swing and so did my siblings and younger cousins!

*   *   *

Mamma and Papaw had a garden in their retirement years; they loved those fresh vegetables and shared with us. They had a nice pond on their property, and our family would go there to swim. It also became a baptismal place for our church.

Linda and Dan Welch, Don and Sheila Higgins, and their families came to Naples often, and we had many happy times together eating and visiting. There would always be a domino game! The younger grandchildren, Mary Evelyn and David, had fun playing with their cousins, Tamie, Tim, and Angie.

Mamma was a very attractive lady and looked especially pretty in pink or blue. My grandmother had never learned to drive. Her sister, Esther, had retired in Naples; she and Mamma had fun going places together, including The First Methodist Church, The United Methodist Women, out to eat, and shopping. One time after Bill and I married, Aunt Esther, Mamma, and Papaw made a road trip together, and they came by our house in Oak Grove, Louisiana to see us. That was special.

One humorous thing about Mamma is the way she responded to jokes. Someone would tell a joke at the table, and nearly everyone would laugh. Then the subject would change. Shortly thereafter, the punch line would hit Mamma, she would start laughing and throw her hand up in the air in excitement! Then everyone got a second laugh!

Mamma not only had good clerical skills, but she was also a great letter writer— she was the family correspondent and record keeper. She made me feel loved with her birthday cards, money gifts, her good cooking, and cherry vanilla ice cream. After I got married, it was a special day when her newsy letters arrived in our mailbox. She told us of family visitors in her home and the activities in which she, Papaw and Aunt Esther were involved. These letters were always appreciated and enjoyed by my family. We loved it that she took time to sit, and handwrite a letter, which is nearly a lost art today.

Mamma was a cheerful and compassionate lady. She and Grady celebrated their 50th Wedding Anniversary in February 1993 with a beautiful reception given by their children at the First Methodist Church parlor. He died a few months later in June.

Mamma was in a lot of pain because of osteoporosis. She was not physically able to live at home by herself. So, she spent the last ten years of her life in a nursing home. Mother went several times a week to see her mother and to see that she had the things she needed. When I was able to visit Mamma, she always had a smile for me.

Mamma loved and welcomed each one of her grandchildren and great-grandchildren, Elizabeth and Bill; Emily and Andrew Beasley; Mary Evelyn: Matthew and Joel Thomas, and Stephen Hudgens; Tamie Higgins Trammel; Payton and Tanner Kendrick; Tim and Sarah; and Claire Welch.

My grandmother went to be with the Lord in September 2003. Besides sharing her middle name, I think I'm like my grandmother in that I like to type, write letters, and learn family history. Because she was a Christian, we will meet her in Heaven.

Mamma's family continued to grow after she went Home. More great-grandchildren were born into her family: David and Sharmaine Moore had Dominick and Hannah; Tim and Sarah Welch had Nick and Lucas; Ali and Andrew Beasley had Drew, Jackson, and Avery; Emily and Jason Blais had Abigail and Luke; and Angie and Greg Deeke had twins, Alaina and Alyssa.

CHAPTER 4

FAMILY LIFE - OUR FOUNDATION

"And you must commit yourselves wholeheartedly to these commands I am giving you today. Repeat them again and again to your children. Talk to them when you are at home and when you are away on a journey, when you are lying down and when you are getting up again. Tie them to your hands as a reminder and wear them on your forehead. Write them on the doorposts of your house and on your gates." *(Deuteronomy 6:6-7).*

One of my favorite poems was printed in the *Guideposts* magazine sometime in the early seventies. The few lines I know by memory are, "So long as there are homes where women work and children play, where men return at the close of day..." It goes on to explain what a better world it will be as long as those kinds of homes exist.

My parents taught Deut. 6:6-7 by the way they lived their lives each day, walking in love with each other and their fellow man.

I distinctly remember that they talked to me a lot about purity. From their instruction, I began to believe that I was "set apart for God's purposes." Their love and respect for the *Holy Bible* and The Church was instilled in our young minds regularly. By their actions and words, I learned wisdom. My parents prepared the "soil" of my heart and mind for the gospel, making a clear and firm path for the Lord's presence in our home.

Daddy got up each morning for nearly thirty years (lacking two months because they laid him off) and went to Lone Star Steel Company to do the same job— interviewing applicants to become employees of the plant. Mother arose before Daddy, lit the gas heaters, made him breakfast to go and packed him a lunch. He reminded her of things he wanted her to take care of, such as phone calls and banking. She kissed him goodbye, and out the door he went, returning each afternoon around 5:00 p.m.

Often, when Daddy came home at the end of the day, I would greet him at the car or door, give him a hug and ask him about his day. Then he would change into his coveralls and go to the farm to feed the cows and do the chores before dark would catch him. Arriving back at our house later in the evening, about dusk in the summer or after dark in the winter, he would eat dinner, go to bed, get up, and do the same routine over again. He worked two jobs, the plant and his cattle, to take care of us. I remember him always working at something. I don't remember Daddy watching TV when I was growing up, and we didn't even own a TV until I was in the sixth grade.

The sound of Mother's voice saying, "Elizabeth Ruth, it's time to get up," was my alarm clock for twelve years of school. She had a tasty breakfast cooked for me—fried egg, bacon or sausage, and toast. Many mornings, I got up early to finish the reams of homework I could not get finished the evening before. For some reason she never got us an alarm clock, which would have been a great teaching tool.

I loved my young siblings and enjoyed watching them grow and play together. Mary Evelyn always loved animals, especially puppies and kittens. When she was about two, Daddy got her the cutest little pet goat, which she would lead around with a rope. Mother curled her hair in ringlets that she called "Buffy Tails," named after Buffy, the freckled-faced little girl on "Family Affair," one of our favorite television shows. Occasionally, I would play dolls with my little sister, but mainly, I was the big sister taking care of her.

David was such a cute little boy. He was a very "easy to be with" child. It seemed like he came here making the sounds of a truck. To have him, a little brother, and a son for Daddy in our home, truly made our family complete. He and Mary Evelyn spent many hours playing together. Like most brothers and sisters, sometimes they squabbled, and Mother, who had never before dealt with sibling rivalry, didn't like it!

In the fall of 1971, Mary Evelyn started Mrs. Martha Carver's Kindergarten Class. I started Ninth Grade at Paul H. Pewitt High School. I was a bit nervous about my new adventure but was excited about the driver's license in my future! My classes and schedule, with piano practice and church activities, kept me very busy.

One sunny day, September 24, 1971, I arrived home from school to learn that Mama Vissering had gone to be with Jesus that afternoon! She was walking in the yard from their car into our house to play a game of dominoes with our pastor, when her heart stopped beating. Dr. Leeves said if he had been there, he could not have done anything about it. She was 93, had a sharp mind for playing dominoes, seldom even had a cold, and still attended church nearly every Sunday morning. She was a Christian wife, Mother, Grandmother and Great-grandmother who lived a long, good life She and Papa had well over 100 descendants! After Mama's funeral service, it felt like she just left us and went HOME! And she did!

Gran was grief-stricken after Mama died. Daddy didn't want her to stay in that big house at the farm by herself. She would go there during the day and sleep at our house at night. She missed Mama so much that when she was outside working at home, she said she imagined that she heard Mama's voice calling her.

Exactly a month to the day later, October 24, 1971, Gran seemed very preoccupied as she came to church that Sunday morning. Mother sang a song written by the late Dottie Rambo, "The holy hills of heaven call me to those mansions far away, where loved ones wait, and crowns are given, and the angels set my spirit free." After church, Gran came to our home to eat lunch with us. Then she hurried to drive out to the house, unlock the doors, and meet her sisters, brothers, nieces, and nephews, who would traditionally be there on Sunday afternoon.

A new STOP sign at a new intersection on the road to Mama's house was one that Gran had never heeded; she would just slow down, look both ways, and keep going. When she crossed the intersection that day, she failed to see the car that was in a curve, a blind spot she missed by not coming to a complete stop. That car broadsided Gran in her door, and she was not here for long. The loss we felt can only be understood if you have said goodbye to someone you have loved very deeply.

Gran was buried in the "VISSERING FAMILY" plot near Wheatville Cemetery where Mama had been laid to rest only one month earlier. II Corinthians 5:8 says, "We are confident, I say, and willing rather to be absent from the body, and to be present with the Lord." Because of that great promise, we did not sorrow as those who have no hope. We know that our loved ones are waiting for us in heaven, where, one day, we who know Christ as our Savior, will be forever with Him and them! I know Gran and Mama will be there in heaven to greet us.

Adjusting to life without those two precious ladies was very difficult for all of us. Knowing they were with Jesus brought us comfort and gave us just another reason to go to heaven too! However, I remember crying at the cemetery because Gran would not know my future husband or be at my wedding!!

My freshman year was a big year academically for me. I was a high school student for the first time, studying some new solid subjects, like Physical Science and Algebra I, cheering with the pep squad and traveling to all the Friday night football games, and making new upperclassmen friends.

Mother stayed busy taking care of her three children and being a wife. She was there for me at the end of my school day. She had a snack for me, and we would sit and talk about our days. Then I would go to the piano and practice one hour five days a week. Evenings were filled with homework, and lots of it. A short time after I began to study, Mother would call me to the kitchen for the good, hot dinner she had prepared for us.

It was my first year taking Home Economics. Our high school had just built a new, modern building that looked like a house on the inside, with several kitchen areas, a large, beautifully furnished living area, spacious sewing, and dressing rooms. I believe that home economics is as important for a high school girl as English or math. Making a home is much easier when one has been taught in the arts of doing so! It is tragic that in our sports-driven culture, schools have moved away from teaching young women domestic engineering. While each subject has its own place of importance, making a home is something that a woman will be doing her entire life. Someone must inspire us to do the thing we've never done before! I'm glad that God put many great homemakers into my life when I was young!

In that freshman home economics class, I learned the vocabulary and steps to planning and making my first garment on a sewing machine. It was a green, dotted Swiss dress with elastic around the waist and a white collar. It was only the beginning of a great skill that I learned to master over the next several years. I liked sewing so well that I took two more years of home economics.

Mrs. Alicia Hampton was an inspiring teacher. Sewing benefited not only my wardrobe, but that of siblings, friends, and many years later, my children.

As we approached Christmas 1971, we started asking the question: Where will the Vissering Christmas celebration be held, since Gran and Mama are gone? Aunt Rose volunteered to host it at her house. We drew names and celebrated in her love-filled home at Christmas for several years in a row. In addition, Aunt Rose took Daddy, Mother, and us kids "under her wing" and did her best to fill in the empty spots created by the loss of Gran and Mama. Since Daddy was an only child, it meant a lot to feel included in her family.

It was a cold, cold January day in East Texas in 1972. In fact, there was snow on the ground. Daddy was already a cattleman, but he became interested in this "new" French breed of cattle. They were famous for their tender meat. He contacted

Mr. Oxenburro from Huron, South Dakota, and bought several heads of the "red" cattle. They were delivered to our lot at the farm by an 18-wheeler, and we were there to welcome them to our ranch. It was the beginning of a dream Daddy had to own these cattle and work to breed them to get a pure-bred Limousin. Over the next years, he was able to use his knowledge and time to achieve that. What he did not know on that January day was how much time and money it would take to accomplish his goal. That was the downside of his endeavor. In his later years, Daddy answered the question, "What has been your greatest contribution to the world?" His answer was, "I introduced Limousin Cattle to Northeast Texas!"

Horseback Riding, My Favorite Pastime!

My favorite hobby was horseback riding. Daddy kept me a horse in the four acres behind our house. Naples Boots and Saddle Club held an annual parade and good rodeo every summer in

July. I looked forward all year to dressing up in boots and western outfit, and saddling up Stroller or my younger mare, Candy. We would ride to the Naples motel where the parade would begin on an early, very hot summer evening and move down the long main street through downtown Naples, and end up at the Naples Rodeo Arena. Horse owners in the Vissering family nearly always participated in the parade. I remember Uncle Jack Vissering, his two sons, John Paul and Wesley, Ikey Harte, who was The Boots and Saddle Club President for several years, Glenda Vissering, Pat Tomberlain, and last, but surely not least, my handsome Daddy riding Prince, his beautiful stallion!

Daddy loved to help people. One thing that stood out in my mind as a girl was seeing my dad loan his quarter horse to somebody who needed to ride in the parade and forfeit getting to ride himself! The scenario is unclear to me now, but I think it was Daddy's first cousin, whose own horse was unavailable one summer. Daddy just loaned him Prince and didn't ride himself. I saw that as great generosity!

The Grand Entry was my favorite part of the rodeo, riding horseback around the flag bearers with the music of "The Stars and Stripes Forever" playing in the background. One year, someone handed me a flag, and it was a special experience as I got to sit still on my horse while bearing a flag during the Grand Entry! Daddy usually got us the box seats so our view of everything in the arena was very clear on the front row. My favorite events were bull riding and barrel racing. In fact, I had a goal to become a barrel racer!

When I had free time on a Saturday or Sunday afternoon, I enjoyed riding horses with my cousin, Glenda. The summer of 1972 found me missing Gran and Mama. It was never the same at that old farmhouse after they died. What a reminder that people are the most important treasures in our lives!

Dallas and Expo 72

Aunt Lois Brown lived in Dallas with her teenagers, Cathy and Steve. "Expo 72" was a special event for Christian youth during that summer where we were taught in Bible Studies across the city during the day, and met for worship and church in the Cotton Bowl. A highlight of my high school years was to attend that timely youth conference with my cousins and enjoy the love and hospitality of my Aunt Lois, who taxied us around the city to all our destinations. I will never forget worshiping with the 50-100,000 American youth in the Cotton Bowl, all holding candles and singing "They Will Know We Are Christians by Our Love." It was during that decade when many hippies found Jesus. We were also changed and given a greater vision for growing and building His Kingdom on the earth!

What parents say or do, good or bad, will most likely be repeated by their children. My parents were tithers. They gave ten percent of their income to the Lord through the local church. Then when there was a special offering for a missionary who visited or someone who had a special need, they gave in that as well. We grew up knowing that tithing was the thing to do, according to Malachi 3:10. When we would get some money through our work efforts, we knew that we were to give ten percent of it to the church. God says, "Bring ye all the tithes into the storehouse, that there may be meat in mine house, and prove me now herewith, saith the Lord of hosts, if I will not open you the window of heaven, and pour you out a blessing, that there shall not be room enough to receive it."

We gave, and God blessed and took care of us. There have been numerous times in our lives that we saw the hand of our Lord taking care of our needs, that the outcome of some situation with our finances, our health, our car, the operation of our appliances, and our safety, was different because the Lord had blessed us, taken care of and provided in that situation. God is faithful to keep his promises "to the third and fourth generation of them who believe." My parents' lifestyle of tithing has influenced my husband, children, and I to be tithers.

We had certain traditions that we looked forward to. Daddy made Valentine's Day one of extravagant love! He would come in with a big heart-shaped box of candy for Mother and candy for the three of us children. There was a card for each of us that would make us cry as we sat and read them out loud to each other. Then we would exchange hugs.

Some of my favorite memories are of Christmas when Uncle Bob, Aunt Liz, Janet, and Sally actually spent Christmas Eve and Christmas Day at our house. We girls were expected to go to sleep early in our room, while our parents stayed up! One year, when Mary Evelyn was only about three, Aunt Liz bought Janet, Sally, and I a sleeping bag for Christmas and gave them to us on Christmas Eve. We put them all on our bedroom floor, and the four of us had a bunking party!

The next morning, we all gathered in the living room and opened what Santa Claus had brought each of us. We were so excited! There were many Christmas times when we were not with my uncle and aunt. However, Aunt Liz got us wonderful gifts and shipped them to us in a big box! That was a highlight of the season for us, and Mother would allow us to open it as soon as it arrived before Christmas!

Daddy loved to have a good time, so it was a tradition at our house for many years to have a bag swing. A large mulberry tree stood near our back door; it was so sturdy that it was nearly the perfect place for the special swing. However, it was not the perfect place for a mulberry tree! My parents had very few arguments, but that tree was a source of contention. Summer was the fruitful season, and those little berries would fall off all over the ground, covering the path to our back door! Kids and adults would track them in so we would use a broom to sweep a "berry-free" path. Mother hated that tree during the season and threatened to cut it down. Daddy wanted to keep the tree because he loved trees—and his bag swing tree.

Using a ladder, he would climb up the tree to the large limb that was perfect for holding the rope to the swing. Then he would tie the rope, get down, and tie the tow sack (feed sack made of burlap), which was stuffed with more feed sacks. This was a comfortable seat for many of us kids to straddle and swing and swing. Daddy would push us way up in the air. Sometimes, we would put three kids on the swing at once! It was where we spent a lot of time. Daddy loved to play with us, and he would talk, laugh, and tease us as he pushed us way up into the air! Most people have to leave home and spend money for that kind of fun!

My parents loved people. I don't think a person could have grown up in the home of Vic and Wanda Moore and not think about others. Their love extended not only to family members, but into the community, the church and the marketplace. My parents always prayed for those in need and reached out in a tangible way when appropriate. In his book, *The Quest for Character*, Charles Swindoll says, "There is no more significant involvement in another's life than prevailing, consistent prayer. It is more helpful than a gift of money, more encouraging than a strong sermon, more effective than a compliment, more reassuring than a physical embrace."(Page 132).

Hardly a Christmas could pass without my parents thinking of someone less fortunate and blessing them with toys for the kids or with some money for the parents to do their own shopping. Also, I can remember Mother and Daddy traveling great distances through the years to support my cousins who competed in tennis, gymnastic meets, or other sporting events in another city. If they could not go, they would call.

The gift of hospitality flowed in the Moore home. We enjoyed having family and friends come into our home to visit for the night or just to eat a meal. Daddy helped Mother plan their special recipes and buy the groceries; they met in the kitchen together and stirred up all kinds of great dishes to serve our company. I have many good memories of friends and family members who came to our house for a big meal and fellowship. We always thanked God for our food.

The main negative at our house about having company was that Mother wanted everything to look perfect, which frequently created some tension and pressure in us as we cleaned, cooked, and prepared for our guests. My jobs were to vacuum the floor, dust the furniture, and clean the bathroom using *Comet*. I was always glad when the company arrived because that meant we could quit cleaning and just have fun. There would be good food, a game of dominoes, music, much conversation, love, and laughter.

CHAPTER 5

FOLLOWING GOD, FINDING A HUSBAND

"Delight yourself in the Lord, and he will give you the desires of your heart. trust also in Him and he will bring it to pass." -Psalms 37:4-5

As a young girl of twelve or thirteen, like most my age, I dreamed of being a bride—my wedding day, of marriage, of being a homemaker and mother. I remember that Mother and I had a discussion about that unique person God would make just for me. She told me that "just as God had prepared Eve for Adam, he had created someone special for me." In my wildest dreams, I could not have imagined that just four miles away, in Omaha, Texas, he was doing just that!

I found thirteen to be a difficult age. Unfortunately, Dr. James Dobson had not yet written his wonderful book "Preparing for Adolescence" (2005) how to survive the coming years of change. God was faithful to watch out for me and hear my prayers for his direction and provision.

In June of 1972, having finished the ninth grade, I was part of a group of officers from our Future Homemakers of America chapter, who were traveling to Wilke's Lodge in Avinger, Texas for a leadership meeting. I happened to find myself as a passenger in the car with Pennie Beasley, our chapter president, her brother, Bill, a college student who was our chauffeur for the weekend, and three other FHA officers. Pennie wanted me to sit in the front seat, between her and the preppy brother. Usually a very serious person, I remember acting very silly that day. I thought of our driver as Pennie's older brother, and nothing more.

In the fall of 1972, I ran into Bill again on two different occasions at or in connection with football games. The first time was on our homecoming night before the game, at The Dairy Bar in Bill's hometown. Pep Squad members and officers had to be at the stadium early to make pictures and prepare for the special festivities of the evening. I rode with Penny's friends to get something quick to eat, and when we went inside, there stood Bill waiting for his order. By this time, I had developed a crush on him! He spoke to one of my companions by name and just said "Hello" to me. My first thought was a discouraging one: "He doesn't even know my name." Bill was a zoology (pre-dental) student at East Texas State University in Commerce, Texas. His sister, Mary Kay, was in our high school band, and I was in the pep squad. Our team, The Brahmas, were in the playoffs that year, and we met our rivals at ET's stadium. Bill came to the game, I thought, to see his sister. As I got off our bus and started toward the bleacher area, I saw him, and we spoke. When the game was over that November night, I hoped to see Bill again before leaving the stadium, and I did.

We "just happened" to meet and walk out of the stadium together, and we talked about how often he came home to Omaha. I began hoping he would ask me out as I learned he came every weekend!

When school resumed in January 1973, after the Christmas holidays, my friend Pennie had an engagement ring from her longtime boyfriend, Tommy Knight. They planned a June wedding, which would fall immediately after her graduation. During a lunch conversation one day, four of us girls were discussing that we didn't understand why she wanted to get married. I made the comment, "I don't even have a boyfriend." She replied, "I'll give you my brother."

Two months later, on a beautiful Sunday afternoon, March 10, 1973, something very special happened for me! My routine was normal, except that we were looking for a new pastor for our church. As an elder, Daddy was responsible for interviewing, inviting, and providing lodging and lunch for the pastoral candidate and his wife.

I was sixteen, and it was during those stretching, adolescent years that horseback riding was an outlet for me. While my classmates were getting cars and dates, I enjoyed my equestrian pursuits via a mare named "Candy." I could saddle her when I had some free time, and off I would go down the road to our farm about two miles out of town. As I sat in the saddle atop my brown mare riding down our street that afternoon, I had no idea of the special visitor who was coming!

Arriving back at my house, I turned Candy loose in the pasture, set my tack up, and walked over to the car where the prospective pastor's wife was sitting. She was looking through some music for the evening service and getting some air through the open car door. I was standing there in my white jeans, making small conversation with our guest when I looked up and saw a bronze Ford Falcon drive past my house. I commented to her, "There goes a guy I'm crazy about, and he doesn't even know it."

Bill Beasley drove past my house to the neighbor's driveway. Was he going there to visit? But then he turned around, came back, and drove into my driveway! Now, I really had it all figured out for sure! Since my daddy hired college students as summer employees for Lone Star Steel Company, Bill must be coming to our house to inquire about employment.

As he stopped and stepped out of the car, I approached him and said hello. He said he wasn't sure he was at the right house. I said, "Who are you looking for?" He immediately answered, "You." To say that I was taken aback would be an understatement. Could a dream of mine be coming true? In my excitement I replied, "Good!"

He proceeded to ask me if I had plans for the following Saturday night. I thought to myself, "I can't think of anything, but if there are, the plans will have to be changed!!!!" He asked me what I liked to do. After a brief discussion about his spring break plans that week, we agreed to go out to dinner the following weekend.

When he drove away, I was on cloud nine as I ran into the house to tell Mother of my news and try to get my feet back on the ground so I could get dressed for Sunday evening church! Although she was very happy for me, she was quick to give me advice. "Don't go to church and school and tell everybody you have a date on Saturday with Bill Beasley. They'll find out after it happens." I knew, however, I had to tell my closest friend, Paula Elrod, who knew I was interested in Bill, and she would be at church that night!

There was much anticipation in my heart about the upcoming weekend. Mother and I shopped on Monday for fabric and pattern and had me a new, hot pink dress made for the occasion. When Bill came to pick me up, he was wearing a hot pink shirt and a multicolored pull-over sweater. Without any planning, we were color coordinated from the first date!

That first evening, Bill was surprised to meet my very young siblings. Mary Evelyn was six and David was nearly two. Off we went in his clean, shiny car to Mt. Pleasant, Texas for a delicious dinner which consisted of chicken fried steak, cream gravy, baked potato, salad, bread, and tea. After riding around awhile as we made non-stop conversation, we drove to visit with Bill's parents, Thomas and Marie Beasley, in their nice and comfortable home. Just weeks before that first date, I had won third place at a talent show held at our school, so Bill asked me to go into their living room to play the winning song on the piano. We started our relationship with much conversation. A strong friendship has been the foundational glue of our lifetime relationship.

Bill was nineteen, and I sixteen, when we started dating that spring evening, March 17, 1973. We were both Christians; he grew up in the Baptist Church and I in the Assembly of God. Since I was the pianist there, he would come with me most Sunday mornings. Because his study of science led him to put everything in a test tube, he struggled with believing miracles still happen today.

Occasionally, I would take a Sunday away from my home church and go with Bill to his home church, First Baptist Church of Omaha. Years after we married, Bill told me that when he was a young boy, his dad would go into the living room late at night to pray. Bill's room was on the other side of the wall, and hearing his father pray made an indelible impression on him. At the age of about thirteen, Bill also started praying that "God would provide him a godly wife who would stay home with his children and train them to know Jesus." Years later, Bill shared his story with our son, Andrew, who wrote the song "Dynasty" in honor of his dad.

Sunday was a special day for us. Regardless of where we went to church, it was a family tradition to have lunch with Bill's grandparents, Murl and Sybil Beasley. Grandaddy Murl and Grandmother Beasley lived on their farm, west of Omaha in the Concord Community. I know Grandmother loved to prepare for us because she went all out with a full table of home cooking for her family: Fried chicken, cream potatoes, peas, sweet pickles, cornbread, sliced tomatoes, walnut cake (Bill's favorite), and iced tea. That was a typical, but flexible menu on any given Sunday.

Granddaddy and Grandmother Beasley took me in like their own granddaughter, and I loved them in return. Both my grandfathers had died when my parents were just babies; Bill had a special relationship with his Granddaddy Murl that I had always wanted with a grandfather. Funny stories and love filled the air each time I was privileged to be a guest in their home, and I will always cherish the times we spent with them.

That first summer after Bill and I started dating, my family left Naples for about ten days to drive to Alexandria, Virginia/Washington D. C. to visit Uncle Bob, Aunt Liz, Janet, and Sally. I rode the 1500 miles in the back seat with my two-year-old brother and six-year-old sister. David's favorite things were tunnels and airplanes, and he was able to view a lot of both on that trip. Our uncle and aunt always rolled out the red carpet for us each time we visited them. Aunt Liz is the "Queen of the Kitchen" so we had wonderful meals. I have visited her only a few times when we didn't go for a picnic somewhere.

The Whitehouse, The Lincoln Memorial, The Washington Monument, Monticello and Mt. Vernon, George Washington's home, were some of the places we visited; of course, there was a wonderful picnic lunch that Aunt Liz brought for us to eat in Lady Bird Park! We even attended a musical at Ford's Theatre. It was a great trip, except for one thing: I already missed Bill. By the time we got back to Naples, Daddy had introduced us to more produce stands than I cared to meet between Virginia and Texas! I was ready for some elbow room after sharing the seat with two young children for 1500 miles! I put in my request for a station wagon (that was before minivans), and Daddy got them one the year after I left home for college!

The truths we teach our children will affect the rest of their lives and our grandchildren for generations. We may feel that they are not listening, but they are. Daddy always taught me that "the more you have in common with the man you marry, the less you have to overcome."

Bill and I had similar backgrounds. We both were from two-parent Christian homes. Our dads knew each other as they both worked at Lone Star Steel Company for most of our lives. Our stay-at-home moms were there to teach us in the preschool years and at home to greet, guide, encourage, and listen to us after school, even when we were teenagers. They kept our home neat and clean, cooked balanced meals, and washed and ironed our clothes. Bill's mother sewed most of his clothes in high school, college, and professional school.

Our dads made the money, but our moms made our homes what they were—happy, peaceful, clean, and orderly. They created for us an atmosphere of security and love. Titus 2:3-5 (LB) says, "Teach the older women to be quiet and respectful in everything they do. They must not go around speaking evil of others and must not be heavy drinkers, but they should be teachers of goodness. These older women must train the younger women to live quietly, to love their husbands and their children, and to be sensible and clean minded, spending their time in their own homes, being kind and obedient to their husbands, so that the Christian faith can't be spoken against by those who know them."

Although four years apart, we both attended and graduated from Paul H. Pewitt High School. We knew the same students and learned from the same teachers. We lived in the same communities and had both been greatly influenced by our grandparents. A college education was a goal we both pursued, which broadened our perspectives and prepared us to make a living for our family.

Because our mothers stayed home with us, we wanted that same blessing for our children. They taught us by example and used the power of words, a belt, and prayer as their main tools. Our dads both were loving faithful providers for us; even in difficult days, they did not run away from their responsibilities. We both were firstborns with two siblings. Attending church and Sunday School was a lifestyle for our families as we grew up, with our parents serving as teachers and leaders in our home churches at different times. Bill's goals were to have a job where he could provide well and spend time with his family, and his wife could stay home with his children. We were in agreement on that before we married.

We were socio-economically compatible. Since Bill was a full-time college student when we were dating, his dad provided the money for his education along with some spending money. Bill worked in the summers at Lone Star Steel company where he made money to spend and save. From the simple pleasures of just riding in the car and talking, to eating out at a nice restaurant for dinner, the good times rolled when we were together.

In August 1973, I began eleventh grade. I was excited about being the President of the Pep Squad for the upcoming football season. Using my leadership skills was something I enjoyed. There were home games, away games, pep rallies, and signs to paint! My friends and classmates, Pam Roberts, Debra Higgins, Glenda Foster, and I enjoyed some special times together through the year. My favorite subjects were typing, bookkeeping, and home economics, and I anticipated seeing Bill every weekend. His sister, Mary Kay, was a senior that year and we ate with the same group of friends at lunch. Sometime during the spring semester, Mary Kay became engaged to Ralph Cline. They had dated for four years.

In September 1974, Mary Kay and Ralph were married at First Baptist Church in Omaha. My mother sang, and Bill and I were honored to be the candle lighters for their beautiful fall wedding.

The one thing in the back of my mind, however, was the question: Do Bill and I have the same spiritual goals that will unite us in marriage? We were both Christians, but at that time Bill had a career success ladder in mind that consisted more of material achievement. Matthew 6:33 states, "But seek ye first the kingdom of God, and his righteousness; and all these things shall be added unto you."

The year was 1975, and Bill and I both were about to experience some big changes. He was a senior at East Texas State University, taking classes, working as a graduate assistant in the biology department, and waiting for an acceptance letter from Baylor College of Dentistry. His strong desire to become a dentist took him on several visits to Baylor's admissions office, where he kept his face and his name before them, hoping they would see his persistence and select him for a position in the Baylor freshman class of 1975. Waiting...Waiting...Praying...Anxiously waiting... Working...Waiting...

I was a senior. We had received our senior rings the previous May before school was out, and it was official. Highlights of that year for me were playing the piano for the high school choir and learning tailoring in home economics class, where I actually made Bill a suit coat. Also, preparing and performing a senior piano recital in Barbara's home in May was a big event.

The academic challenge came as my training as a writer was carried a step further through my senior English teacher, Mrs. Hampton. She taught me English IV and Composition. Our first writing assignment, due at the end of class that day, was "to describe an orange" in one page! A requirement for graduation was the familiar and often dreaded "Senior Research Paper." After more than 45 years, my particular subject escapes me now, but those daily writing lessons and challenges prepared me for all the college assignments that followed.

I graduated from Paul H. Pewitt High School on May 29, 1975. It was with feelings of pride and accomplishment that I wore my royal blue cap and gown that evening, marched in with my Class of 1975 to the song "Pomp and Circumstance," and walked across the stage at the football stadium to receive my diploma. Twelve years is a long time to be with the same people every day, and I was only sad to think that my classmates and I would never be together again. Each of us would go our separate ways, living our lives and making decisions based on the values that had been instilled in us by our parents, our teachers, and for some of us, our church.

At graduation, I felt confident and prepared, emotionally and academically, as I anticipated and made plans to leave home and begin college in August at East Texas State University, my daddy's alma mater! That night after graduation, Bill and I celebrated with dinner at Johnny Casey's Seafood Restaurant in Longview. My graduation gift from him was a beautiful watch.

I got a summer job at the Morris County National Bank in my hometown where I filed and helped prepare bank statements for mailing. That was in the day when people got their canceled checks back in the statement! It was during that summer that the new Morris County Bank building was complete, and we got to move into the beautiful modern facility.

In June 1975, Bill turned 22 and received his acceptance letter to begin classes at Baylor College of Dentistry! That was truly a milestone accomplished through hard work, persistence, and God's right hand! My parents and I honored him with a surprise birthday/going away party at our home. Guests were Bill's parents, Pennie and Tom, Kay and Ralph, Grandpa and Grandmother Beasley, Grandmother Reeves and Mr. Reeves, Bill's uncle and aunt, W.C. and Rowene Beasley, Mary Evelyn, David, and the honoree, Bill. We hid the cars and were able to truly surprise him, which made it extra special.

Shortly thereafter, my boyfriend and his parents traveled to Dallas, where they found him an apartment near the dental school, and he began classes in July 1975. It was obvious to him from the start that he would be very busy and would not be leaving Dallas often. Our dates would be fewer and farther between. The telephone and U.S. Mail became our lifeline to continue our thriving relationship.

College life began for me the following month, August 1975, when I became a student at ETSU. Smith Hall was home to me and my new roommate, Suzanne Henderson from Ore City, Texas. We got along well, encouraged each other, and enjoyed talking and laughing. We had wonderful Christian suitemates who introduced me to the Baptist Student Union on campus, and I was encouraged in my faith from fellowshipping there. We enjoyed sharing, laughing, and eating dinner together in the evenings at the cafeteria. I loved my classes and dorm life and did a lot of walking back and forth from dorm to campus to class and cafeteria as I had no car my first year—proof that people can go to college without an automobile! Suzanne would take me anywhere I needed to shop in the area.

Bill would give me a ride about once a month, and we would travel home together to visit our parents. On most other weekends, Bill drove from Dallas to ET to see me on Saturday, or on Sunday for church and lunch together. We attended church at First Baptist in Commerce or First Assembly of God in Greenville. Then we went for lunch at a wonderful buffet there.

I was thankful that so much preparation had been given to me. Life can be so much better and enjoyable when someone has taken time to "prepare" us for what lies ahead. As an English student, I encountered an old liberal professor, who some said was an atheist. Since I was contemplating marriage, I thought it would be interesting to research it and see what I could learn. I wrote my paper for his class on "How to Have A Successful Marriage." Sometime later after completing his class, I ran into the old teacher on campus, and he obviously remembered me because he said, in jest, "Let's see, Miss Moore, how many times have you been married?"

By the summer of 1976, Bill and I had dated for over three years, and I had become discontented with our relationship. Even though we had a lot of time together invested, I questioned if Bill was the one for me to marry. It was time to step back and take a serious look at where I was going. I had finished my first year of college and he had completed his first year of dental school. His attitude and moodiness began to annoy me. I'm reminded of the scripture that begins, "If the Lord had not been on my side..."

because I believe God allows or even causes some discomforts in our lives to bring about good change. It may seem all bad initially, but good will come from it.

As I thought and prayed about our relationship that summer, I knew I needed to know for sure if Bill was the one God had for me to marry, or was there someone else? God has a way of bringing people and circumstances into our lives to help us to seek and find answers. He was really stretching me and getting me out of my comfort zone. Besides "letting go" of a three-year plus relationship, he was leading me to change colleges in the fall for one semester, at least, and enroll in Southwestern Assembly of God College in Waxahachie, Texas, about thirty minutes from Dallas.

In August, I broke the news to Bill that I needed some space: an opportunity to date other people and time to sort things out. He was devastated! About a week or two later, I began the fall semester at Southwestern. I left the friends I knew and the familiar surroundings of the campus and routine at ETSU for a totally new environment at SAGC. Maybe God would have a husband for me there, I thought.

It was during that difficult valley that God taught both of us. Bill was so at the end of himself over losing me that he began to pursue the Lord in a deeper way just to survive. It was a difficult time. He was so upset that he was afraid of failing in dental school, and with all the money he had invested, he could not afford that. The Holy Spirit had ministered especially to him as he attended Lakewood Assembly of God Church, near his apartment in Dallas. He said when he went down for prayer, it was as if the pastor knew what he was going through.

He called me on the phone and told me that he was setting some new spiritual goals. I could tell by listening to him that he was growing, even through his pain, and so was I. I began to realize that Bill was the best choice for me. I learned to make quiet time a priority, even above doing my homework; that really was a hard change to make. It's neat about God, that when we put Him first, he helps us get everything else done!

God gave me a special roommate at Southwestern; Reva Franklin was a year younger than me, and we had grown up together in church. That fall of 1976, we shared each other's burdens in our basement room of that old Southwestern dorm and on the road to Naples because I had inherited the used family car!

By semester end, I knew that Bill Beasley was the one I wanted to marry. When Christmas came, I was expecting an engagement ring, but it didn't come. Before our holidays were over and it was time to go back to school, Bill told me he had some questions about us, and he needed more time himself. I told him I would be waiting when he made up his mind.

That spring semester, 1977, I went back to East Texas State University. That time of "waiting" was an opportunity for me to press into God to draw closer to him. At Southwestern I had learned a real love for the Word of God, and I began to claim key promises for my life and future. In March, I became a Resident Assistant in Smith Hall and had my own private room. It was a special time with the Lord. One of my favorite verses during that time, and I encourage young people with this, "Delight thyself also in the Lord, and he shall give thee the desires of thine heart. Commit thy way unto the Lord; trust also in him; and he shall bring it to pass" (Psalm 37:4-5). That semester was literally spent delighting myself in the Lord, making Him the love of my life. I "set my face like a flint to do his will." I posted my own encouragement of Bible verses and poems on my walls and mirror and drew strength from keeping them ever before me.

In July 1977, Bill came from Dallas to ET one Saturday to take me on a picnic. It was on that day that he asked me to marry him! I said yes, and the wedding plans began. September 24 was our wedding date because Bill would have a week off from school before beginning his senior year. I was a summer school student at ET taking Intermediate Accounting and two other subjects. After Bill popped the question, my concentration "went out the window." We decided that after we married, I would work to pay the rent and groceries, and after his graduation the next year, I could resume my college studies. I withdrew from school and moved to my parent's home to plan our wedding.

God is such a personal God. One of the highlights of our wedding preparation was the way he blessed us with my engagement ring. We had looked a year earlier and found a ring I liked at Adelstein Jewelers in Dallas. When we began to seriously shop for rings a year later, we looked at several jewelry stores, but I never found one I liked as well. When we returned to Adelstein's to look at their selection, the same mounting was not on display. We described it to the nice red-headed lady who was helping us. She remembered they had just received some new mountings that day. When she put the tray out on the counter, there was the exact mounting I had admired a year earlier!

Mrs. Beasley, Mother, and I went shopping for wedding dresses. I found the one I liked, and Mrs. Beasley sketched it off. She sewed my beautiful white wedding dress, complete with seed pearls and lace. We were blessed with two miscellaneous showers, a lingerie and kitchen shower. The rehearsal dinner was hosted by Mr. and Mrs. Beasley, at the home of Pennie and Tom.

After four and one-half years of dating, Bill and I were married in September 1977, in a beautiful, candlelight ceremony at First Baptist Church of Omaha. As I took my Daddy's arm that evening to begin our walk to meet Bill at the altar, Daddy said, "We're going to have fun!" Entering the candlelight setting and beholding the candles glowing in the full church of about 350 people, I caught a little glimpse of heaven !

Because we knew that the Lord had truly brought us together, we wanted Him to be glorified during our wedding and throughout our married life. Together, we had chose the scriptures we wanted shared during our double ring ceremony, conducted by our pastors,

Reverend Don Couch, who led us in our vows, and Reverend Clifford Longino, who served our communion. Bill's Uncle, W. C. Beasley was his best man; Paula Elrod was my maid of honor. Our attendants were Bill's sisters, Pennie and Kay and their husbands, Tom and Ralph, and then our college friends, Suzanne Henderson Hampton and Phil Pittman. Mary Evelyn was a junior bridesmaid, escorted by my cousin, John David Tatum, a junior groomsman. My brother, David, was young enough to be our ring bearer; he walked with our flower girl, my young cousin, Kristin Mills.

They say that at every wedding, something will go wrong or something funny happens. Our interesting story is of three parts. At one point, I could see people coming into the building bringing jugs of water to the kitchen for the reception. The water in Omaha had been turned off that evening and water had to be brought in. It was a hot September day, and one of the air conditioner units had gone out in the sanctuary. We had so many candles around us during the ceremony that several of us in the wedding party felt we were melting! A key line in our vows to each other where we almost laughed was the part about "with all my earthly goods, I thee endow." We thought that was funny because all we owned at that point in life was a bean bag chair, a stereo, and Bill's Ford Falcon!

Besides having the Lord's presence there, a special part of the ceremony was when my mother stood at her seat and sang the song, "Sunrise Sunset"— "Is this the little girl I carried, is this the little boy at play? I don't remember growing older. When did they?" The organist was my cousin, Barbara, and other love songs were sung by Cousin Charlotte. Ushers were Mike Anderson and David Brown. Bill, my dashing prince in his white tuxedo, and I, pledged our lives to one another forever. We had a beautiful reception with bride's cake, a chocolate groom's cake, punch, coffee, nuts, mints, and a host of friends and relatives to support us. Our honeymoon was a trip to Eureka Springs, Arkansas.

Are You Still Looking for Mr. Right?

This advice is for all those still looking for "Mr. Right": I know that if I had leaned unto my own understanding and followed my preconceived ideas about the kind of husband I thought I would marry, I could have easily missed God's will in a husband for me. Girls and women can be in love with just a figment of their imaginations, someone who doesn't even exist! God is the only one who knows the man who would "just get finer with age" and be faithful for a lifetime. He also knows the man who will be the best father for your children. Only God can know that. Let your heavenly Father guide you, girls, because he will give you His best! Don't get in a hurry and make a decision you'll regret for a lifetime! Pray, and God will lead you and him.

> *"For I hate divorce!" says the Lord, the God of Israel. "It is as cruel as putting on a victim's blood-stained coat," says the Lord Almighty. "So, guard yourself; always remain loyal to your wife" (Malachi 2:16 NLB).*

When God brings two people together in the covenant of marriage, he is planning to produce something to build up The Kingdom of God. As two people live together, day after day, year after year, working, making decisions, forgiving, sharing a bank account, overlooking each other's mistakes, building a life together, through the good times and the bad, giving birth and raising children, it is the bitter and the sweet that we share. Like that grain of sand under the oyster, a pearl is being made! Marriage is a picture of Christ and his love for His Bride, The Church. It was by following God that I found the right husband, and you can too!

In honor and memory of our parents, grandparents, and great grandparents:
Wanda and Victor Moore—married for 55 years

Marie and Thomas Beasley—married for more than 60 years
Ruth and Grady Higgins—married for more than 50 years
Sybil and Murl Beasley—married for more than 60 years
Lillie and H.J. Vissering—married for 45 years
Martha Virginia Beasley and Shepherd Ivy Beasley—married more
than 60 years
Stella Kate and Charles Jones, Sr.—married more than 40 years
And in celebration of mine and Bill's 45 years of marriage,
I dedicate this song, recorded by Suzy Lessinger:

"That's When the Real Love Starts"
A long white dress, A warm summer night
Flowers in the church, In the candlelight.
They proclaimed the love
That was there in their hearts
But they found out later
When the real love starts.

When the rains didn't come,
And the crops didn't grow
There's more mouths to feed
Than seeds to sow,
They stayed together
When their dreams fell apart.
That's when the real love starts.
I was just a kid
That was long ago
But I learned more from them
Then they'll ever know.
So, when the money's running out
And the bills are rolling in
I just hold you close
And I think of them.

It all seems so easy
When things are going right
But the true test of love
Lies somewhere down the line.

When the rain didn't come
And the crops don't grow
With more mouths to feed
Than seed to sow
You got to stay together
If your dreams fall apart.
That's when the real love starts
That's when real love starts.

CHAPTER 6

MARRIED LIFE IN LOUISIANA

"Through wisdom is a house built; and by understanding it is established; and by knowledge shall the chambers be filled with all precious and pleasant riches." (*Proverbs 24:3).*

"...but by love, serve one another."(Galatians 5:13).

After a wonderful honeymoon, we stopped in Naples to get our wedding presents en route to our first home together, an apartment in Dallas. Bill began his senior year of dental school the following week, and I began my daily routine as a wife and homemaker.

Adjustments always go with a change in life. Keeping balanced meals on the table and writing ten thank you notes each day for the first month kept me busy! How blessed we were to know so many generous people who showered us with wonderful, useful gifts to start our married life.

In addition to my homemaking duties, I needed to find a job, keeping in mind that we had one car. I gained employment at Baylor Medical Center in the Medical Records Department. The office manager told me I was overqualified for the job, but we knew that the following year Bill would graduate, and we would be moving. It was a temporary way of making some money, having the same daytime hours at school and work, and sharing the transportation.

My new job was to sit at a desk nearly all day and check the charts to make sure each doctor signed and dictated in his patients' records. Considering the size of Baylor Medical Center, one can imagine the stacks of charts that came through that office each day. The work that I did became very monotonous but needful, and the pay was helpful and appreciated.

I made enough money to pay our rent and buy our groceries, which at that time was about $500 take-home pay. Since my parents had always taught me to tithe, I asked Bill if we could tithe on what I brought home. He had been taught to give an offering at church or money to those in need. He went along with my desire to tithe because I was the one making the money, and he wanted me to be happy.

For entertainment in Dallas, we had little extra to spend, but enjoyed going to the mall window shopping and to the museums, etc. One of our favorite things was to go at night for a hot fudge sundae to Swensen's Ice Cream Parlor! We lived in a furnished apartment and had a small black-and-white TV that his parents gave us. The shows we liked were *The Beverly Hillbillies, Mash, Andy Griffith* and *I Love Lucy*.

Our first argument was because Bill thought I was telling him too many details. He assertively told me that, "he was not my parents." My parents had always made me feel free to talk to them in detail. I soon learned that husbands don't always want all the details, just the bottom line. For the most part, we got along very well, and our home was peaceful.

Bill and I agreed from the beginning that we both needed to pursue our own individual interests, and that we did not always have to be together to do that. That gave us the needed space to grow and develop as individuals as well as a couple. Bill loved reading, and there was much of it required for his education. After work and school each day, I prepared our dinner, we ate together, and Bill went back to the dental school to do lab work.

Bill had already begun attending Lakewood Assembly of God Church, located in a beautiful sanctuary nearby; it became our church home during the next eleven months. Our pastor, Reverend F. M. Fyordbak, was a very dynamic and loving, fatherly man. We also found fellowship in our couples Sunday school class.

Our first Christmas was memorable. Daddy brought us a small, live Christmas tree. Bill had a school holiday, so he shopped and chose all red glass ornaments and lights. We had fun decorating together. I had made Bill a special stocking before we married and had to make me one to go with his. We played Santa Claus to each other with special little gifts. A "doll" ornament Bill gave me that first Christmas still hangs on our tree every year more than forty years later! Traditions are the glue of life!

In January of 1978, we began deciding about where we would live and work after graduation. The Public Health Service program sent dentists to understaffed rural areas and paid their salary for two years or more. Bill and I thought that sounded like a good opportunity for us because we would not need any start-up money to equip an office. We could just begin practicing in the location we chose. We looked on the map at the PHS available locations; they were in remote towns in Oklahoma, the coast of Texas, and two towns in Louisiana— Oak Grove and Tallulah. The government would pay Bill's expenses to travel to one site, and we chose Oak Grove.

In March, we flew together from Dallas to the airport in Monroe and rented a car. We then drove to Oak Grove, a rural delta farming town about sixty-two miles from Monroe. The long, straight road from Delhi to Oak Grove, with its scrubby scenery at that pre-planting time, made us really wonder where we were going and what Oak Grove would look like!

Upon our arrival to the small town, we stayed the first night at Mike's Motel, which was the only one in town and brand new in the 70's. The next morning, we drove down Main Street and stopped there for breakfast at a country cafe where the waitress gave us both a bill! Then we went a few streets over to meet Dr. Armstrong, the dentist. He and his wife showed us the very modern colonial dental office, introduced us to some local people, and we looked over the town as a possible place to live and work.

When we returned to Dallas, Bill kissed the ground and was not interested in going back to that "little farming town" in Louisiana. He was a Texan and was looking for "the good life" in his native state. As the weeks progressed, we prayed, and we shared the Louisiana opportunity with our parents. Bill began to change his mind. He decided he was interested in the Oak Grove opportunity if we could find decent housing, and communicated this to our contact, Jack Irvine, the hospital administrator.

In April 1978, while still in Dallas, we had a special surprise visit! Mary Kay and Ralph stopped to see us on their way back home from San Antonio, where they adopted their new son and our first nephew, Paul !!!! How excited we were for them and for us. He was a beautiful baby and so welcome into our family! Paul made us "Uncle Bill" and "Aunt E!"

In May, Bill graduated from Baylor Dental College. It was a grand event, and our parents and siblings came to support him. He had worked very hard for seven full years—four of college and three in dental school— to accomplish his goal of becoming a Doctor of Dental Surgery! We celebrated the occasion with pictures, dinner at a fine restaurant, and visited with our family members who came.

Bill earned his dental degree, but to practice dentistry he had to pass the Texas State Board, which was a critical three-day event.

He was very anxious, but he studied, worked, and we all prayed. About a week later he received a letter stating he passed! YAY! We were very thankful to God and hopeful about our future.

In July, we traveled back to Oak Grove to finalize our housing arrangements and were blessed to rent a brand-new house from the West Carroll Builders. Bill was Commissioned as an Officer in the United States Public Health Service. The government would pay his salary and the Police Jury (under the direction of the hospital board) of West Carroll Parish would provide the dental office. The PHS hoped that we would like it there and become a private practitioner after two years.

I continued to work at Baylor through the summer while Bill worked at home to prepare for our move. We were excited about a new beginning in a new state.

Marriage is an adventure created in the heart of God! It is meant to be a lifetime relationship between two people who make a commitment before God to be faithful to each other until death parts them. When I was growing up, divorce was a very uncommon thing. Today, our culture teaches people that marriage is designed to make one happy and when one is not, then one needs to find someone who will make them happy.

I have found that God has used Bill to strengthen me as a person and push me to grow. Growth is painful and happiness is not always a part of that growth. However, staying together and working it out produces something in both man and wife and for the Kingdom of God! God intends to produce something that we could not produce by ourselves!

We are so thankful to come from a line of people who stayed the course! We have seen true love lived out on a daily basis in the lives of those who came before us. I am talking about commitment.

On August 1, 1978, we made our move from Dallas to Oak Grove The small town is also one hour from Greenville, Mississippi, about one hour and fifteen minutes from Vicksburg, and seventeen miles from the Arkansas line. The Public Health Service provided a moving van and workers to pack our household furnishings. The large Mayflower truck stopped in Omaha to load some furniture our parents were giving us.

Bill's mother traveled with us to help us get settled in. Our first night in Oak Grove, Bill and I slept on the floor in the new house we had leased. When the large Mayflower moving van arrived, it was a very hot and humid summer day. Just married for eleven months, we had purchased a dining room suite in Dallas with Bill's graduation money. My parents had given us an antique bedroom suite that my grandmother had left for me, and Mrs. Beasley had refinished it. The rest of our furniture, besides the bean bag chair and the stereo that we started married life with, was mainly "attic provincial!" We were in a brand-new house, but it did not come with window treatments. Mrs. Beasley gave me some very old curtains for privacy, and I greatly looked forward to having the money to order something new and modern to replace them very soon!

We realized how very blessed we were to be in the new house, to have a good job, and to know that God had truly led us there. As we unpacked the boxes and put everything in its proper place, the new responsibilities of beginning work were on my husband's mind. Working together helped us to get organized in a short time so that we could begin work at the dental office the following week.

The modern colonial office with its brick facade and white columns was an attractive building. Located just across the street from Oak Grove Park and down the road from the hospital, the dental office was easily accessible to all who would come to Billy C. Beasley, D.D.S.

I was my husband's first dental assistant, and our first patient was a local man who dropped by for an extraction before we were fully ready to begin. We gave him an appointment, at which time he returned, and we removed the tooth he was complaining about. The local newspaper, *The West Carroll Gazette*, came, took a picture, and wrote a small article about the new dentist in town.

We enjoyed meeting the people of the community, who made us feel welcome. Jack Irvine, the hospital administrator, taught us the business office systems. He and his wife, Alease, became our first friends. We did not have a lawn mower, so they loaned us their riding one. We also had just one car, so Jack loaned Bill his Jeep. Soon, we hired an experienced dental assistant who had worked for Dr. Armstrong. I became the receptionist/office manager, scheduling patients and doing the bookkeeping.

We were so thankful to have a regular paycheck, one that would pay all the bills. After gaining a job, Bill decided he would continue tithing from what he made doing dentistry. As we have made tithing a part of our lifestyle, God has blessed us over and over again and rebuked the devourer many times (Malachi 3:10).

We were invited out to dinner by several couples in the community. Bill joined the Lion's Club, which met for lunch once a week at the school. Our new friends, Jack and Alease, were members of First Baptist Church and invited us to attend. Although we never officially joined, we were as active as we could be in Sunday School and with music ministry, and that was our church family until 1983.

Bill began to meet the specialists in the area very early that fall of 1978. Dr. Lee Engel, an orthodontist in Greenville, Mississippi, became one of our dearest friends and like a brother to us. As Bill referred patients to him, they would enjoy talking, and he invited us out to dinner. It was in 1979 that he became my orthodontist, and I was blessed with the straight teeth without spaces that I had always wanted! Each time I went for my checkup, the three of us enjoyed dinner, visiting, and some special entertainment together. One time we had a great adventure when Lee had the idea that we three would go to Belzoni, Mississippi one Saturday for their annual Catfish Festival and craft fair. Although they had other foods there, Lee said "you can't go to the catfish festival and not eat catfish." So, we did. The fish was great, the crafts and people were in abundance, and it was a memorable time, one of many we enjoyed with our friend who loved his patients and enjoyed life. His enthusiasm was contagious!

In Oak Grove, we lived almost five hours from our biological families, so God brought special local people into our lives. The Berry Family became very dear friends during the early years we spent in Oak Grove. T.F. Berry, a lifetime farmer in West Carroll Parish, and his wife, Oree, were faithful members of First Baptist Church where he was also a deacon. They had raised their five children on their farm. They took us under their wing and made us feel like we were an extension of their family.

We would go to their house to eat, fellowship, and play music. I guess it was there that I was first introduced by Mr. Berry to boiled peanuts. Daddy had always parched our peanuts in Texas, but Mr. Berry boiled his. Mrs. Berry, a very dedicated and loving mother, was also a guitarist. She loved to invite several musicians in the community to her house for an evening to make music together. Her son Scotty and Ed Prevost would bring their guitars and sing with us.

Mr. Berry always planted a big garden in the spring. Mrs. Berry and her daughters would can vegetables and fill their freezers with good things for their winter pantry! We were recipients of peas, tomatoes, or corn at random times when we were there to visit.

I'll never forget that one time when I was about to have a garage sale and needed something to hang clothes on. Mr. Berry welded me a long clothes rack, which he built on wheels that made it easily moved. We have used that in our storage room for years and still own it to this day. It was the kind of deed that a loving father would do for his daughter!

Pete Berry, and his wife Libby, were also special "Berry" friends of ours. A beautiful lady, Libby, always had a smile, a positive attitude even in times of difficulty, and was one of my favorite people to see and visit with in Oak Grove.

Our Oak Grove "grandmother" was Mrs. Elsie Whitten. "Granny Whitten," a lady of great faith and God's Word, was one of the oldest members of First Baptist Church. Granny told me that she had read the Bible about 36 times! We enjoyed talking about our Lord each time we got together. Granny and her husband lived in a small brick house just a few doors from our dental office.

Psalm 139:17-18 reminds me of Granny Whitten. "How precious are your thoughts about me, O God They cannot be numbered! I can't even count them; they outnumber the grains of sand." Granny compared the length of eternity to the grains of sand on the seashore. She would say, "If a bird moved one grain of sand at a time from all the seashores, eternity would still be going!" What a great analogy and reminder of the great importance for each of us to trust Jesus as our Savior and live for Him! Eternity is forever!

Every summer, Mary Evelyn and David came to Oak Grove and stayed with us for a week. We did all sorts of fun things together like playing badminton in the backyard, going to the movies, picnicking, and introducing them to new friends. As David grew, he usually found a way to make money at our house, either by mowing the yard or working in the flower beds at the office.

God blessed us with many dental patients. Referrals from our patients built our practice. We advertised very little throughout our twenty-two years in Oak Grove. People said they wanted Dr. Beasley to provide their dental care because he treated them gently and communicated well with them.

My husband took a personal interest in his patients and their families. He learned about their hobbies, trips they were taking, and about their children and grandchildren. He prayed for his patients and asked me to pray for them.

Bill set goals to make the office better than he found it. He equipped a third exam room so that he could bring in a dental hygienist. Because we were in such a rural area, he was concerned that it might be hard to secure one. God sent us our first hygienist named Charlotte, who was married to a cable television technician who moved into our area to work. Besides being a Christian, Charlotte was an excellent hygienist, and having her as part of the dental team made Bill's job easier.

A number of his patients would bring him something good to eat. Those who had gardens would bring fresh vegetables. Those who liked to cook would bake something: Mexican cornbread, cookies, cake, pie, and jelly, to name a few.

One time Bill had a patient who told him that her daughter was sick and actually needed a miracle to get well. We had an evangelist coming to our church who operated in the gift of healing. He told her to get her daughter to attend one of our evening services and be prayed for. At his invitation, the lady took her adult daughter for prayer, and she was miraculously healed!

Bill was blessed with good staff members. After working for four months for Bill, I turned the job over to Gloria, our new receptionist. I started back to college in January 1979, to study Office Administration at Northeast Louisiana University (now the University of Louisiana at Monroe). With two years of college already behind me, it would take me two to finish. It was a round-trip, daily commute of 120 miles per day to Monroe. I enjoyed my classes and attending the Baptist Student Union. The caring teachers in my department made the difference. The classes I took prepared me to work as a medical/legal secretary.

Sometimes in the afternoon after school, I would go to visit with Mrs. Berry. She was like a second mom to me. After our visit, as I was about to go home, she would give me some of her home cooking to help me with our evening meal.

A Second Nephew

Early in October of 1979, our second nephew was born. Pennie and Tom had their first son and named him Jeff. He was a beautiful child with dark hair. We enjoyed going to Texas to see this new life God had sent to our family.

After commuting to college for a year and a half, I became very tired and visited my doctor. I started to feel better, but decided to take the summer of 1980 off from school and take a break from the 2 ½ hour daily, round-trip commute to Monroe.

That summer, Mary Kay and Ralph adopted Beth Ann, who was born two months early. She was very tiny, and her dedicated parents had to handle her very carefully to get her through those fragile months and even the years that followed. They were so thankful to have a little daughter to go with their son, Paul, and we were excited to have our first niece.

While I was resting from school that summer, Mr. Donald K. Carroll, an attorney, was taking applications for a secretary, and I applied for the job. September 1980, I started working as his legal secretary and very much liked the variety of my work, which included typing real estate deeds, loan papers, wills, etc.

Because we had agreed that I would stay at home when we started our family, we never depended on my income to live. We lived on what Bill made and used the money from my job to furnish our home and take a vacation. I learned so much as a legal secretary and liked meeting our clients.

At First Baptist Church, we especially enjoyed being members of the Couples' Sunday School Class. As it grew in number, Mrs. Willie Ruth, a retired schoolteacher, was our teacher, and she cared about each of us. Dr. James Dobson says, "Women need to find other women to talk to, and not expect their husbands to listen to every word they say." God sent some special friends into my life from that class, especially Kathy Britt and Betty Strong.

In the winter of 1981, the Public Health Service Conference was held in Denver. We learned that some changes were being made that would affect Bill's employment benefits. The future policy decisions caused him to begin thinking of leaving government employment to become a private practitioner in Oak Grove.

In the spring, Pennie and Tom had their second son and named him Kris. He was cute with light brown hair. The Beasley family was growing by one new baby each year!

Dr. Beasley became a solo dental practitioner in Oak Grove in June 1981. The original goal of the Public Health Service in sending us to the small rural town had been reached—for us to stay permanently and continue to provide dental care to the community. Bill continued to build the practice and improve it any way he chose. Another X-Ray was added, landscaping, more concrete for parking, and a new sign. Later on, paint, carpet, wallpaper, new furniture, pictures, and lamps made the inside more inviting and comfortable for the patients and staff. We were grateful for the great opportunity God provided for us and for the nice office and furnishings too!

In September 1981, we shared with our parents and friends the exciting news that we were expecting our first child! Our new baby would be born in May 1982!

A few things Bill has taught me in marriage:

1. Be on time: "It takes time to do things."
2. Overlook annoying occurrences like spilled milk: "Accidents happen."
3. Unconditional love and commitment can be powerful.
4. Faithfulness holds great value.
5. Love is apologizing and moving on, forgetting what is behind.
6. Work first, then play.
7. Cleaning up as you mess up makes life at home easier.
8. Organization is the springboard to success!
9. Save for a rainy day because it's coming!

10. Pay your tithe first, then save something!

11. Sacrificial love is when you give even when you don't feel like it.

12. You can make yourself laugh by what you do and say, even if you don't feel like it.

CHAPTER 7

EMILY, GIVER
OF SUNSHINE AND SONG

"Lo children are a heritage of the Lord: and the fruit of the womb is his reward. As arrows are in the hand of a mighty man; so are children of the youth. Happy is the man that hath his quiver full of them: they shall not be ashamed, but they shall speak with the enemies in the gate."(Psalm 127:3-5).

As Bill and I prepared for the birth of our first child, it was with much anticipation. I had a wonderful pregnancy. I was working as a legal secretary for Hamilton and Carroll Law Firm.

One day during those first three months, when I was so tired, we closed a home loan for a lady named Jessie and her husband Willie, who had moved to Louisiana from Ohio to be near her sister. Jessie had been the housekeeper for several people; she knew the ropes and wanted part-time work. Bill said, "Let's hire Jessie to help you until you get your energies back." She became not only an employee who helped us maintain our home, and take care of our children, but also a special friend who worked for us for the next thirteen years!

As my May due date approached, I chose yellow gingham fabric for sheets, bumper pad, and bed skirt. The crib assembly caused the reality of fatherhood to hit Bill! We went shopping together and purchased a very large Paddington bear to set in our new wooden baby bed. We did not know if we were having a boy or a girl because ultrasounds were not done routinely then.

In April, I worked my last day, was presented with a beautiful gift by the staff and went home to prepare for the baby to come. It was a time to get rested and put the finishing touches on the preparations needed for bringing our first baby home.

My friend, Dotty Berry, hosted our baby shower in her lovely home in Oak Grove, and we received many beautiful, useful gifts from our church family and friends. Our parents came for the weekend so our mothers could share the special evening with me.

Early one Friday morning in May, I woke Bill up and told him it was time to go! He jumped into the shower while I called Dr. Jarrell in Monroe, who seemed to be sitting by the phone. He said he would meet me at St. Francis Hospital. Quickly, we were on the road; Bill turned the flashers on for the 62-mile trip. As it turned out, there was really no reason to rush. Dr. Jarrell decided to induce labor and get the baby here by late afternoon. They do call it labor for a reason! Bill stayed by my side!

My parents and young siblings came from Texas to be with us that day. Emily was born at 4:20 p.m., weighing 8 lbs., 12 ounces, and was 21 inches long. A healthy, baby girl with a head full of dark hair, she reminded us of her Aunt Pennie. It is very difficult to explain the deep emotion and love I had for my first child as I began to hold her there in my hospital room.

The next day, Bill's parents came to see her. By then, there were about twenty babies in the nursery! Mr. Beasley told the nurses

"To move that Beasley baby to the front where, after driving so far, he could see her!"

We carried Emily home the following Tuesday. She was a perfect baby, except for some jaundice; Dr. Dyess, her pediatrician, wanted to check her bilirubin level every day until it went down. Mrs. Beasley drove me and Emily the sixty miles to the hospital lab every day for five days so they could take some blood. By that time in May, the Louisiana humidity had risen, and the daily trips to Monroe were difficult.

Both our mothers came and stayed with us for a week. Mrs. Beasley came first and cooked delicious, nutritious meals with bread pudding for dessert. I had gained so much weight with my pregnancy that she helped by starting me on a Weight Watchers diet. My wonderful mother-in-law washed the clothes and kept the house as if it were her own, and would not go to bed at night until everything was neat and in its proper place.

Because of my experiences with taking care of much younger siblings, caring for a baby was not foreign or scary to me. However, it's a totally different role to be the mother rather than the big sister. Mrs. Beasley taught me how to give Emily her first bath. That was not my favorite part of the morning because it was impossible to keep her from getting cold. She laid on the changing table, and I carefully bathed her from head to toe. I cleaned her tiny ears with Q-tips and then proceeded to bathe her tummy and not bother the rest of the naval cord that remained for a few days.

Mother came the second week, cooked, washed, and took good care of us too. By the weekend, Bill and I were ready for an afternoon outing to Greenville, Mississippi, which we enjoyed.

After two weeks, our mothers were back home in Texas, and it was just our family of three. Bill went to the office every day, and I was at home with little Emily, just as we had planned it. I couldn't have been happier as our new little girl brought me so much joy and fulfillment. I was so blessed that Bill wanted me to be there with her, and I loved nearly every minute of it!

From her entrance into the world, Emily brought us sunshine. She was a beautiful baby girl, the gift from God to us laying in her nursery, surrounded by our love and yellow gingham. One of my favorite things about having a little girl was dressing her in beautiful dresses and sun suits. When she would wake up in the night or early in the morning, I was so excited to jump up and go into her room to see about her, and she seldom ever cried.

In June, our friends, Kathy and Don had Holly, and she became one of Emily's special playmates. The following month, Glen and Betty had Lindsey, and she too became a playmate and friend to Emily through the years. The three mothers, Kathy, Betty, and I would get together frequently and visit while our daughters played together. As friends do, we shared joys and sorrows through the years, watching, training, and guiding our daughters as they grew up to become productive, young Christian women.

We attended First Baptist Church in Oak Grove when Emily was born, and because she was so good, they called her the "queen of the nursery." Our good friend, Dotty, worked there every Sunday, and she and Emily bonded. It was at First Baptist that we dedicated Emily to the Lord on a Sunday morning. She was a beautiful bundle of white in her new christening gown and bonnet purchased just for the occasion. My parents and siblings came from Texas to be part of the dedication ceremony.

Bill and I had a vision for Emily. We treasured her as a gift from God, created in His image and an eternal soul. We loved her so much, and we planned to teach her about Jesus. We nurtured her, took care of her, hugged and kissed her, talked to her, and made her feel safe and loved. When she was old enough, we would teach her to obey us. As she grew, we would read her books and nurture in her a love for learning and singing. We would teach her modesty, purity and how to be a lady. Most importantly, we would teach her how to pray to God and trust that through the atmosphere of faith and love we would provide that she too would in her childhood make a personal decision to follow Jesus!

During Emily's first year, I started going to the dental office every Thursday to help Bill with the business. We found a wonderful lady to take care of Emily one day a week in her home, Mrs. Bert, who got our little daughter to take her first step. She spent a lot of time with her, talking to her, building up her self-confidence and caring for her needs. Our babysitter was also a gardener who taught Emily how to shell peas and shuck corn, and she loved it!

At an early age, Emily showed great intelligence. She loved books; we read a story at naptime and then a Bible story at bedtime. She also loved her dolls and stuffed animals. Our baby girl radiated a special excitement and boldness in her personality at an early age. Jessie gave Emily a large ragdoll dressed in a pink dress as a gift, and she made up the name "Shray Cray" for her.

Another special Christian couple who reached out to us in love and became our friends were Blanche and Lee Lamb. They lived on a farm and always planted a garden. We especially enjoyed the fresh vegetables they brought us in the summer. At Christmas, Mrs. Blanche would bring us a gift of some of her special canned goods like "Strawberry Fig Preserves." One time I bragged about it, so she invited me over to her house where she taught me how to make it in her kitchen.

Mrs. Blanche told me that she would keep Emily for me sometime when I needed to get away. I knew that our baby girl was in very good hands. I could feel the love of Christ as Mrs. Blanche and Mr. Lee lived their lives unselfishly.

A New Church Home

Although Bill and I had attended First Baptist Church since our move to Oak Grove in 1978, and we loved the people, we had never joined. When we talked with the pastor about joining, he said that I would have to be rebaptized. Bill and I did not agree with that, and we prayed about what God would have us do. I had been immersed in water as a girl, and I was satisfied with my experience.

As we sought the will of the Lord, we visited several churches. Bill visited with a patient who told him about Providence Baptist Church, a new fellowship of believers where he was a member in Lake Providence. We decided to visit in June of 1983. The pastor, Brother Don, and the Body of Christ gave us a warm welcome. We had been praying about this important decision and within two weeks we knew that was where we wanted to worship and work.

Second Child on the Way!

September 1983 brought us the happy news that Emily would be getting a brother or sister for her birthday the following May 1984. She was sixteen months old and would turn two right after the new baby's birth. Thoughts of taking care of "two" babies made me feel a little overwhelmed at first. I didn't fully realize at the time how being very close in age would allow them to enjoy growing up together!

The nine months went by very quickly. Realizing our baby would be here before Emily's birthday, we had her party a month early, and invited her three closest friends, Holly, Lindsey, and Murray. Bill had spent a busy week after work assembling her brand-new swing set in our carport! The girls had fun swinging and playing together as we all celebrated Emily turning two!

When Andrew was born in May, Emily became the big sister, and what a great sister she was! The first big word I taught her was "fragile." She learned to be careful and quiet. As he grew and they played together, Emily was the leader, and he loved following her.

Before Emily could read, Bill decided he wanted us to buy a set of Encyclopedias. Dr. Smith, my college professor and friend, sold Encyclopedias, and he presented the idea to us. I think they were $500 at the time. I thought it was an investment too early, but Bill said he enjoyed reading them as a boy, and he wanted to provide them for our children.

Emily attended Wee Care, a preschool sponsored by the First Baptist Church of Oak Grove. She especially enjoyed her teachers, Mrs. Betty Rose and Mrs. Cherry, one day a week while I worked at the dental office. She graduated in their commencement exercises in May 1987 and was very excited about starting school!

Emily really thrived in Mrs. Sheila Hudolin's kindergarten class at Oak Grove Elementary School. She and Emily loved each other, and there was much knowledge from books and drama imparted to that young student during a year. Our little daughter loved to sing "Mr. Tom Turkey" and many Sunday School songs.

The Girl Scouting experience was something I wanted for Emily, so I organized a Daisy Girl Scout Troop, and the cutest little girls joined. We continued that troop until the girls began the sixth grade. During that time, we made new friends, worked, played, hiked, camped, traveled, and sold a lot of Girl Scout Cookies. During Emily's first year in Brownie's, she sold over 500 boxes and won a black-and-white TV. That was a lot of cookies to deliver! Those Girl Scouts from Troop 97-Silver Waters Girl Scout Council still have a special place in my heart.

In second grade, Emily gained a love for books and reading through the influence of her second-grade teacher, Mrs. Deborah Hawthorne. She read to her students and challenged them to "dive into books "and develop their writing skills. Both helped to lay an early foundation in Emily for becoming a diligent student.

It was during the second grade that Emily became a piano student. She had several teachers through the years, but the teacher who developed her the most was Mrs. Laurie Thompson. We drove every week to Bastrop to Mrs. Laurie's home where student-teacher bonding occurred and Emily advanced. At the National Piano Guild competition for two years, Emily scored a superior rating, being the first of the young teacher's students to ever do so.

There are many lessons that we get to teach our children as we parent, but I remember one especially. Emily was an easy girl to raise, but she was a normal child who had to be trained. One day I caught her in a lie. I spanked her for it, and she never told me another one. Good parenting is teaching by example. I cannot expect my child's actions to be better than mine.

One of the ways we taught Emily the power of prayer is through our shopping trips together. When she was just an elementary student, and needed clothes, we would discuss the items she needed—jeans, dresses, etc.—and then we would pray together that God would lead us to the items we needed that day at the right prices. At the end of our trip, we could look back over the day, the items we found and the price we paid, and we would invariably see that God had truly guided us. It was a real faith builder for both of us.

Emily enjoyed singing through her Girl Scout troop and during the summer at King's Camp in Mer Rouge. When she was in the fifth grade, she sang her first solo at church with my accompaniment on the piano. The song title was "Mountain Top," with the message, "I love to live on a mountain top, fellowshipping with my Lord. But I must come down from the mountain top to the people in the valley below, or they'll never know that they can go to the mountain of the Lord."

After that first solo, Bill did something for Emily that surprised and blessed us. He went to Radio Shack and purchased a small PA system with a microphone for Emily to use in her room to practice. What an inexpensive, yet huge investment that was in training her toward her "bent." From then on, she was planning and learning the next song.

Although she continued her piano lessons, Emily was very comfortable with a microphone. In sixth grade, she entered the West Carroll Farm Bureau Talent Competition with a solo to "Sing Your Praise to the Lord"; she won third place, a trophy and had her picture in the paper. In the ninth grade she entered again singing "Via Delarosa" and won second place. From that night came an invitation to sing for the Miss West Carroll Pageant.

Dr. James Dobson declares that seventh through ninth grade is the hardest age for a growing adolescent. I agree with him. Emily felt very alone at that age, with very few friends who thought or had values like hers. I spent time with her and consoled her with the fact that it was just a phase of life, and those struggles would not last forever.

It was during her seventh-grade year that she had such a heavy load at school, played junior high girls' basketball, took piano lessons which required much practice, and found her schedule to be exhausting.

In eighth grade, she chose not to play basketball and focused more on her piano music and attending Immanuel Christian Fellowship on Wednesday nights. It was there that she received a strong dose of God's Word from Pastors Stowe and Kaki Harbin, who were also our neighbors and teachers in our public school. Agape love flowed from the congregation to Emily and back to them as they encouraged each other in the Lord. She began praying about being a member of the 1997 Summer Mission Team with Mr. and Mrs. Harbin.

The summer after eighth grade, Emily took her first voice lessons from her piano teacher, Mrs. Laurie, who also had her master's degree in Vocal Music. Six weeks of lessons helped Emily considerably. We were told to expect a bigger change and improvement by the time our daughter was sixteen.

In August, as Emily began ninth grade, a prophet named John Nelson came to our church for the first time. He had never seen Emily before but gave the following prophetic word over her: "I see you as part of a team, but then later, individually, as an evangelist. You have the ability to influence people to move."

During her ninth-grade year at Oak Grove High School, Emily was invited by her teacher to play for the high school graduation in May. The song was a duet, which she learned with Nathan, a classmate, and they worked all nine months on it. By March, Emily had become a team member preparing for the 1997 mission trip to

Ozamis, Philippines. They met weekly with the Harbin's in their home to talk and pray and plan for their June departure. They would be gone for a whole month, including travel time.

Graduation time arrived. Emily and Nathan played their wonderful duet at the piano there on the Oak Grove High School football field. The graduates marched in and out to their impressive piano number.

Right before Emily was leaving for the Philippines, she was able to share with Providence Church about the goals of the mission and sing a solo: "Here I Am, I surrender my life to the work of your hands..." My heart was filled with feelings of joy and pride in this daughter who had given herself to the Lord and was always singing His Praises!

Our Daughter, the Missionary

Bright and early on June 1, 1997, we met Mr. and Mrs. Harbin at the Monroe Airport where they would begin the long trip to the other side of the world. Our fifteen-year-old daughter, Emily, would not be home until June 29. As I stood and watched that huge silver bird split the sky, it became clear to me that she was truly in God's hands. It's easy to dedicate our babies to the Lord as we hold them in our arms, but when we can no longer hold them, we find out if we have really given them to Him!

We could not talk to Emily very often, but we prayed faithfully for her.

I include here Emily's own testimony about her Philippines mission trip, which she submitted in 1999 to *Guidepost for* their Young Writers' Contest.

"Flight to Faith"
By Emily Beasley

Cock-a-doodle-doo...my eyes popped open as my alarm clock cried out in its rooster voice that it was 3:00 a.m. and the day I had prayerfully anticipated for over a year! In approximately four hours, I, a fifteen-year-old girl, would depart with my mission leader, Mr. Stowe Harbin, and seven other teammates. We would journey from Monroe, Louisiana to Ozamiz, Philippines to share the Gospel of Jesus Christ. God would change my life forever in that summer of 1997.

Our team set out with the purpose of working in the many ministries of Happy Church, which enrolled 8,000 members. Some of these ministries were: Happy House, Sunday School, home-based outreaches, and building houses for the poor. Happy House, home to over one hundred people taken in from the streets or abusive situations, was our temporary residence. Every person living in the house was taught about Jesus Christ and given a job to earn their stay. The home-outreaches, where we preached, sang and prayed for the sick, were designed for those who could not come to church; many received salvation! Happy Church...not only God's mouthpiece but also His hands and feet, has contributed to the Kingdom's rapid growth in Ozamiz.

After one full week of air travel, we reached the tiny Ozamiz airport with joy and anticipation. Many smiling, brown faces welcomed us with a banner, leis, and songs. I had never experienced such appreciation in my life.

Upon my arrival, I felt self-confident and prepared, but God was yet to change that. The first shock wave hit hard when I discovered the bathroom facilities of Happy House. Bubble bath times were very sacred to this American girl. After almost two days, I could stand the filth no longer. Soap, a faucet, cold water, and a bucket describes the experience best! Living for a short time with the inconvenience and scarcities prevalent to the Filipino lifestyle has transformed my worldview and created in me a more content and thankful heart.

With each passing hour, the hideous voice of fear, doubt, and insecurity screamed more loudly in my ears. After leading morning devotions, I realized that those who had depended on God for each meal knew Him and His word better than I did. Doubt struck a blow! Is it God's will for me to be here? I'm not prepared. I can't handle this. I could get a disease. Did I miss God? My self-sufficiency had been stripped from me...physically, spiritually and emotionally. As my fears closed in to devour me, I called out to God. Shortly thereafter, Mr. Harbin, also having been on his knees, tapped on my door. God had revealed unto him my struggle; he quoted to me Romans 8:1 & 2. "There is therefore now no condemnation to them which are in Christ Jesus, who walk not after the flesh, but after the Spirit. For the law of the Spirit of life in Christ Jesus hath made me free from the law of sin and death." The Word of God cut straight to my heart, reassuring me that I was in His hands. However, praise God that He chose to take the refining process yet further.

That night, Mr. Harbin was to preach at a youth service and invited me to sing. Though I felt I had nothing to give, I went. God spoke to me that humid night through the story of the rich man in the Gospel of Matthew. The altar call was given for those who had not surrendered everything to the Lord. I knew that I had been trying to rule my own life...a task too great for my human frame. I, the missionary, swallowed my pride and took the steps to the altar, which have changed my life. The Holy Spirit filled me as I surrendered all to Him. From that night on, I had peace about the mission. I knew that I was still inadequate, but the God of the universe living in me was my omnipotent Father!

"This is it!" said Pastor Elvie Go of Happy Church, as she pointed to an eight-by-eight, one-room building with a dirt floor and exterior walls made of rusted tin. This dilapidated structure was to be home for Marilyn, a pregnant woman abandoned by her husband and left with nothing but her three sons. Pastor Elvie quickly informed our team that we would renovate this house for this single mother. Later we ripped off the corroded tin, built a floor, and finished the inside walls. After laboring for three days, the house was complete. In preparation for Marilyn to move, Pastor Elvie took us shopping for household necessities. We female team members were taking great pains to color-coordinate everything. Pastor Elvie interrupted our decision process as she laughingly stated, "The color does not matter, as long as her needs are met." This statement taught me a great lesson. We color-coded Americans so often focus on trivial things when we should be grateful as long as we have basic necessities. We surprised Marilyn with her new house and gifts. When she arrived, we serenaded her. Elvie provided lunch for them in their new home. As tears fell, Marilyn said she had many problems, but she thanked God that we had solved one.

Pastor Elvie Go lives out her name; she "goes" wherever God sends her. When she gave her life to Jesus Christ, her fiancé let her know that Christianity was not good for him. Elvie was finishing a law degree when God called her to Happy Church. She said she would have gladly given the job to a man, but no man would take the responsibility. As a result of her obedience, thousands of people have received Jesus. Elvie had a "just-do-it" attitude! She would point to people on the streets, insist that we witness to them, and they would receive Jesus. Though it was difficult for me, I now know that I must always be ready to share my faith. Elvie Go has taught me by example to be "instant in season and out of season."

Cock-a-doodle-doo...back home in Louisiana my alarm clock crowed at 1:00 a.m. after two weeks of silence. As my mother approached my bedroom door, the rooster's beckoning ceased. PRAY! My parents immediately interceded for my safety. Little did they know a storm was approaching our tiny boat in the South China Sea. We sailed back to shore on their prayers.

The Philippines mission was, for me, a flight to faith. What God began in me through the power of prayer has become a continual lifestyle. I can truly say with the Apostle Paul that "He who has begun a good work in me will be faithful to complete it."

*   *   *

Emily returned home to us a different girl than the one we knew the month before! She had a thankful heart, was more humble, and had a greater desire to follow God. That night during the Youth service in the Philippines, The Holy Spirit filled her with the evidence of his presence— her personal prayer language. Emily literally saw and felt the power of prayer, and it became a greater part of her life and ministry on the home front thereafter. She had more compassion for others after seeing the people, conditions, and faith in action in the Philippines on a daily basis.

1997: Emily Began Homeschooling Too

When she began homeschooling the following fall in 1997, she would begin her morning in her room with her own quiet time. She exuded tremendous patience in the home as she began a totally new approach to the high school experience. Her ability to love and study with a sometimes-stressed mother was amazing. We would pray together about our needs and direction and watch God provide. I marveled frequently at the patience, joy, and love that Emily possessed. They were fruits of the Holy Spirit in her life! The work God did in her in the Philippines truly prepared her for the next three years. Being together with family under one roof, twenty-four hours a day, seven days a week, studying together, depending on each other, working together, not only to run our household smoothly, but also to accomplish a high school diploma, is not easy. We grew in our relationships with each other and with God! That could not have been accomplished without faith and the work of the Holy Spirit.

Christians deal with the same struggles as non-Christians, but we pray and trust in God to help us, and He does. When God comes into our lives, we relinquish our control for His. Just as we must trust our earthly father and mother to provide a roof over our heads, clothing, etc., we must trust our heavenly Father for all things, even the daily, unexpected things that come up. He is a faithful God and is so personally involved in our lives.

Some things Emily has taught me:

1. The gift of peace that rests on her is desired by many and possessed by few.
   She has taught me to seek after the peace of heart God has promised to believers.

2. Her diligence to take time to absorb what she reads and learns has inspired me to be more focused.

3. She lives by the phrase, "Wherever you are, be there."

4. Her honesty has inspired me to be a better listener as she is.

5. Her gift of encouragement about my writing has helped me in valuing and using my own gift as a tool for building up God's people.

6. Her perseverance in difficult situations through her college years and in the workplace, and her ability to handle conflict, have helped me in areas of weakness.

7. Although I will always be her mother, the friendship Emily and I enjoy as adults is also a precious gift that I treasure. Though miles may separate us since she is married with a home of her own, what was established in our hearts, especially during those precious home-schooling years, can never be diminished by distance. We can always pick up where we left off. That is the mark of true friendship.

CHAPTER 8

ANDREW, MANLY MUSICIAN

"A wise son heareth his father's instruction..."
(Proverbs 13:1).

O ne evening when I was twelve years old, a young Christian woman came over to visit with my parents. She spoke a prophetic word to me that I have always held in my heart and believed. She said, "Someday you will have a son, and he'll be a great man of God."

On a wonderful and very memorable day in May of 1984, our son, Andrew Thomas, was born to us! Andrew is the only son to carry on the Beasley name, and we wanted to honor Bill's dad, Thomas Beasley.

Andrew was born two years after Emily, and it was déjà vu! I woke up at about 3:00 a.m. on Friday morning and told Bill I thought it was time to go to the hospital. He jumped in the shower, and I called Dr. Jarrell. He said he would meet me at St. Francis Hospital in Monroe as soon as I could get there. Bill put the flashers on and away we went...

Weighing in at nine pounds, one ounce, and measuring twenty-one inches long, Andrew was referred to by Dr. Jarrell as the "blockbuster." Bill and I were so thankful for our beautiful baby boy. My parents, Mary Evelyn, David, and Bill's mother were also there to welcome him. Emily came with her daddy the next day to the hospital to see me and look through the nursery window at her new brother, whom she loved quickly.

Because my mother still had children at home, Mrs. Beasley came again and took care of all four of us for two weeks. She cooked wonderful and nutritious meals, kept the house clean, washed the clothes, and helped me with the children. The first two weeks went swiftly by, and I remember the Monday morning after Bill's mother went home and Bill left for work. I was alone with Emily, two years old and Andrew, two weeks old. The reality of my calling to motherhood had begun to dawn!

In Andrew's baby book, I recorded the prophetic message, and claimed Andrew to be that son God had promised me sixteen years before. A few months later, we dedicated Andrew to the Lord at Providence Church. Pastor Don Boyett officiated the sacred dedication, and John and Rhonda Parker did the special music. My parents and siblings came to support us.

Bill and I considered our work as parents an assignment from the Lord! We took it very seriously; it was a top priority for us. I read a lot of parenting books when I was training my children. We loved Andrew and took good care of him. We would teach him to obey as he was old enough to understand, and we would read to him too. We would get him together with children and adults of like minded faith and character so that he would have godly influences. We would take him to church regularly and teach him how to pray to God. We hoped and prayed ourselves that he would choose to follow Jesus at an early age—in childhood.

It took a while to settle into a daily routine with a baby, a toddler, and a self-employed husband to care for. I dearly loved being a wife to Bill and mother to my young children. Although my lap was full, my heart was happy and content! ! I gave myself fully to my calling of motherhood! I would get Bill off to work, get Emily dressed, give Andrew his bath, and before we knew it lunchtime would arrive, and Bill would be home to eat with us. It was a very busy morning, so we would eat a sandwich or leftovers for lunch, and I would cook a big meal in the evening.

One day when Andrew was still a baby, Bill came home and said, "I need a good, big meal at lunch. That is when I'm working, and I need energy during the day. A sandwich just doesn't hold me." That was when I began cooking a large, hot lunch every workday. I found it to be a discipline and a juggling act to fit in all I needed to do as a mother, and then to have a hot lunch ready between 12:00 and 12:30 every day when Bill came home from the dental office. The good things about it were that it met Bill's nutrition needs, and ours too, and it let me get the big meal behind me, so I didn't face it in the evening; leftovers for dinner freed up time at the end of the day. I continued the habit of cooking a hot lunch on weekdays for the next fourteen to sixteen years. Bill says that nutritious lunches instead of fast food has probably kept him healthy all these years! I must admit that I didn't really like having to cook a hot meal every day at lunch. I submitted to what Bill wanted and needed, and it was a healthy lifestyle decision.

I continued to help Bill with the dental office on Thursdays, which gave me a change of pace from the home front. I enjoyed interacting with adults and using my office administration skills too. Emily and Andrew both went to Mrs. Bert's house for a while; when Andrew was about one, they started staying at our home with Jessie. She would come to clean our house on Monday and come back on Thursday to take care of the children. She loved them, and we loved her.

Emily was a very doting big sister. As Andrew grew and they began playing together, she was the "boss." She did all the thinking, and he submitted to all her many ideas—for just so long! On Christmas morning, she would look at his toys and tell Andrew,

"I knew you were going to get that!" He loved "Emee," and they spent many, many happy hours together.

One day when Emily and Andrew had an appointment in Monroe with, their pediatrician, we were sitting in her waiting room when we met some Lake Providence people who would become our special friends. Rhonda was there with her little son, Jake. We started talking, and soon afterward, Rhonda, Lamar and Jake began attending Providence Church. Andrew and Jake became buddies, and Rhonda and I became friends.

Andrew was a very cute, loving little boy. I would tuck him in each night and listen to him talk before he said his prayers. He said his top three best friends were Jesus, Bill, and me! Then he said his prayers, and I prayed for him.

Our children got a new cousin to play with in July 1986 when Matthew was born to my sister, Mary Evelyn, and her husband, Greg, who had married two years earlier. We were so excited to have this beautiful little boy, our first nephew and cousin in the Moore family. Despite our age difference, my sister and I now shared the common bond of motherhood.

When Andrew was a preschooler, we were very close. He was a compliant child, wanting to do the right thing. Proverbs 20:11 says, "Even a child is known by his doings, whether his work be pure, and whether it be right." One day Bill was saying goodbye to us before going to Texas to his step-grandfather's funeral. Andrew, about three or four, told us he was going to pray; he went to his room and closed the door.

My husband went to church a lot on Sundays when he would rather just be outdoors soaking in the sunshine and breathing in the fresh air. We would drive past the "swamp" between Oak Grove and Lake Providence, and he told me that he often thought, "I'd be better off out there like those hunters." But he continued to be faithful to attend church with us, instead of just taking us, knowing he was role modeling for his children.

Andrew also attended Wee Care at First Baptist Church one day a week, where he loved his teachers and his little friends. He was so cute in his little graduation cap in May 1989. Kindergarten was in full view!

Three years after Matthew was born, our second nephew and cousin on the Moore side, Joel Ross Thomas, was born to my sister. He was a beautiful baby, and I was privileged to help bring mother and son home from the hospital. A welcome banner hung cheerily on the front porch and big brother, Matthew, and my parents were there to welcome their fourth grandchild!

On a hot August day in 1989, Andrew started Kindergarten at Oak Grove Elementary School. He was very excited about going, but I had mixed emotions about him leaving. After seven years at home with children, I would be there alone. What would I do with all that time? In my adjustment process, I found there was still plenty to keep me busy.

Andrew loved school! He was a very good student! He liked his elementary teachers. He enjoyed spending time with his friends, Kyle, Luke, and Jake.

When the Cub Scout troop was organized, Andrew joined. He sold popcorn to raise money, and we attended the Fall Mom and Me Campout at Camp T. L. James in West Monroe. I looked forward to this mother and son event that we attended every fall.

By second grade, our son especially loved to hang out with his dad. Bill spent time with Andrew at home, building Pinewood Derby cars and attending his Cub Scout ceremonies.

A significant bond occurred between Bill and Andrew during the summer after third grade. They packed up the bicycles, the tent, the camping and fishing supplies, the groceries, and traveled to northern Arkansas to canoe The Buffalo National River! That was the glue that began to knit this father and son tightly together. Bill said "When I get outdoors, I start feeling life come back into me!"

Andrew and the other boys in our church had a special, dedicated Sunday School teacher named Mrs. Estelle. She put her heart into teaching them every Sunday and providing special treats! Once a year, Bill planned and carried out a Saturday bicycle ride to Vicksburg National Park for Andrew's third and fourth grade Sunday School class.

At eight and nine years old, Andrew wanted to play the guitar. Our pastor, Brother Don, played the instrument very well and agreed to give Bill and Andrew lessons. The two men went to Monroe together one day and bought a wonderful Alvarez guitar. Bill was beginning to play praise songs. Andrew could make the chord, but he would fret out because his hands were too small. We could see that he needed some time to grow physically before he was ready for that instrument.

By the time he was a fifth grader, we had a young, gifted worship leader at our church by the name of Jonathan Wiggins, who played the keyboard. Andrew told me one day that he wanted to play the keyboard also. I said, "You learn to play the grand piano in the living room, and I'll get you an electronic one." He began to take piano lessons that year from Mrs. Laurie Thompson. He caught on very quickly and played well but hated to practice. I prodded him for most of the two and a half years that he took lessons. Finally, seeing the writing on the wall, I told my son he could quit piano lessons. Then, in sincere honesty, I added, "Andrew, I don't want to put you on a guilt trip, but if you don't find an instrument to play, you will be burying your talent."

Andrew entered seventh grade as a homeschooler. He got his daily assignments quickly and had time to work on other things like building a dog pen for his golden retriever, Trevor, and music. We had to ask the question, "How will God accomplish what he has promised us?"

I began to look at the life of King David and heard a song that struck a note: "When others see a shepherd boy, God sees a King, even though his life is filled with ordinary things. In a moment, you will touch him, and everything will change. When others see a shepherd boy, God sees a King." I looked at Andrew and the other young boys in my junior high Sunday School Class and knew they were very special in God's Kingdom. In later chapters I will discuss our life as a homeschool family in greater detail, but I want to address some key points in this chapter about how to raise sons versus raising daughters.

Our society has tried to make us believe that women and men are created equal. It is true that women should be paid the same wage as a man for doing the same job. However, God did not make men and women alike for very good reasons. Therefore, we cannot use the same techniques to raise our sons and daughters. We will not produce strong, godly men without using the right approach. Hopefully, the principles I learned will make the path smoother for parents who come behind us raising sons. Mothers, if we treat adolescent sons the way we treat girls, we will produce men who are underachievers in two ways: either they will be wimps or resentful.

It is imperative that the father truly "step up to the plate" with a son's training during the age of adolescence. I saw Bill do that in numerous ways. He taught him to speak respectfully to me. He taught Andrew how to work. Today, Andrew is a very hard worker, and has worked two jobs at one time to take good care of his young family. He is very much a multi-tasker too.

At the beginning of tenth grade, I believed God was leading me to design Andrew's curriculum myself. The first subject the Lord guided me in was the Bible. He led me to the course entitled *Experiencing God* by Henry Blackaby. We both had a workbook we studied separately, then sat together to discuss our answers. It was a very rigorous Bible Study.

God showed me that every time Andrew said or did something that was against God's word, that I was to discipline him with the Word of God. II Timothy 3:16-17 says, "All scripture is given by inspiration of God, and is profitable for doctrine, for reproof, for correction, for instruction in righteousness: That the man of God may be perfect, thoroughly furnished unto all good works." When Andrew was unkind, I would tell him to write for me twenty-five times, "Be ye kind one to another." He would say, "I don't have time to write any sentences!"

The fall of 1999, Andrew Eastmond, a favorite psalmist and evangelist, was invited to our church to minister to the worship team. Because Andrew was the drummer and Emily was a singer, I was the taxi. I carried my paperwork and was prepared to be in another room while they had their meeting. Our worship leader, Jonathan, saw me and invited me to join the meeting.

After the message, the minister went around the room praying for each person. When he got in front of me, he said, "I see you teaching children. There is an arrow you are hitting on the ground. Keep doing it because you are getting through." That was God's confirmation that correcting Andrew by using scripture was working, and I was to keep doing it. Afterward, I questioned the minister about the scriptural passage he was referring to, and he explained about the passage in II Kings 13:18.

While training Andrew to become a godly man, I wanted to talk to another mom who had walked my path. Some of the mothers of famous godly people went through very difficult years with their children because they were in rebellion against God. I remember sitting in my room one morning and telling God, "I am not willing to work this hard and see my son go the ways of the world!" I asked God to send me some help, and I know that God not only heard my voice that day, but he also saw my heart. According to Mr. Webster, the word "help" is a broad term which means "Aid, assistance, a source of aid, remedy, relief, one who is in the service of or who assists another."

No doubt, God was helping me on a daily basis, but something was missing. Weary from the responsibilities and the battle, Bill and I attended the January 2000, Northeast Louisiana Homeschool

Conference. It was that weekend that the Lord ministered to me some answers through the speaker for the evening, Reverend Norm Wakefield. He was a former pastor and youth leader who had previously attended a church in California whose focus was to disciple men to lead godly families. It was from his personal experiences that he came to write *Equipped to Love,* which is about idolatry-free relationships. His lessons on *Equipping Men* spoke the Father's Heart to us that winter weekend during Andrew's sophomore year of homeschooling. I believe the truths he shared are one of the keys to winning back the young men and women of this generation for God's Kingdom. The following truths he shared, and I applied, turned the tide on my relationship with Andrew.

I learned and began to apply these thoughts and principles:

1. A young man gets his identity from his father. A father must affirm his son as a man, or the son will look to women, his work, and addictive lifestyles to get this basic need met. As mothers, if we are the most influential one in our boy's life, we must begin to release and delegate more of the control and decisions of his life to his father. If your son does not have a father who can do this, a godly man in the church can be called on through your pastor to do this important task. As mothers, we continue to cook for him, wash his clothes (it is OK. to teach him how to do his own laundry), nurture him, encourage him, but we should go to our husbands with more and more of the training and even discipline that our sons need as they enter adolescence and manhood. I believe that with Andrew, this was a key factor in his maturity. When I let go of "control" and released Bill to oversee more of Andrew's guidance, then more peace came into our home. It is not an easy thing for us mothers to let our boys become men, but with God's help, we must do it!

2. When a boy reaches the age of 13-15, he will begin pulling away from his mother, which feels to her like rebellion or insubordination. This is a natural part of his design because God has made him to leave father and mother and lead his own family. We mothers must use wisdom when this process begins, or we will squelch what God is doing in our young men.

3. When a boy becomes a young teenager, thirteen and fourteen years old, he perceives things we say to him the way a man does. That means that we women must communicate to him, keeping the fact that he is a male in our minds. We can no longer talk to him as we did when he was a boy or the way we do our daughters. His filtering system is made like his father's because he is developing physically and emotionally like a man, although his stature and age may not fully indicate it. Example: Bill says that on his day off, if I have a chore at home for him to do, tell him in advance the list of things. He doesn't want me to tell him throughout the day another thing I thought of for him to do. He wants to plan his day, doing what is on his "list" so that he can do some things he wants to do. When Andrew was a teenager, I would mention to him from time to time throughout the day the things I wanted him to do. He would get very frustrated with me. A knowledge of treating him as a young man helped me to communicate with him on that level.

It is important here to mention that "teenager" is a relatively new or modern term, one that our grandparents did not have to deal with in raising children. It is our culture that has hindered parents and children. Several years ago, young men who are now considered "teenagers" were working and taking their place as the man of their family. The same thing is true for girls; they were thinking about and experiencing the tasks required for making a home— cooking, washing, having children, and pleasing a husband.

4. Part of loving our son is beginning to release him to be a man. I recommend the book *Wild at Heart* by John Eldridge, along with his other books. Every woman needs to understand the way a man thinks. I believe this "lack of understanding" about men is the reason for many divorces as well as lost sons. If we try to train our sons to think the way we do, we will not achieve our goal. That is a tragedy, not only for God's kingdom, but also for the contribution that men make to our world!

5. As mothers of sons who are junior high and older, we must allow God to work in their hearts. I thought being "in control" of Andrew was doing the godly, most "spiritual" thing for him. I believe fear keeps us from letting go; we think that our husband will not see and do the best thing for our son or that our husband will be too hard on our "little boy," which is really a deception. Our controlling spirit throws up a wall between us and our husbands as well as our sons. It's as if we are exalting ourselves above husband and son. I was able, with God's help and his grace, to release Andrew to Bill and the Lord; that helped him to grow and bloom. It was more peaceful in our home because I wasn't always in the middle. We must release these young men to their fathers or godly men who can mentor them in the things of God, imparting to them Biblical truths, discipline, a strong work ethic, masculine knowledge, and wisdom.

Just like a mother knows how much pressure to put on a daughter, a godly father knows how much pressure to put on a son to produce somebody who can take his place as a leader and a man in his own family. Mothers tend to be soft on our sons and hard on our daughters. God gave children a father and mother because He knows that we balance each other!

6. Besides unconditional love, the best gift we can give our sons is prayer support. Amazing things will happen in your son(s) when you start talking less and praying more. As Andrew finished his ninth-grade year of home schooling, I attended the Northeast Louisiana Homeschool graduation in West Monroe. It was during that ceremony that I heard the Holy Spirit say to me, "The last three years you have physically worked very hard training Andrew. The next three years are going to require much prayer." Our children never get too old or "arrive" at a place where they no longer need our prayers or moral support.

7. We humans can learn a lot from watching animals with their young. Watch how a mother hen reacts if you try to bother her chicks. She will flog you. In that same way, we must watch over our sons and daughters as it relates to "the enemy of their souls—Satan himself." As I prayed for Andrew, I was also the "watchman on the wall" over his life. I watched out for the friends he chose. I knew that he was "set apart" for God and that if he spent time with the wrong influences that "bad company corrupts good morals." I pushed him toward that godly calling on his life and reminded him of it!

I'll never forget that one summer day when he was in high school, he ate lunch and was planning to go to town with a new acquaintance from work. I told him he could not afford to hang out with someone who might be using drugs or alcohol. It just takes one time in the wrong place, with the wrong person, and a son or daughter's reputation and life can take a wrong turn.

As we raise sons, we must watch out for the girls who will come along to seduce our sons! Don't be naive and think it can't or won't happen to your baby boy! Many mothers, especially, and fathers, have trouble "seeing" that their son or daughter are young adults; this blindness keeps them from acting wisely. The enemy comes along and deludes their young person; the parent is sitting there saying, "I can't believe that happened." I Peter 5:8-9 says, "Be sober, be vigilant; because your adversary the devil, as a roaring lion, walketh about, seeking whom he may devour: Who resist steadfast in the faith, knowing that the same afflictions are accomplished in your brethren that are in the world." Understand the season of your child's life!

It is unfortunate that girls and women of our culture have become forward and aggressive. They will "present" themselves to your son! So, be wise and alert to watch out for the temptations and snares that Satan will send to entrap your son to change the course of his life away from the Kingdom of God. The Proverbs is full of warnings to young men to stay away from women who are luring them to their bedchamber. Our culture is constantly bombarding your son with lustful, sinful thoughts. Parents must teach our sons how to be a godly man, to live a pure life and abstain from all appearances of evil.

8. Sons compete with their fathers for their mother's attention. Moms, if your husband is not your son's father, you need to be especially aware of this.

9. Dress modestly in front of your son.

10. When our kids were growing up, there were no personal cell phones. However, the internet was still loaded with things kids don't need to see. Today, young parents deal with the good and bad about cell phones. Talk to your kids about the dangers, and then give them the boundaries you expect of them. Each parent must ask God for direction

and build in as many safeguards as possible. Pornography causes addictions, broken hearts, and broken marriages.

11. When you are training a son, remember that you are preparing a husband for a special young woman and a father for your grandchildren. Andrew and I had numerous conversations and specific moments where we had an understanding that he would respect me as his mother and as a woman. I also underlined "kindness."

12. Last but not least: Christian parenting is very hard work. The fruit is sweet. Remaining faithful is a gift to God, your children and yourself for the rest of your lives and through eternity. One life fully committed to God can change the world!

    Recently, I saw part of a television documentary entitled *Billy Graham, America's Pastor*. What if somebody had not impacted Billy Graham for Christ? He has led countless millions to Jesus. You may be training up the next great evangelist or statesman!

With the information received from Norm Wakefield, I had the knowledge to begin to change my attitudes. It can be a painful and emotional experience because we are giving up "our will" for God's will. God began to soften my heart and helped me to "rebuild" my relationship with Andrew. I endeavored to show him unconditional love, even when he did something I did not like. I started looking at what Andrew did right instead of what he did wrong!

Andrew's life has taught me:

1. When God makes a promise, he always keeps it.

2. When God gives you a promise, the devil will attempt to thwart God's plan, so be alert for the enemy as you work for the Lord.

3. What we spend our time doing each day is what we become good at.

4. Humility is the precursor to God's favor and growth.

5. The devil hates a man-child. Scripture tells of evil men who killed boy babies in their attempt to kill a Champion for God — the story of Joseph, the story of Moses, the story of Jesus!

6. God is faithful, and he blesses faithfulness.

7. "Be who you are, nobody is better qualified" –(Mary Englebright). When Andrew started working, he gave me a journal, the front cover of which bears this quotation. It speaks to me each time I see it. Most of us need a reminder in this world of trendy look-alikes that the best person we can be is ourselves.

CHAPTER 9

MIXING SUNSHINE AND MUSIC

"Therefore, whoever hears these sayings of mine, and doeth them,
I will liken him to a wise man, which built his house upon a rock:
And the rain descended, and the floods came, and the winds blew, and beat upon
That House: and it fell not, for it was founded upon a rock."(Matthew 7:2-25).

Anyone who has ever built a house knows that after the house plans themselves, the foundation is the first and most important thing you want to build well. If it is not solid and secure, then everything else is insecure. When two people marry and begin building a home together, there are some foundational things that must take place for those relationships under that one roof to stand the test of time. Now we were mixing our marriage and our children, and there were some key, foundational ingredients that we blended to make everything, and everybody work well together. I believe our relationships today are good because of the foundation we laid back in the 80's, but also because we have continued cultivating our relationships with our children at each stage of their lives.

Our Words

Any two people can choose to get married and buy a house to live in. However, not every married couple builds a house using wisdom and good sense.

God used His Word to speak our World into existence. We are created in God's image. He says that "Life and death are in the power of the tongue." Think about the words that have been spoken to you. The words that were positive and good built you up and spurred you on to success, growth, and good works. If you have some personal cheerleaders in your life like I do, you know how much this means. The negative words caused you to doubt yourself and may have caused you to withdraw. That's what Satan wants—to silence us and cause us to withdraw from our journey and our influence. Think before you speak. You can't take your words back! Our words build up our family members or tear them down. Be a builder!

I have found that most of the success of marriage depends on communication. No matter how long you have been married, if you have trouble talking through things with your spouse, go together to a Christian counselor who will give you tools to help you. If there is one thing that I would have changed in our marriage in the early years, it would be learning to communicate better. That is a very key and vital ingredient for success and contentment in your marriage first, and then to train your children.

Our Money

1. It's one thing to date someone and love being together, but it's quite another to share a home, a bank account, a kitchen, a car, and children. Every couple should talk about their

views about money before marriage. Each of us brings from our family of origin their view about money. I recommend Dave Ramsey's book "Financial Peace."

2. When we married, Bill was starting his senior year of dental school, so we had little discretionary money to spend. But we made ourselves a budget to live on from the beginning and still do after forty-five years of marriage. Making and living on a budget makes all the difference because you have established your goals, where your income is going, where you are giving, and what you have left over.

Habits

We had fun at home together, playing a game, watching a movie, reading a story, sharing meals and conversation together around the table, talking and praying for the needs of our family and for others, or just being under the same roof but individually enjoying our own hobby.

We enjoyed our yearly family vacations using our timeshare, making a road trip and happy memories together. We regularly attended our church together on Sunday morning and Sunday night. Each of us attended Sunday School.

Discipline

Proverbs talk a lot about discipline. It was written to teach young people how to live and how to stay pure. There is a discipline of obtaining knowledge, of work and of disciplining our children. Bill was the sole breadwinner for our family, and I worked one day a week at the dental office. I was at home with the children all the other days. Bill modeled a disciplined life in getting up every day and going to his office to see patients, whether he felt like it or not. That spoke volumes to Emily and Andrew, who learned to be disciplined students at school and in their music education.

I cooked many, many meals that I didn't want to cook, but I did because of love, commitment to my family, and the budget. I read Emily and Andrew a Bible story nightly and prayed with them before they went to sleep. I remember feeling extremely tired, but I wanted to instill the love and knowledge of God and His word into my children. I wanted them to learn to pray. We taught our children to obey us. When they did not obey us, we spanked them or took away a privilege. They learned there are consequences for their disobedience. We were teaching them to obey us first so they would follow God and obey Him.

Working in the Right Season to Reap a Harvest

So much of success in life comes from doing the right thing in the right season. The Bible is full of passages that relate to "the season" of a person's life. If we sow in the spring and summer, we will have something to harvest in the fall. The enemy's ammo is to keep us distracted during the sowing season so that we will not have a harvest.

In past generations, whether a family had food to eat was determined by what they planted, the rain and sun that came to cause it to grow, their hard work in the hot summer and their hard work to harvest it in the fall before winter came. That was their food during the winter. Today, we can easily lose sight of the importance of the seasons, except for whether there is a football, basketball, or baseball game!

As Christians, we must discipline ourselves to live in the season we are currently in, not in the past, not in the future, but in the present and planning. Likewise, we must sow seeds into our kids while there is time. A preschooler must learn to obey his/her parents, to respect his/her elders, and to tell the truth. Children/ teenagers must learn to work and save for the luxuries they want. Teach your children to live in sexual purity before they start dating!

Work on your marriage and being the best spouse you can be through the years. Don't grow apart because you're putting all your time and energy in on your kids. If you do, you may find yourself together in an empty nest and don't know or like each other! Don't let that happen to you. Work on your marriage every day. Save something from every paycheck through the years so that when you get too old to work, you'll have more than social security to live on. You'll be glad you did.

Bill Enjoyed Serving His Country

Having been a commissioned officer in the Public Health Service from 1978 until 1981, Bill still had an attraction for the military. He joined the Louisiana National Guard as Dental Officer in the 2224 Medical/Dental Detachment in January 1989. One weekend every month for about four years, he traveled from our home in Oak Grove to Baton Rouge for his weekend drill. He enjoyed and benefited from the camaraderie with the other doctors in his unit.

I was able to travel with Bill on several occasions as we would make it a weekend getaway time, sightseeing in Natchez, Mississippi, and St. Francisville. In the summers, Bill's two-week camp took him to Fort Sam Houston in San Antonio. The children and I were able to fly to visit Bill and visit with Uncle Bob and Aunt Liz too. We all relished our time together and swimming in their pool.

Desert Storm took Bill's Guard unit to Fort Polk, Louisiana for two weeks in December of 1991. They were there to screen soldiers for the war zone in Iraq. Bill missed Emily and Andrew's Christmas programs at school. He returned home to us just in time to celebrate Jesus' Birthday with us and open all our gifts.

The Louisiana Dental unit was attached to the 82nd Airborne out of Fort Bragg, North Carolina. They missed being called to active duty in Iraq by three weeks if the Iran/Iraq War had lasted. We felt very thankful and blessed when the war was over.

*   *   *

A Good Singer Needs Strong Lungs!

A very embarrassing, yet somewhat humorous experience occurred when Emily and Andrew were about six and four. Emily went through a stage of life where she would scream loudly when something uncomfortable happened to her.

It was early fall, sometime in September. Our dear friend, Granny Whitten, our "adopted" grandmother, and I started celebrating our birthdays together by going out to dinner. Bill was out of town at a dental meeting, so Granny, Emily, Andrew, and I went to Mike's Fish House. We went through the buffet line and sat down and enjoyed our meal. The children finished first and went just around the corner from our table to wash their hands.

Suddenly, I heard a blood-curdling scream, and so did the other customers! I went to see what in the world had happened. Emily had splattered water all over herself! I came back to the table to tell Granny what was going on. She said, "The people at the next table asked me if that child got a bone in her throat, and I said, "She couldn't scream that loud if she had a bone!"

I decided that Emily was just developing her good vocal cords for singing! About the time we were ready to start spanking her for that screaming stage, it ended!

The Largest Wrapped Christmas Present!

I never checked The Guinness Book of Records, but I'm sure my Daddy's Christmas gift for his grandchildren in 1989 was the largest wrapped Christmas present! Mother, David, Mary Evelyn, and Daddy went outside to wrap up the mystery surprise gift. We stayed inside with the young children. We could not imagine what it would be!

When we got the "Go," we went to the front yard to see the biggest wrapped gift and stood and watched as they slipped the lid off. Underneath the wrapping paper was a real live Shetland pony! Naturally, Emily, Andrew, and Matthew (Joel was a baby) were very excited and wanted a turn at riding. Their Grandaddy led each of them around in the yard as they took their turn on their one-of-a-kind wrapped Christmas present!

Emily and Andrew Make a Decision to Follow Christ

Emily prayed to receive Jesus as her Savior when she was about eight years old at Vacation Bible School at our church! At the age of seven, Andrew prayed to receive Jesus as his Savior at home ! This is what we worked and lived for–to see our children follow Christ! Both were baptized on the same Sunday morning by our Pastor, Don Boyett. My parents and siblings came from Texas to be with us for that great milestone. We were very thankful that our children had chosen to follow Christ. God would bring other people into their lives to help us disciple them so each of them would grow into a mature Christian.

Grandparents are Influential

Although our parents lived five hours away in East Texas, we managed to see them about every three months. Emily and Andrew grew up spending time with both sets of their grandparents because they lived four miles apart. Their names for my parents were Mom and Granddaddy and for Bill's parents, Mawmaw and Pawpaw.

When Andrew was about to turn one, Daddy had decided that we needed a Collie puppy. We split the cost and got another "Corky" on Andrew's first birthday. His name was chosen because we had several registered Collie dogs when I was growing up, and we named each of them Corky!

Our puppy grew very quickly and in just a few months was much bigger than both children. He was our special family pet and even sired two litters of puppies during the eight years we had him in our fenced backyard. We decided to find Corky a new home in

1993 because he had bitten a couple of children who were visiting in the neighborhood.

Daddy was responsible for seeing that Emily and Andrew had their own large sand pile in our backyard. He borrowed a truck from our friend, Gene Edmondson, and he and Bill went near the river and got some sand. With a few pieces of timber, he and Bill were in business with everything they needed for construction. Andrew, Jake Perry, Emily, and friends enjoyed hours of fun in the big sandbox.

My parents would get the children in the summers and keep them for a week at a time. They would watch movies, go swimming, fishing, and play games together. Mother's kitchen was the heart of her home, so she always had the next good meal, and Cokes, chips, and popcorn for a snack. The grandchildren have fond memories of "Mom's Marvelous Munchies!" Mawmaw and Pawpaw had Emily and Andrew over for fun and a visit with their first cousins, Paul, Beth, Jeff, and Kris.

Mrs. Beasley was a very good cook too, and would prepare peas and cornbread, vegetables, and meat for the kids. I'll never forget that one year when Emily was in high school, and she came home from church camp and said, "I want some Mawmaw food!" Bill's Mom sewed beautiful dresses for Emily when she was a little girl. After our kids started school, Mr. Beasley started a generous and thoughtful tradition with his six grandchildren of sending each of them $5 for every report card! They loved getting that money in the mail!

Christmas with Extended Family

The Beasley Family always had our Christmas celebration at Bill's parents' house on Christmas Eve night. The menu was always breakfast food: scrambled eggs, bacon, ham, biscuits, red-eye gravy, ribbon cane syrup, and tea. Emily and Andrew had fun playing with their cousins again. We would sing Christmas carols together in the living room, and Aunt Rowene and I took turns playing the piano. We had a fun gift exchange because we drew names before Christmas. Mr. Beasley always had eggnog for us to drink afterward. Then, the phone would ring in the hallway, and it would be Santa Claus! He was calling to talk to each of the six Beasley grandkids before he would arrive later that night! Bedtime always went easier because each of them wanted Santa to come soon!

Special Friends to Help

When Emily and Andrew were growing up, there were times when Bill and I wanted and needed to get away. Our special friends, Libby and Pete Berry, blessed us several times when they had our children come to their home for a couple of nights. They spoiled them like their own, and I always knew my young treasures were in good hands.

During that same season of our lives, we had our front yard professionally landscaped. I wanted to make some flower beds in the back, as well. How could I do that with just a hoe and a rake? Pete Berry came over one day and brought his big, heavy tiller to our backyard and tilled the soil all along the back of my house! That was an amazing labor of love that he did with a smile, and I was so grateful.

Another special Christian couple who blessed us with keeping Emily and Andrew were Jo and Gene Edmondson. Their daughters were grown, and they took a special interest in our children. They took care of our kids in their home for a couple of nights so we could get away, and it was a gift to us as young parents!

Rules of the House

Our guide for living is The Bible. We would always say either aloud or to ourselves, what does the Bible say? What is the right thing to do? The right thing to do can be found in the scriptures.

The standard we seek to uphold is purity and godliness. We were very conservative about television and movies, those at the theater and those rented. Why? Because Philippians 4:8 says, "Finally brethren, whatsoever things are true, whatsoever things are honest, whatsoever things are just, whatsoever things are pure, whatsoever things are lovely, whatsoever things are of good report; if there be any virtue, and if there be any praise, think on these things." The Apostle Paul is talking here, and he goes on to add, "Those things, which ye have both learned, and received and heard, and seen in me, do and the God of peace shall be with you." Many people wonder why they don't have peace. What are you taking into your mind?

When our kids were in the Kid's Choir and Vacation Bible School, they sang many wonderful songs. One song that I'll never forget had these lyrics, "My mind is like a computer, daily programming it in. It eats whatever you feed it. So let the feeding begin." One of my favorite Christian bookstores was in Hot Springs Village; they had a little quote at the bottom of every receipt, "What goes into a mind comes out in a life!"

Another standard in our home was that our children did not entertain someone of the opposite sex in their rooms. They weren't allowed to have friends over if Bill and I were both gone from home. Many young people fall into temptation because they are allowed too much alone time with a boyfriend or girlfriend. We parents are responsible to God for our children and for what we allow to go on under our roof. I am the gatekeeper for my family.

"There's No Place Like Home"

One time when we were on vacation at our timeshare, I bought a little sign that I hung in the garage beside the door. When we would arrive back home after a trip, Andrew would say, "There's No Place Like Home." Every child should believe that!

CHAPTER 10

FINDING GRACE
AND GROWING

"For by grace are ye saved through faith; and that not of yourselves: it is the gift of God; Not of works, lest any man should boast."(Ephesians 2:8-9).

This chapter of my life began in the summer of 1989 when I was about to turn thirty-three. A series of struggles and wrong thinking brought me to a place of anxiety that I could not overcome on my own. I was depressed. The months went by, and the depression got worse.

God is working on our behalf, even during life's storms. He sent a special lady to my church named Millie. She was a nurse and had been delivered from the pit of depression. It was hard for me to imagine that smiling, peaceful lady the way she described her past. She recognized that I was going through a similar struggle. She told me, "You will come out of this and be able to recognize the devil when he comes; you will tell him to get out!" Besides her frequent encouragement, she prayed for me.

The Christmas season had arrived. As I read the Christmas story, I began to think about the life of Mary and what she told Gabriel. She responded to his message with these words, "Behold the handmaid of the Lord; be it unto me according to thy word."(Luke 1:38). In other words, she agreed with God's will, even though she did not fully understand it. She surrendered to His will. The Lord began speaking to me and undergirding me with those truths.

A few days before Christmas, Andrew came down with pneumonia, and he was very sick. We could not go visit our relatives in Texas. It was extremely cold outside, so we built a fire and put on a holiday movie—*It's A Wonderful Life.* God can use anything he chooses to encourage us. As I watched that movie, I reflected on what a wonderful life I had, even in my miserable state of mind and doctoring a sick little boy. It was a December of frigid temperatures in Louisiana, and a hard month for me.

January 1990 appeared on the calendar, and I was still praying and seeking God for help. Through the past months, a couple of my friends had mentioned the name of a Christian counselor who lived in the next city. The day I decided to call Molly, it seemed there were angels all in my house! I had never felt anything like that before, but I knew there were a lot of people praying for me. Depression had been my companion for too long. I heard Molly's voice for the first time on her answering machine and left her a message.

She returned my call and gave me an appointment time to come and talk at her office the following Friday. Bill went with me, and we both talked with Molly about my struggles. She wanted to see me twice a week. My friend Millie called that weekend, and I told her about seeing Molly. She was really thankful that I was seeing a professional counselor.

As I would go to Molly's house two times a week and sit in her den waiting for my appointment, it began to feel like a safe place. Molly was a wonderful, godly woman, who had a major handicap herself—she was blind. Although her physical vision was impaired, through the eyes of her spirit came forth godly wisdom, along with her knowledge of the Bible, and her professional expertise. I could talk frankly with her, and then she would give me the truth to replace my wrong thinking.

Although I asked Jesus into my heart when I was five years old, I had never understood the part about grace. I had been taught the works side of Christianity but missed the part about "Jesus plus nothing makes me born again," Elizabeth's paraphrase for "by grace are you saved through faith, not of works lest any man should boast." I couldn't work hard enough or jump high enough to get it right. Through her counsel and through prayer, Molly began to help me rebuild the foundation of my faith. It was a long, difficult, emotional process. I cried, felt shaky, insecure, frustrated, and depressed often.

My godly counselor told me that when people serve God out of legalism, they eventually come to a fork in the road. At that point, they either find grace and come into the freedom that Christ died for, or they just go wild because they can't get it right!

By March, she decided I needed to get some medication to help me finish processing my problems. It would help me stay focused and finish talking through my questions and confusion. She referred me to a doctor who could help me with the medication! It was a difficult journey, but the new prescription helped me feel better in about two weeks. Molly's love and patience with me, her availability and the truth she gave me began to set me free from depression.

I came to understand that my faith in Jesus and what He did saved me, not my good works. A simple child-like faith in Jesus and his finished work on the cross was what I needed. I had always aspired to be perfect and learned that perfection can only be attained in trusting in His perfection. Focusing on the grace of God that came to me through Jesus' shed blood, His death and resurrection, and my faith in HIS FINISHED WORK, brought me a new freedom. That is the only perfection I can ever know in this life. My works only come because of my love for Him. Grace—greater than all my sin.

A contemporary song I know has the lyrics, "Jesus with skin on." All of us need to know personally a human being who models the life of Jesus. God used my own wonderful husband, Bill, to show his love and grace to me during those long months of depression and pain. One day he came home from work and just laid down on the narrow couch beside me. With his arms around me, he said, "We're going to get through this. I'm here for you if you need me." The enemy had used fear against me saying, "You're going to lose your husband and family because of your condition." Bill's words that day gave me assurance and confidence that he was committed to me for the long haul—no matter what came, he would be there for me. That is just like God's love—UNCONDITIONAL!

The neat thing that happens in Kingdom living is that God's times of testing are never wasted! It is first for our benefit and then we must pass on what we learned to help somebody else.

Have You Experienced God's Saving Grace Through Faith in Jesus Christ?

Maybe you too have learned a legalistic way of trying to reach God. I want you to know my Risen Savior! All religions except Christianity are individuals reaching up to God, trying to work their way to heaven through good works. Christianity is not a religion but a relationship. Christianity is God reaching down to sinful, fallen man by sending His only son, Jesus Christ, to come to earth as a human being, die on a cross for our sins, defeat death and hell, and rise from the grave! Though perfect and without sin, Jesus saw the great chasm that separated sinful me from God, and He said, "Father, if it be your will, I will go to the cross so Elizabeth can be your child. Through my death, she can not only have the abundant life here on earth, but she too will rise on resurrection morning and can live forever with us in heaven."

When I heard that love story, my answer was yes!!!! I cannot have abundant life or eternal life in heaven without saying yes to Jesus Christ. Jesus said, "I am the way, the truth, and the life. No man can come to the father except through me." There are many religions who claim that they are praying to God. The only way to know God and be heard by God is by trusting in the Son. Jesus revealed the Father to us.

Will You Trust Jesus to Be Your Savior and Lord Now?

If you answered yes, then pray the following prayer:

> *"Jesus, I know I am a sinner, and I believe you died on the cross for my sins. Please forgive me of my sins and transform me into a new person. I surrender control of my life to You today. Help me to obey you and serve you faithfully until it is time for me to be with you in heaven. Amen."*

If you prayed this prayer, begin to grow in your walk with Jesus by reading the Bible, beginning with Matthew, Mark, Luke, and John. These books tell the life and words of Jesus. Obey all that is written in His instruction book. That is the way to have an abundant life. Then find a Bible believing church where you can make your decision to follow Christ publicly so you can be discipled. Then you can use your gifts to build up The Body of Christ there. Choose a time that is best for you each day to read the Bible and Pray. He will speak to you through his Living Word because he has given you His Holy Spirit to illuminate it to you. If you personally know another Christian, share with them your decision to follow Christ so they can encourage and pray for you in your new walk with the Lord. God does not intend for us to live the Christian life as a lone ranger!

Finding our New House

For several years, Bill had been wanting to buy a nicer house and move to another neighborhood, but our house would not sell. In the fall of 1990 we found a large, pretty house with two acres of land. Bill did all the paperwork and made all the phone calls to get our loan approved.

We brought home the boxes to begin to pack. We were so excited. The weekend before we were planning to move, a telephone call came from the Seller. He was backing out on selling the house! We were disappointed.

After talking about it, we had to trust that God had something better. Romans 8:28 says, "And we know that all things work together for good to them that love God, to them who are called according to his purpose."

Someone said, "God's delays are God's opportunities." About two and one-half years later, we found our house. Our house hunt began on Easter Sunday of 1993 as we were hunting eggs in the yard with Emily and Andrew. We would hide the eggs so they could find them, and then they would hide them so we could find them. We were sitting in our lawn chairs enjoying the beautiful weather, when I said to Bill, "You know, if we are going to have another house while Emily and Andrew are still at home, we had better get with it. God knows what we need; let's get the house He wants for us."

We knew of two houses that were for sale in town. Bill set up the appointments with the owners, and we went the next evening to see the first one, which would have required a great deal to update. The next day we went to look at the brown cypress house on Ridgecrest Drive. It had three bedrooms, tile floors, lots of storage, and a special bonus: a very large swimming pool and deck. For years, Bill had said he wanted a house with a pool. We decided that was the one for us!

Our Lord sent us a couple to lease our first home that we had tried so hard to sell, and we bought the new house on Ridgecrest

Drive in June 1993. Emily was eleven and Andrew was nine. As the days and years went by, the pool for exercise, family fun and company, the great floor plan for our family and the future homeschool years, and our special neighbors were some of the benefits of living in the brown cypress house. We even lived so close to our dental office that Bill could walk to work if he wanted to.

That summer of 1993 was the year that expenses definitely came in huge bunches. Life is like that sometimes. We are able to achieve a dream, which is so fulfilling. Proverbs 13:12 says, "Hope deferred makes the heart sick: but when the desire cometh, it is a tree of life." Bill had worked very hard, and we were so excited about finally moving to our new house. But, I had been suffering from chronic sinus infections. We had invited Mary Kay and Ralph, Paul and Beth to meet us at Disney World to share our condo. Before our trip, the doctor told me that I just needed to have surgery to correct my sinus problems. In July we went on to Florida and had a great time with our families there visiting and seeing The Magic Kingdom, Epcot, and MGM Studios.

But, on our return home, I underwent sinus surgery to correct a deviated septum, etc. It was a very stretching time of recovery, but I have a faithful Lord, a great doctor, a wonderful husband, children, and a church family who prayed and helped me.

One day while I was recovering, it started getting hot in our new house. The electrician came and gave us the bad news. The cooling/heating unit is worn out and must be replaced! So right from the get-go there was a large expense to our new house, but God provided.

A New Nephew

In October 1993, we welcomed Stephen, our sixth nephew and another cousin for Emily and Andrew. He is my sister's third son. God gave Stephen a sharp mind and he excelled academically!

One of my very favorite songs:
"The Little Things"
I used to pray God would part the sea
That he would be there standing, looking back at me
There would be a sign, a miracle or two
And I would know exactly what He wanted me to do.
That's how I would pray, until the day
I looked at the sun shining in the sky
I heard the birds he'd sent to sing a lullaby
I felt a gentle breeze blow across my face
Then I realized that every day I know His grace
Lord, I stand amazed
Chorus:
It's the little things that I can't live without
It's more than just miracles God is all about
It's the little things that hold my life together
I don't need a parting sea
Every day I wake up, I ask God for more of the little things
Once I sought to see the face of God
I prayed with all my might He'd let me see
Then I saw some children playing so alive and carefree
And I heard God softly whisper, "That's Me"
Once I understood, I began to see
That with everything God was reaching out to me
In a helping hand or a loving smile
He was showing me that He was right there all the while
With me every mile...showing me
It's the little things that I can't live without
It's more than just miracles God is all about
It's the little things that hold my life together
I don't need a parting sea
Every day I wake up, I ask God for more of the little things.
Every day I wake up, I ask God for more of the little things.

Words and Music by Brian Arnold and Recorded by "Chosen Few"

GROWING

"But grow in grace, and in the knowledge of our Lord and Savior Jesus Christ. To him be glory both now and forever. Amen " (II Peter 3:18).

"Then we will no longer be immature like children. We won't be tossed and blown about by every wind of new teaching. We will not be influenced when people try to trick us with lies so clever they sound like the truth. Instead, we will speak the truth in love, growing in every way more and more like Christ, who is the head of his body, the church. He makes the whole body fit together perfectly. As each part does its own special work, it helps the other parts grow, so that the whole body is healthy and growing and full of love." (Ephesians 4:14-16).

According to God's Word, we are commanded as Christians to grow up and become mature in Christ, no longer being like babies who take a bottle. We must put our roots down deep so we can know God better by reading the Bible, spending time in His presence, sharing His love with others, and thus bearing more fruit for His kingdom.

I believe that I really began to grow up in Christ after my foundation was rebuilt on grace. I then had the SOLID ROCK on which to build because everything else is shifting sand. I'm reminded of the old hymn, written by Edward Mote and John B. Dykes, that says, "My hope is built on nothing less Than Jesus' blood and righteousness, I dare not trust the sweetest frame, But wholly lean on Jesus' name. On Christ the Solid Rock I stand– all other ground is sinking sand... After I found God's grace, he put several people and truths into my path to help me grow and mature in Christ.

I began to pray more. God began to call me to be an intercessor. One of the main areas emphasized in our church was prayer. Because God has given me compassion for people, I began to pray for those he placed on my heart. I prayed more for my own husband and children. I began to go and anoint their rooms with oil while they were at school and pray for them to surrender to the call on their lives. d I would worship the Lord with songs at my piano, which would turn into times of intercession.

More Tools

It was during those years of growth that God brought different books across my path to bring a better understanding to my mind and spirit. I read *This Present Darkness,* by Frank Peretti, which opened my eyes to spiritual warfare, and what possibly happens in the realm of the spirit between the forces of good and evil. *The Perfect Heart,* by Jeri Williams, was a great explanation of how the fruits of the spirit in our lives causes us to be able to walk in our house with a perfect heart and how to pass it on to our children in the home. The Shaping of a Christian Family by Elisabeth Elliot t is the beautiful story of how her parents taught their children to live the Christian life in the home.

Hettie Lou Brooks, My Teacher of God's Kingdom Living

Vickie, my beautician, would always tell me about attending Hettie Lue Brooks Women's Seminars in Hot Springs, Arkansas, and she gave me a brochure.

My first seminar, *The Lion and the Lamb,* in the fall of 1993, was my first time hearing Hettie. God's Word says that we grow precept upon precept, and that is what happened as I attended each seminar twice a year. Hettie and her late husband, Don Brooks, and their family own a 500-acre ranch and Brookhill Ranch Camp (summer kids camp) near Hot Springs Village. That is where she held the seminars which became an oasis for me to get refueled for running my Christian race.

Hettie said, "Come up Higher, Girls!" As I listened, laughed, cried, and applied myself each weekend, a confidence in who I am in Christ continued to rise up in me. I gained courage and stamina to go home and be a faithful, positive mom and wife. Hettie always gives us gifts that we take home to remind us of what we learned. When we get back into the trenches of life, those object lessons remind us to take action and to be vigilant in our walk with the Lord.

These seminars have done so much for me that I began to invite other women, including my church family, my friends, my mother, and sisters. My neighbor attended one weekend with me, received healing for pain in her body, and rededicated her life to Jesus. We have all been touched by the power of the Holy Spirit!

Learning the Power of Worshiping Jesus

Another step of my growth involved learning the power of worship in a believer's life. Our church began to emphasize worship, and I got hold of it. Hettie taught us about worship. I began to worship God for who He is. As I did that at church and at home in my quiet time, I began to hear His voice as I would come into His presence. God's word says, "He inhabits the praises of His people." There were times at church when I was needing encouragement or seeking direction, and the Holy Spirit spoke those comforting words or gave me direction or an answer during our worship service. It makes sense that if He is present when we praise that He speaks to us.

Fruit of Evangelism

As I applied these new tools, those evangelism seeds my mother and daddy had sown in me as a girl began to grow. I became more sensitive to the Holy Spirit about the people I saw at the post office, at the bank, at the grocery store, and at the ballgame. God would give me words of encouragement to speak, a testimony to share with someone who was struggling, or I would just pray for that person as I went on my way. I began to write encouraging notes to people God would place on my heart. When they got the note in the mail, the common response I would hear from the recipient went something like, "That's just what I needed on that day." "I will keep this in my nightstand where I can read it again." The Holy Spirit guided me to write them!

One of my favorite witnessing experiences was sharing the Gospel with a man who worked in our neighborhood. His name was Mr. M. (abbreviated) He walked to and from work, and he passed by our house to do so. I frequently asked myself, "I wonder if that man is saved?" One day as he was walking by our house on his way home from work, I asked him that important question, "Are you saved? If you died tonight, do you know you are ready to meet Jesus?" He said he was not; I asked him if he would like to be. He said yes, so Andrew and I invited him on our back porch, where we led him in the sinner's prayer. What excitement we felt in our hearts at being able to lead that precious soul to Jesus!

We don't live in that neighborhood anymore. As we were moving to Arkansas from Louisiana, God impressed on me the importance of making the most of every season of our lives. Jesus was on his way somewhere when he touched the people in his path! God wants us to just reach the people who are in our path on the way to get groceries, to get the mail or to earn a living. He only asks us to give what we have, not what we don't have!

Growth at the Dental Office

Karla was just a little girl of about twelve when we moved to our parish. She became our babysitter. She was a very gifted student who graduated from Oak Grove High School as valedictorian, received her degree from Louisiana State University and went on to LSU Dental School in New Orleans.

In 1993, as she was anticipating graduation the following year and making plans about where she wanted to practice, her heartstrings were pulling her back home to Oak Grove and West Carroll Parish. Bill was still dreaming of making some changes in his life too, and we began to pray about whether we should bring Karla in as a dental partner. The only dentist in the parish at the time, we needed an answer to the question, "Could our area support another dentist?"

God will allow our faith to be tested. In December of 1993, trying to decide whether to bring in a partner the next year, we had just such a financial test. We paid our employees and our bills but did not have the money in our checking account to pay ourselves. I found the promise to stand on in Habakkuk 3:17-18, "Although the fig tree shall not blossom, neither shall fruit be in the vines; the labor of the olive shall fail, and the fields shall yield no meat; the flock shall be cut off from the fold, and there shall be no herd in the stalls: Yet I will rejoice in the Lord, I will joy in the God of my salvation." As we were praying and trusting in God's timely provision, one of the largest checks for dental work completed came in the mail, and we could pay ourselves!

The following year, with the assistance of AFTCO Practice Management Consultants, it was determined that our dental practice could support two dentists. In August of 1994, Dr. Robertson became the dental partner of Dr.Beasley.

The office growth of bringing in a second dentist created the need for another office staff member and God sent us Margaret. She and our loyal bookkeeper/office manager, Mrs. Nell, made for a great business office team. A long awaited and much needed computer system was purchased. With our two dental assistants, Linda, Carrie, and a hygienist, the partnership was off and running well in August of 1994!

Life was busy with home, parenting, work, and church. Emily and Andrew were in the seventh and fifth grades. The school year went by quickly with homework, music lessons and sports.

May is a little like December at our house because there are so many occasions to celebrate and activities to attend. There was Mother's Day, piano recitals, end of school activities, and last but not least, two special birthdays to celebrate. We always enjoyed having Emily and Andrew's friends over for some food, fun, swimming, music, and laughter as each of them were growing a year older. Andrew was promoted to 6th grade and Emily to 8th.

A Significant Summer

As our children grew in stature, they were growing in other ways as well. In the summer of 1995, Emily and Andrew both attended Brookhill Ranch Camp for the first time. Andrew carried his friend, Jake, and Emily decided not to take anyone with her and meet some new people. They loved their counselors, Hettie, the Founder and Leader, and all the great activities offered there. When we picked them up at closing ceremonies on Saturday, they had so many wonderful experiences to share with us. Brookhill Camp food is always so good, but after the closing ceremonies, our campers were hungry and always chose Red Lobster. They both came back home happy and with better attitudes. From time-to-time Andrew would preface his remarks with, "Mrs. Hettie says..." My favorite quote from Andrew about his experience at camp was, "Brookhill is the closest place to heaven on earth!"

"Jesus" Helps Us Find Our Van!

It was the Summer of 1996, and we had been shopping for a new van. That summer, we booked a timeshare week in Hot Springs for us during the same week that Emily and Andrew were going to Brookhill Camp. We arrived at South Shore Resort on

Lake Hamilton on Saturday. There was some time for fun with the kids before they checked into camp on Monday.

Bill and I enjoyed Hot Springs. One morning, Bill went looking at the car dealerships and came back in a beautiful, emerald green luxury car. We drove it around for a few hours, but decided to keep looking, especially for a van. At another dealership we met a salesman who rode with us to try out several vehicles. We learned that he played the part of "Jesus" in Hot Springs outdoor Passion Drama, "The Witness." He referred us to a one-year-old green Town and Country Van with leather seats; just what we were looking for. That week we bought our van from "Jesus" and surprised the kids at camp when we picked them up on Saturday! That "new used" van served us for nearly 250,000 miles.

God is interested in every detail of our lives, from cars to careers, and as we seek him for his best, he will lead us and give it to us. He knows everything about our future and our needs, including our children's needs. He will provide if we will give up control and "not lean unto our own understanding"; his best is ours when we ask him, trust him, and wait on His timing.

As I have grown in Christ, I have been especially blessed to watch my family mature in Christ as well. In I Corinthians 3:6-7, Paul says, "I have planted, Apollos watered; but God gave the increase. So then neither is he that planted anything, neither is he that watered; but God that giveth the increase."

CHAPTER 11

THE ADVENTURES OF HOMESCHOOLING

"And you must commit yourselves wholeheartedly to these commands that I am giving you today. Repeat them again and again to your children. Talk about them when you are at home and when you are on the road, when you are going to bed and when you are getting up. Tie them to your hands and wear them on your forehead as reminders. Write them on the doorposts of your house and on your gates."(Deuteronomy 6:6-9).

Homeschooling was the avenue God used to touch each of us individually, to bind us together as a family, and to mold us more into His image. It was the glue that God used to solidify our relationships with Him. The adventure required us to rely fully on Him. Through our experiences, we learned to know Him more intimately, to hear his voice, to understand his ways, even in the fellowship of his suffering. We became bonded as a family during that four-year period, something that nobody can take from us.

Seeds for homeschooling began when Andrew was twelve years old and finishing the fifth grade at public school. I became very concerned about his discontentment in school, and I began to notice a pattern. He was unhappy during the school year. He was an A student with good conduct. His teachers were good and cared about Andrew. During the summer he would attend one or two Christian camps where he would get built up, but shortly after school would start in the fall, his attitude was not always good.

About the last week of fifth grade, I decided I had enough!! I was going to visit his teacher. After I described Andrew in about two sentences, she interrupted me and said, "Andrew is bored. He finishes his work before everyone else and then has time on his hands while others finish." We talked with the principal, as well. He reasoned that Andrew needed more of a challenge and recommended testing him for the gifted program at the beginning of sixth grade; he projected that as Andrew got into the higher grades he would automatically be challenged by the more difficult subjects as well as having more choices in his classes. The parent-teacher meeting gave me new hope, and I could have a better summer believing that the gifted program was the next step for my son.

The following fall, at the beginning of sixth grade, Andrew tested for the gifted program and made it! It did give him an outlet. The teacher was a sweet Christian lady; she exposed her students to the computer and to writing a research paper. However, the time allotted for the gifted class at the elementary school was only about 45 minutes a day. Except for that time, his routine remained fairly the same as before.

About two weeks before Andrew's sixth grade year was completed, a particular action by someone else at school caused me to go and visit the principal. He was very cordial and listened very attentively. I shared with him why I was frustrated. The whole experience caused me to analyze if I wanted to stay on the public-school path or blaze a new trail for my pre-teen son.

I took a walk and prayed and listened. I felt the Lord was stirring homeschooling in my heart. As Bill pruned some trees in our front yard that day, I shared with him about my meeting with the principal. We continued to pray about Andrew's future education, and I asked some friends from church who home schooled to agree with me in prayer for guidance. Little did I realize that God was about to prune me as I would soon set out on a pioneering effort to home school my junior high son!

The missing link in my decision-making process to homeschool was to find out how we would handle higher math. Math was my weak subject in school. The Christian Home Educators Association of Louisiana, put me in touch with a former homeschool dad who taught two sons in Baton Rouge. He told me of their success as grown young men and recommended Saxon Math. Emily said they used Saxon Math in her Algebra I class. She had mentioned that the book was so self-explanatory that she could figure out the new concept from reading before the teacher could get it on the board. That was my confirmation.

After Bill and I decided that we were willing to provide the opportunity for Andrew to school at home, we wanted to discuss the pros and cons with both children. Emily was going into ninth grade and was not interested in homeschooling. She looked at school as her mission field but thought homeschooling would be great for Andrew. When we talked to Andrew, he liked the idea, but we agreed to take a little time to pray about it together. That week, as I went to say goodnight and pray with him, he said he thought the best thing about homeschooling would be having more time with us.

The decision was made, and the curriculum was ordered from Christian Liberty Academy Satellite Schools. They would choose the curriculum for my student, and issue the report card and diploma; three things I did not want the responsibility for. After a few weeks, we received our textbooks, instructions, tests, and a required library book, one of four he would read and report on during the year. I liked it that Andrew would be encouraged to read books.

Homeschooling-Year 1

After Labor Day, we started our new adventure with faith, enthusiasm, determination, and peace. Since Bill came home at lunch for a hot meal, I got Andrew involved helping me cook lunch. He seemed to enjoy it and became comfortable preparing food in the kitchen. The three of us would visit together around the table as we ate. Then Emily would come home after her school day and again we had great food and conversation around the table.

Soon after school started, Andrew quickly figured out that he would have extra time on his hands if he focused on his schoolwork first. One fall day he decided to do two days of school assignments. The next day he built a large dog pen for Trevor, his new energetic golden retriever. He wrapped goat wire around some posts behind our storage room and built a wooden gate from scratch. I was as proud of him as he was of himself.

I felt good about what I was providing for Andrew and what the home environment was doing for him. However, I hit overload very quickly. Andrew's curriculum required me to make out lesson plans for every day, which I enjoyed. There was much grading, and tests to schedule and keep up with. Also, several of his subjects required some of my help. Andrew's good education was very serious to me because it would help determine his ability to provide for his future family. One day the Lord spoke to me and said, "If you can teach Andrew about me, you can teach him about the world I have created." That was just the encouragement I needed!

Andrew wanted to have fun while he studied. I would get frustrated that he frequently was distracted while studying English, for example. I explained to him many times that he could not clown and learn those subjects. There were times of punishment for disobedience. One day he said that he was just trying to make me laugh!

As the first year moved along, I became more and more stressed. It became a harder task than I had imagined. I sought the encouragement of other homeschool moms who had been doing the job for years. My friend Karen responded, "You must remember that we started homeschooling with a kindergartener and you're starting with a seventh grader." I frequently remembered another friend and homeschool mom saying, "It's a laying down of your life!"

I started realizing that to be successful, I would have to learn to delegate some of my duties to the kids and to Bill. I did most of the cooking, involving Andrew sometimes, and delegated the dishes and clothes folding to the kids. They would rotate between the two jobs every other week. Bill hired a lady to clean my house every two weeks, and he took over the job of paying the bills.

I felt bad about feeling bad but felt God had called me to the labor of love. But I was frustrated with God. I felt inadequate, tired, and angry; doing the job required totally trusting the Lord with many questions, which challenged my pride and my faith. Each morning I would pray before we started school. I always felt like I was in work mode. I knew that the Lord was allowing us to deal with some attitudes in Andrew as a 12-year-old rather than seeing them later when he was 16. Bill and I discussed it often, but he really could not help me with my feelings and frustrations. I took my struggles to God in prayer. There were mornings when I would sit in my room having my quiet time and say, "Lord, if you do not go in there today with me, I might as well stay in here, because I cannot do this without your help."

In October of our first homeschool year, we picked up Emily at school one afternoon to travel to Monroe for music lessons. When she got in the car, she said, "I may not go back." I said, "What do you mean?" She went on to share that she was unhappy there and did not think like the other students. I told her she would finish the school year and pray about homeschooling the next year. Her plans for the following June 1997 were to travel to the Philippines as part of a mission team. I said that when she returned from that trip, we would make a decision about whether she should home school.

The Lord sent a wonderful Christian lady across my path to encourage me when I attended Hettie's Seed Sowers meeting at Brookhill Ranch. When I told her about my home-schooling experiences, she said, "The only way you can fail is to quit." Those words rang in my ears many times, thereafter, giving me courage to keep walking! Her encouragement was an answer to my prayers.

Homeschooling-Year 2

In the fall of 1997, we began our second year of homeschooling, with Emily as a tenth grader and Andrew as an eighth grader. It was doubly challenging because with Emily beginning homeschool, I had two sets of lesson plans and each child had eight or nine subjects, including art and P.E. I would make out a schedule for the day for each of them. Emily was a very strong reader, with much attention to detail. She needed very little help from me, mainly to review for a test or with difficult literature assignments. We hired Sandra, a former full-time math teacher, who so graciously agreed to come to our home several times a week to help Emily and Andrew with their Algebra I and II assignments and test preparation.

There were very few homeschool families in our area, but we did have a small "co-op" of families who got together for parties from time to time. I was so under the load of my responsibilities that I experienced very little of the fun of home schooling that year. However, I could see the peace and freedom that schooling at home brought to Emily and Andrew. That brought me fulfillment, assuring me that I was doing the right thing, in spite of the load I carried as the mother and teacher/administrator.

One of our outlets that year was going to Monroe every Tuesday evening for music lessons. Emily was established with a piano teacher, and Andrew, an eighth grader, began drum lessons in West Monroe. Afterward, we would eat, run some errands, and get home about 9:00 P.M.

A Wedding in Our Family

The fall of 1997 found our homeschool family on a trip to a very special wedding. On November 16, in Los Colinas, Texas, my twenty-six-year-old brother, David Moore, married Sharmaine Orlando in a beautiful ceremony. A wonderful dinner followed, along with a solo to the bride by her father and a love song for the couple, sung by our mother!

It was a great time of celebration and visiting our extended family members. The newlyweds left for their honeymoon in a boat that was waiting for them in a canal just outside the restaurant.

A Great Youth Convention

God is so faithful to help us as we train and teach our children because He is with us. He brings other people and circumstances along to guide us. Our pastor's wife, Linda, received information about the Eastman Curtis Youth Convention that was coming to a large church in Jackson, Mississippi, only two hours from us. Bill and I decided to investigate it and organized a youth trip to go to the weekend conference in November 1997.

While we were there, Emily became interested in attending Oral Roberts University. We had never thought about her going that far away to college before. Part of the excitement at the Convention was the $20,000 scholarship they were giving away in a drawing.

Emily and Matthew, a member of our youth group, both hoped to win it! The seed was planted in Emily's heart that weekend to attend ORU.

Matthew received a supernatural healing when he went forward for prayer. It was a real miracle!

Back to the home front and the everyday routine of homeschooling. While the school was in session, so was the need for a good meal. It was inconvenient for me to continue to cook a big meal at lunch, and I resented doing it at that time. I felt that I was obligated because Bill expected it. During the morning schedule, Emily or Andrew would say, "What are we having for lunch?" I resented their question because my work seemed endless, but I felt bad about my attitude. As I began remembering that Jesus has set us free, I started throwing off the chains and giving myself the flexibility to have a sandwich or something else very easy during the busy school day. Nobody died! Moving past the resentment and feeling good about serving my family, I practiced being thankful that they enjoyed and looked forward to the food I had cooked for them. The blessings I had became more important than the burden; thankful not to be eating alone was the new attitude.

Homeschooling-Year 3

Our third year of homeschooling, 1998-99, brought a little more joy and freedom to me because of the new routine we added. Also, by that time, I was able to start looking back to see what we had accomplished, increasing my confidence level.

Emily and Andrew both auditioned and were selected for the Masterworks' Youth Choir in Monroe. Their choir practice became part of our Tuesday evening routine. It was through Masterworks that we met several other home school students and became involved in the Christian Home School Association of Northeast Louisiana. It was very helpful to be able to socialize and see regularly other high school students and their parents who studied our same books at home. Both kids made some new home school friends, and I found camaraderie with their parents. Our teens enjoyed participating in the rehearsals and concerts and trips that Mrs. Donna Dugas, Director, and her organization provided.

In the fall of 1998, Emily and Andrew were excited to learn that they would be making a choir trip in the Spring to San Diego, California, where they would compete with other choirs from across the nation. They participated in the group's fundraisers.

By September, Andrew had taken nine months of drum lessons. After shopping on the Internet, in catalogs. and consulting with his instructor, our ninth-grade son selected his own set of red Premier drums. With his dad as his benefactor and a promise to pay some of the money back, he ordered his red drums! As a team, Bill and Andrew finished out a portable storage room together, which besides a workout room, was a perfect place for Andrew to practice and better learn his shiny new instrument! I don't remember but one complaint from our good neighbors, and that was because he was practicing too early in the morning!

In October, our worship leader, Jonathan, attended a prophetic worship leader's conference in Jamaica. His first Sunday back at our church, he called our family to the front after the sermon. He charged Bill with the following: "You are raising two generals in God's army." He continued by exhorting about his responsibilities as father and leader. "Just as you have received your convictions about grace, you must extend grace to others who might disagree with you. Emily will have a ministry in grace. Andrew has the ability to really focus or be really unfocused. He will operate in the five-fold ministry and will see things before they happen. God will use this family in the community."

We went home that day feeling especially favored and further affirmed in our responsibilities before God and the job we were doing as parents. There was yet more for us to accomplish in the environment of our home school, which I named "The King's Academy."

One of the most important achievements of our homeschooling years was the work God did in Bill's heart. In April 1996, several months before we began our homeschool adventure, a large group from our church attended the Brownsville Revival in Pensacola, Florida. Bill was the only member of our family who did not go.

When we returned, we "brought back" in our own hearts to our homes and church the revival fires. Because of what he saw in others, Bill became very frustrated and did a lot of questioning. One Sunday morning, the Holy Spirit spoke through me to Bill as we knelt at the altar. "You feel like you are on the outside looking in, but God is going to use you and your quiet personality to mold you into a man of prayer." That is what happened, and I began to see him come into a spiritual maturity and boldness he had never had before.

Bill Started Attending Men's Seminars at Brookhill Ranch

Bill procrastinated on attending Brookhill Men's Seminars because he wanted to avoid the crowd and didn't want to sit for a long time. Finally, after attending camp for a couple of summers, Emily said, "Daddy, all of us are 'Brookhillers' but you, so you need to sign up and go." He listened to his young daughter's exhortation and began about 1998 to attend the bi-annual Men's Seminars where he began to come into a greater freedom in Christ. My prayers were being answered and that motivated me to pray more! Answered prayer for an intercessor is like fuel for a fire!

When Bill would come home after a seminar, he would share the highlights, and we could see him walking in greater peace, faith, love and boldness. He had already begun to do some teaching for the men's class at church and had delivered one sermon to our congregation on "The 23rd Psalm."

Also, in the late 90's, my husband, the dentist, heard that one of his patients had cancer. I asked him, "Do you know if he is saved?" We began praying for the man, who sometime later came into the office. After treating the patient that day, Bill asked if he could pray for him, and he was very receptive. A short time later, we learned that before the patient died, he received Jesus as his Savior!

Bill Obeys the Lord's Voice

In February 1999 on a Friday morning, it was a typical homeschool schedule, and Bill was having his usual day off from work. He called us all into the den and said he felt that to be obedient he had to get rid of the TV! A weakness for flopping on the couch at the end of a stressful day at the dental office, and channel surfing for several hours every evening, were admitted weaknesses for him. He added that one could see some very ungodly behavior in his own home just by surfing the channels.

Emily and Andrew were amazingly receptive to what their father said. Immediately following our talk, Andrew helped his daddy carry the living room TV to the storage room. The one in our den was kept for viewing selected movies.

The result of Bill's obedience produced good fruit. With the free time that Andrew had after his homeschool day, he took the same guitar bought for him in third grade and taught himself to play! Little did we realize that God would use Bill's obedience to groom a worship leader! Emily started teaching piano lessons to beginning students and used her knowledge and influence to make some spending money.

It was also during the "no TV" time that Andrew wrote his first song. He gave it the title "Mary Ann." Since that day Andrew has written numerous songs, and Bill has learned there is great reward in obedience! Jesus said, "If you love me, obey my commandments" (John 14:15).

Emily's First Visit to ORU

Oral Roberts University, in Tulsa, Oklahoma was our destination in March 1999, as Emily was considering her plans for college. A private Christian liberal arts institution, ORU was birthed as the result of a mandate God gave founder Oral Roberts to "Raise up your students to hear My voice, to go where My light is dim, my voice is heard small, and my healing power is not known, even to the uttermost bounds of the earth. Their work will exceed yours, and in this I am well pleased."

While there for College Weekend, Emily decided ORU was where she wanted to be, and didn't really want to go home. Bill told her that he could not write her out a check for the expensive tuition, but "If God orders it, he will pay for it." We began to pray for God's will, his direction and provision for Emily's college needs, which would be in August 2000, only a year and a half away. As we prayed, Bill began to plan and look at investments he could make to send his daughter to her school of choice.

May 1999, Emily and Andrew traveled with the Masterworks choirs to San Diego and won Gold Awards. My home school students were enjoying their new lifestyle. Their joy and fulfillment transferred to us.

The following month found us finishing up Emily's junior year and Andrew's freshman year of high school. I did not feel very well as we made the last push to finish up daily work, take finals, and then send everything to Christian Liberty for our report cards.

Summer 1999

Emily began her summer taking her training and her place as room counselor for King's Camp, a Christian summer camp for children and youth, located about forty minutes from our home in Mer Rouge, Louisiana. Andrew was hired by a local farmer to help for the season at his nearby produce stand.

On June 2, 1999, I visited my doctor who confirmed that I was pregnant. I was very happy because I wanted another child; I was not ready for the empty nest. When we visited that day at his desk, Dr. Jarrell told me that he did not think the pregnancy was one that I could carry to term, and not to tell anybody until we ran some tests.

Bill and I discussed the whole situation and prayed for God to work everything out. As the days passed by, we decided to share the news with Emily and Andrew as we felt they were mature enough to be part of praying with us.

Dr. Jarrell was concerned that there could be a precancerous condition there along with the baby that I carried. He did several ultrasounds, but never could see the baby. He was very patient with me and told me to return on Friday for another ultrasound.

On Thursday, June 10, at home, I miscarried! The next day, blood tests showed that I had indeed lost the baby. I was disappointed and saddened. As we talked with Dr. Jarrell the next day, he was concerned and believed that we needed to do surgery as soon as possible. The following week I had the surgery, with the pathology reports showing no signs of cancer. I received wonderful care in the hospital, and when I went home, Bill was with me for a week.

During my recovery, our church family and friends blessed us with an abundance of food, some housework, and ironing. It took me several months to feel better and begin to get my strength back.

Andrew Graduates from Brookhill Camp

Camp #7 at Brookhill Ranch Camp in Hot Springs was Andrew's destination in August 1999. Having finished the ninth grade, he would graduate after being a camper for five summers. Bill, Emily and I drove him there, checked him in, met his counselor and said our goodbyes at his assigned cabin. As we drove through the beautiful ranch on our way out, we prayed for Andrew that he would receive a special touch from the Lord.

The following Friday, Emily and I drove to Hot Springs so that we could attend Brookhill's closing ceremonies on Saturday and bring Andrew home. He sat in the front with me on the way home and began to tell us about his camp experiences. As he talked, he became emotional and said, "I don't want to go home. I rededicated my life to Christ at the crucifixion ceremony on Thursday night, and I don't want to go back to the way I was. I need a youth leader like Steven Sexton." Steve was not only the camp director at Brookhill, but he was the Youth Leader at Christian Ministries Church. I knew that Andrew had experienced that special touch from God!

Upon our return to Oak Grove, I told Bill, "If you pull a U-Haul up to our back door, I will begin to load it so we can move to Hot Springs." Bill responded calmly by saying that the timing did not seem right to him.

Clearly Hearing God's Voice

About a week later, on August 18, 1999, I awoke about 5:00 a.m. and was praying. The Holy Spirit began to speak to me. When I got up and continued my prayer and Bible study in the swing on our deck, it was like taking dictation as I wrote down what He continued to say:

"...Hard times are coming.
Prepare your hearts and home.
Sell your stocks and bonds.
Get out of debt...
You will move to a place I will show you..."

The Lord continued, and I received the Word as it seemed to be obviously for me and my family. He did not tell me to share it with others, so I did not. It was a sobering but encouraging message for me. I was not looking forward to even sharing it with Bill and kept it to myself until a month later when the Lord prompted me to tell him.

The Lord knows our weaknesses, and as grace would have it, about a month later, Bill and I were discussing our finances. Bill is a saver and does a good job of investing our money through the years and carefully watches over it. I knew the area of savings was a sensitive subject because, like all wise people, he likes to get the greatest return for our investment. I said to him, "Bill, I have something to tell you, but you won't like it." He said, "Well, go ahead and run it by me anyway." I read to him that word from the Lord I had written down the month before on August 18.

Bill received the "message" very well and responded by saying, "I have been concerned about our money and have been praying for some direction about what to do with it." The following week he proceeded to take action to move our money out of stocks and mutual funds and into more conservative places. However, he became very frustrated with me one day as he walked through the kitchen. I just responded by saying, "Pray about this. I'm telling you what I believe the Holy Spirit said to me." Then I prayed that God would confirm His word to Bill. That week we received a letter in the mail from a secular financial advisor in New Jersey who was giving the same advice about the stock market and what was going to happen.

Bill spent the next three or four weeks moving our money. He found it to be a hard and painful experience because he knew that the interest earned would be less. "The greater the rate of return, the greater the risk!" That was about two years before September 11, 2001. Psalms 25:14 says, "The secret of the Lord is with those who fear Him! and He will show them His covenants." The following spring of 2000, the Nasdaq and Dow began to drop, and as you know, it fell down very low after September 11, 2001. Because we were obedient to what the Lord told us, we did not lose anything in the stock market.

About getting out of debt, we took money we had saved and paid off the note on our dental office and our van, leaving us with only our home mortgage. About moving to a new place, we thought that it would probably be some acreage somewhere in the country, but still in our same parish. The following year, 2000, God did "show us that place to move."

Homeschooling-Year Four

Our last year to school our children at home was 1999-2000. Emily was a senior with Christian Liberty Academy Satellite Schools. She braved Chemistry, along with her other senior subjects and her senior research paper. Her diploma would be issued at the end of the year by Christian Liberty.

Andrew was a sophomore, and I put his curriculum together by looking at Emily's sophomore subjects and at God's leading. I considered his musical abilities, and what he would need to get his high school diploma and to be prepared for college. We did a Composer Course, an "Experiencing God" workbook for the Bible, as well as Algebra II, English II, etc. He read several library books, including a couple chosen by his dad.

Both Emily and Andrew were in Masterworks Choir again, and we anticipated our afternoon away from our house on Tuesday for rehearsals and errands. Both teenagers enjoyed seeing their homeschool friends, which really met a need in their lives.

Meanwhile, Emily was still thinking, pondering, and visiting colleges to make her final decision. In September, we took her to Louisiana Tech University in Ruston, about two hours from Oak Grove. She liked the campus, and knew it was more affordable. One Saturday morning in October, as we sat at the kitchen table together, I told her that if ORU was where the Lord wanted her to go, that He would provide, and she was not to settle for something else.

A few weeks later, on November 4, the prophet, Jon Nelson, came back to our church to preach. After he had ministered to several individuals, including Bill, he saw Emily and asked if he had ever met her. She told him yes. He said, "Tomorrow night, I want to speak with you."

The following night, we went back and the word of the Lord to Emily came forth from Brother Jon Nelson:

"God is just about to move for you in a stronger way than ever before. God purposes to bring to you the financial ability to accomplish what you have felt Him calling you to do, especially concerning your education and your preparation for His work. You're going to see that God has brought you a miracle in that area! There has been a desperate need, and there have been times when you thought, "well, maybe I should just give up and go in some other direction, but you just don't feel led to go in some other direction. God will bring it to pass. God will bring it to pass."

We were so excited!!! We began as a family and as individuals to exercise our faith to believe that somehow, someway, God was going to supernaturally provide for Emily to go to Oral Roberts University to get her education. In the coming year, God would reveal His plans and His ways and perform His miracle!

In that same week, Brother Nelson also gave Bill a word. "...I have a way of placing you where I want you..." The next month he was elected a deacon at our church, a position he did not seek, but he was humbled to be chosen and to serve our congregation at Providence Church.

We approached the year 2000, the New Millennium, with great expectations, and questions filled our mind. Bill would be ordained a deacon, and what would he accomplish? How would God miraculously provide for Emily to go to ORU? Where would God guide us for Andrew's junior year of high school?

We welcomed the year with a New Year's Eve party at our home for Emily and Andrew's friends. It was a rather impromptu celebration! Emily said she wanted to have something special to tell her children one day about how she brought in the new millennium and her graduation year. She mentioned it to a few of her friends at church but didn't follow through with planning it. Bill and Andrew went across town to the fireworks stand and saw Ryan, a friend from Youth Group. He said he was planning to come that night to Emily's party! Bill came home and told me and Emily that Ryan was planning to come that night to her party! We were shocked and got in high gear and had the New Year's Eve party that evening!

We enjoyed hosting the event with board games, refreshments, sparkling grape juice, and fireworks, bringing in the New Year with a bang! There was much fun and laughter among the celebrators, especially as Bill attempted karaoke!

By February, our fifteen-year-old son and Algebra II were not getting along very well, and plowing through to completion became very difficult. It was apparent to me that we needed to make some changes in his curriculum for the following year. I prayed specifically for direction and guidance for the next step in Andrew's education!

Valentine's Day was celebrated with a party at our home for our two youth groups, Immanuel Christian Fellowship and Providence Church. Emily and I made decorations depicting God's love, and we served a sit-down dinner to 29 teenagers and chaperones. After the evening of dinner, devotions, and game time, our eighteen-year-old neighbor, Jarrod, told his mother, "I felt like I was on the Riviera!"

Church Men and Youth Travel the Same Weekend to Conferences in Arkansas

When March blew in, Bill rallied the men in our church and a group of them traveled r to Brookhill Ranch to attend the spring Men's Seminar. It was an enriching time for them.

That same weekend, I was a chaperone with the Providence Youth Group to the *Dare to Share Conference* in Russellville. We learned how to share our faith with others and practiced by going door-to-door in a local neighborhood. The power of the Holy Spirit came during a time with our group of about 21, and mightily touched many who gave testimony. We returned home with great expectancy of what God was going to do in and through those precious young people.

Seeking Direction

Attempting to decide about Andrew's curriculum for the next year, Bill and I attended the *Louisiana Christian Homeschool Conference* that was held in April at Louisiana College in Pineville. The encouraging and informative words from the special speakers, computerized teaching tools, and testimonials from other homeschool parents encouraged and gave us plenty to ponder as we returned home. Bill wanted us to purchase something that weekend; I wanted to wait.

Emily and I Enjoyed Choir Trip and Historic Sites

Emily and I had been planning to go on the Masterworks Choir trip together for months. Boston, Massachusetts was the destination for the competition in April 2000. To go on that trip with Emily and be a chaperone was a great time for us both. En route by airplane, we were delayed for a lengthy time, which made the choir director very unhappy because it threw the schedule off.

When we finally boarded our plane, Emily and I had an opportunity to witness to a Jewish man who was impressed to learn one of the choir songs for the weekend was "Hatikvah," Israel's national anthem. We listened to him as he shared his beliefs, and then we were able to tell him about Jesus, The Messiah he has not read about in the New Testament!

I enjoyed getting to know the other members of the choir, especially the two girls who stayed with us in our hotel room. Seeing those places where history was made like Paul Revere's home, Old North Church, the Battle Green in Lexington, the Boston Tea Party site, and the U.S. Constitution were some of the highlights of our visit there. The main reason for the trip was to compete with other choirs from the nation, and find the Masterworks Choirs in true form—bringing home the Gold and Silver awards!

Emily's High School Graduation

Graduation Day arrived in May of 2000 for Emily and six other homeschool students from northeast Louisiana. In a beautiful Christian ceremony held in Cedar Crest Baptist Church in West Monroe, each student was presented their diploma by their parents. Emily gave the speech for her class, sang the folk song "Seize the Day," and was part of a girl's trio singing "Adonai." She was supported by friends and family from Texas and Colorado. It was a great milestone for all of us to celebrate together!

One of the graduates requested the special speaker for the evening, "Emil the Potter," a fine Christian young man from Florida and a potter by trade. He delivered his sermon as he fashioned a pot on his wheel—quite the object lesson for us all!

Finishing and Time for Rest—or So I Thought!

The following week, Andrew completed Algebra II and his sophomore year, and I completed his grades and report card. After such an eventful spring, I was ready for summer and a much-needed rest. However, the coming months proved to be a whirlwind of activity and major changes in our lives.

A week after Emily's graduation, we had Youth Sunday at church. Each of them had a special part on the program of leading worship, a special song, or a testimony. I was so proud of our Providence Church youth. I could see so much growth taking place in them since the *Dare to Share Conference* in March. After the service, we had pot-blessed dinner and cake to honor our youth and to say goodbye to our friend, Sophia. She was moving to Arkansas to go to college. That day our deacon committee had a special meeting to discuss hiring a youth leader.

By the first week in June, Andrew was preparing to work at King's Camp. He would be serving as the drummer through the work-study program for six weeks. He said, "We need to make a decision about my schooling before I leave for camp." I told Andrew that I was willing to do whatever the Lord wanted. Andrew seemed discouraged. Bill came home from work shortly thereafter and brought in an encouraging letter and $100 from Andrew's Grandfather Beasley toward his work-study support.

On Friday of that week, Bill, Andrew, and I sat down together to talk about Andrew's schooling. If we were going to make a change, why not look at all our options? We could continue homeschooling and change curriculums, or we could make a move. We did not feel that returning to public school was an option for us.

We decided to call the principal of Christian Ministries Academy in Hot Springs. After one phone conversation with, Bobbie Foster, I knew their curriculum was what I wanted for Andrew his last two years of high school. To get that kind of education for him would mean making a major move!

We had learned to admire the students from Christian Ministries Academy as we had attended seminars over the past seven years at Brookhill Ranch. We saw something in their students and camp counselors that we wanted for our own children. The year before, Andrew had voiced his need for a leader like Steven Sexton.

It was decision making time. Since we had already been praying about Andrew's next school year, God was giving us the grace and wisdom we needed. Bill and I both felt that God was leading us somewhere else to worship and serve. We wanted His will more than anything else.

Receiving Clear Direction About Andrew's Next School Year

On June 13, 2000, we interrupted Andrew's camp week and took him and Emily with us to Hot Springs, where we toured Christian Ministries Academy and Christian Ministries Church. Bobbie interviewed Andrew, and he was accepted that weekend for the following school year beginning in September! We were so excited! We agreed that we would move to the Hot Springs area provided we could sell our home, our dental practice, and office building. Bill said, "You know, if we do this, it will have to be a God thing."

With Andrew being so quickly accepted into the school, we needed to consider housing that same weekend. We spent the day with the Century 21 realtor who showed us for the first time all around Hot Springs Village, the beautiful, gated community about 30 minutes from downtown Hot Springs and bordering Brookhill Ranch. It was a time of exploring!

Emily's ORU Miracle Scholarship Revealed

The day after we returned from Hot Springs was June 18, 2000, Father's Day and my own Daddy's birthday! Before church that morning, we received a phone call from a former dental associate of Bill's, Dr. Kevin Finley, of West Monroe. He talked to me and began to tell me the reason for his call. He was on a committee to help find a girl to receive a $20,000 scholarship to attend Oral Roberts University! Applications were taken at the beginning of the year, and there was a female applicant he was considering, but she chose another school. One of his employees, Amber, told Dr. Finley that her friend, Emily Beasley, had the desire to attend ORU. After prayer, he believed that Emily was the student to receive the scholarship!

He told us to contact another committee member, Reverend Mark Acres, a 1999 graduate of ORU and associate pastor of the

Upper Room Church in Bastrop, Louisiana. He would gather the pertinent information needed to get a letter about the scholarship from President Richard Robert's office to the Financial Aid office. What a Father's Day gift from our Heavenly Father: He always keeps his promises! We were so grateful and excited!

The next day, Bill talked to his partner about our plans to move to Arkansas. She wanted to buy his half of their dental practice and our red brick office building and land.

The next evening, Bill went to visit Brother Don and tell him of our plans to move. Within two more days, a couple from our church called to say they were interested in purchasing our home; three weeks later we knew Jamie and Margaret would be the new owners of our home. So many memories we had made together there with each other and with friends.

The significance of all these variables coming together in about two months can only be understood through the eyes of God's provision. We lived in a small, rural farming town in the northeast corner of the state, where real estate can move very slowly. Just as God guided and provided for us to move there twenty-two years earlier, he was providing for us to move to Arkansas.

Meanwhile, there were several phone visits with Reverend Mark Acres about Emily's scholarship. One day as we talked, I asked him for the "name" of the scholarship. He replied, "The scholarship does not have a name. Do you know how it came about?" When I said, "No," he proceeded to explain its origin to me.

"Reverend Charles Reed, at Lamb Broadcasting and TV Channel 39 in West Monroe, had a telethon on November 1, 1999, and Richard Roberts, President of Oral Roberts University, was there as a special guest. While they were on the air and talking about how the Christian university trains up young adults and sends them out, Richard Roberts said, "It comes into my spirit now, to sow two $20,000 scholarships into one boy and one girl from Louisiana who want to attend ORU. You send them to us, and we'll send them back to you better." Reverend Reed felt led by the Lord to ask two former ORU students, Dr. Kevin Finley and Reverend Mark Acres, to help him in selecting the two scholarship recipients from among the applicants!" We, the Beasley Family, knew nothing about Lamb Broadcasting or the applications!

Finding a Home in Arkansas

The summer was very busy. Bill was working daily as a dentist, working on plans for selling the office, and seeking a dental license from the State of Arkansas.

About the second week in July, we decided we needed to make a trip to Hot Springs to look for housing. Bill did not have a job yet in this new location, so we chose where we wanted to live based on its proximity to Christian Ministries Academy and Church. We really liked Hot Springs Village and decided to look for a place to lease. God had told Bill, "Like I provided for Abraham, I'll send you out with my best provision." The week we were to go look, the Lord especially impressed on my heart that we needed a house, not a townhouse or a condominium. We knew at Andrew's age we would be having a lot of youth to visit, and he would continue to play his drums. That could be a tall order, but not for our God!

We traveled to Hot Springs Village around July 15 and spent the next morning with a nice realtor from Crossroads Realty. After lunch we went looking again with an agent from Century 21. As we enjoyed Chinese food at The Forbidden City Restaurant that evening, we looked at each other and said, "We leave for Louisiana tomorrow, and we still haven't found a place to live here."

After dinner, we responded by phone to a "house for rent" ad in the newspaper. The owner agreed to meet us and guide us to the house. As we walked in the door, I said, "Bill, this is it!" The house had a cathedral ceiling, which I had always wanted, and a full two-car garage with a window; we could put an air conditioner in to create an extra living area and maintain Andrew's drums.

As we visited with the owners, Norm and Donna, they told us the house "should still be occupied by the former tenants who, back in December, had signed an eighteen-month lease on the house, which is very uncommon. Around June 1, (about the time we called CMA) they suddenly decided to move to Memphis and broke the lease!" After we told Donna and Norm about our reasons for moving, they showed us an electronic gate, which put the house about ten minutes from Christian Ministries Academy! We knew that our God had guided us and provided again! We were so thankful.

The ORU Miracle Full-Tuition Scholarship

The following week, on July 21, Emily was working at her summer babysitting job. We were in Texas visiting our parents. She called us there with some news. Mark Acres had called Emily that day at work to tell her of God's full miracle provision regarding her education! In trying to get the award letter from Richard Robert's secretary to the Financial Aid Office, the ORU President had decided to double the scholarships and award full tuition to Emily and the other recipient, Jason Bowen of Calhoun, Louisiana. Emily had indeed received a miracle scholarship! She did not apply for it; she said yes to what God was calling her to do. We believed that God would do what He said!

Meanwhile, Bill, in addition to making a living, was spending hours putting together the plan to sell his practice, and to get another license to practice dentistry in the State of Arkansas. That process required much time and effort. He was scheduled to meet with the State Board of Dentistry in Little Rock on August 13, 2000, which required him to leave Oak Grove on August 12. We were moving Emily to ORU on that same day.

Before Emily left her native state, we traveled to West Monroe on Thursday evening, August 12. Reverend Charles Reed of Lamb Broadcasting and Channel 39, devoted his hour-long program to the two ORU scholarship recipients, interviewing Emily and Jason Bowen, and men who had helped him with the process, Dr. Finley and Reverend Acres. Reverend Reed presented Emily her framed certificate and congratulatory letter from Oral Roberts University, which reads:

"Dear Emily: Congratulations on receiving the scholarship from Lamb Broadcasting! You are truly blessed to receive such a great gift from God. I am glad that you will now have the opportunity to be academically, physically, and spiritually challenged at Oral Roberts University. I know that God has placed you here for a reason that will affect the rest of your life. You have been awarded a four-year full tuition scholarship. The total value of this scholarship is over $40,000 and is renewable over the next four years of attendance at ORU...I look forward to you starting in the fall..." The letter is signed by the Director of Undergraduate Admissions.

Pondering...

As I reflected on all the Lord had done the year before, I remembered the voice of the Lord to me on August 18, 1999. Bill acted in obedience to the Lord by moving our money out of the stock market. We did not even know Lamb Broadcasting existed, but the following month, Emily's provision to go to ORU became a creative miracle in the heart of God, and to the mind and spirit of Richard Roberts. Three days later, November 4, Emily received the "word to believe" from the prophet at our church. God was truly orchestrating the circumstances and events of our lives. "You will move to a place I will show you." Now, a year later, we were making a major move to a special city, house, church, and school in Arkansas to further Andrew's Christian education!

Moving

With full tuition paid, Emily packed up her college-life furnishings into our van, and we were ORU-bound on August

13, 2000. As we began our trip to Tulsa through "The Natural State," we met Bill in Little Rock, where he had just satisfactorily completed his meeting with the Arkansas Dental Board and was granted his license. He made the trip up to Oklahoma with us. Because we knew that ORU was God's will for Emily, our first child to leave home, we left her there with peace in our hearts.

On August 16, 2000, our brown cypress house in Oak Grove legally became the family home of Jamie and Margaret. Two weeks later on August 29, the huge, orange Allied moving van, loaded with the Beasley household furnishings, pulled out from 301 Ridgecrest Drive and headed for Hot Springs Village. During the course of that same day, we said goodbye to some friends, neighbors, to Karla and our special staff during our lunch together. That afternoon, the two dentists signed the closing papers which transferred ownership of the dental practice and building from Dr. Beasley to Dr. Robertson.

Bill had provided dental care to the residents of Northeast Louisiana and Southern Arkansas for twenty-two years. We had many special patients, dear friends, and wonderful memories. We were grateful for God's guidance and provision there, and our moving dream was coming true.

When God leads us, he always has His Kingdom and our higher good in mind. In the Eighth month—that of new beginnings—He was transplanting us again to a new land!

CHAPTER 12

TRANSPLANTED TO A NEW LAND

"...and go to the land I will guide you to."(Genesis 12:1).

It was August 30, 2000, the first day of our new adventure in Arkansas! So glad to be here, we were looking for the moving van to arrive during the morning. Before that, however, there was an interesting phone call! I answered and realized it was a dental supply salesman who knew about our move to Hot Springs Village and my husband's need for a job.

Bill learned the reason for the call. Two weeks before our move, a middle-aged dentist from Hot Springs had died suddenly and left his widow, three young children, and a dental practice. The dentists of the city had been taking turns filling in to keep the practice running, but the family wanted to find a buyer for it. Bill was immediately intrigued with the opportunity and told the salesman that he could come the next day to meet the staff and hear more about it.

Our furniture and belongings arrived, and getting settled in continued for a while. The most important thing was to get our kitchen functional and get Andrew's room straight where he could begin his new school adventure the following week. It was a

Wednesday, and Andrew insisted that we needed to go to church that first night. After the service ended, he was invited to Tom and Danette's home for fellowship and snacks. Little did I realize that evening, that godly family I was about to meet would be influential in Andrew's life, and the special friends they would become to us in our new home in Arkansas. I want to say that through the years, we have been inspired and motivated to become more like Christ from fellowshipping with Tom and Danette and their children, Joseph, Daniel, Katie, Mary Ann, and Suzanna. They serve our Lord through the offering of their home, their food, their musical talents, their humility, and their love! That knowledge not yet attained, I decided to taxi Andrew and Tiffany, a friend from King's Camp who was also a new transplant. I wanted to meet the "host family."

Bill Investigates New Dental Opportunity

The next morning, dressed for work, Bill took his briefcase and went to town to investigate the dental practice opportunity. He enjoyed meeting the office staff, the dentists, and the businessmen who were handling the sale of the practice. After a few days, he wanted me to go and meet the staff and see the office, which I did.

Emily came home from college the first time for Labor Day weekend. She had a lot to share with us about her new adventure and how she was enjoying ORU very much, just as she imagined. We loved being together again as a family of four, eating, talking, catching up, and showing Emily for the first time ever our new home. She liked it and began to meet the college-age people in our church.

The day after Labor Day, Andrew began his junior year in his new school at Christian Ministries Academy's Fall Retreat, which was held annually at Brookhill Ranch Camp. The Fall Retreat allows all the staff and students to get on the "same page" before beginning the new year. Soon our son was off and running with the uniform, classes, new friends, new teachers, and a basketball team. He even had Steven Sexton as his youth leader! It was such an exciting time in our lives! God is good to us. In the coming months and years, God used Steve to mentor Andrew. "Leaders are not born; they are made."

The day came for me to visit the dental practice Bill was considering purchasing. I went to meet the staff, see the facility, see the location, and have lunch with my husband. It was an amazing experience. The office and staff reminded us of our dental practice many years ago in Oak Grove. What was God doing, we had to ask? Bill was inclined to "go for it" since he needed a job. We hadn't celebrated selling our other practice; let's not jump into the next one so quickly, I thought.

Everybody around Bill, including the other dentists, the accountant, and bankers he consulted with and even our parents, believed it was the perfect "made to order" opportunity. They thought we should buy it.

The day before the practice was to be legally in our name, we could not get any peace. We were wrestling in our spirits and couldn't sleep well. Bill had already gone to the office of the specialists in the city, including the orthodontists and oral surgeon. One or two of them had already sent beautiful flowers welcoming him as a dentist to the community!

While all the arbitration about the sale of the practice was going on, Bill agreed to just be at the office and see the patients until the deed could be signed. About September 27, the day before the office was to be ours, Bill dressed for work but expressed before leaving that he just did not have any peace about going through with the purchase. Bill Beasley is a man of his word! He didn't have peace about buying it, but he had given his word; all the groundwork had been laid for purchasing the practice, and we were close to signing on the dotted line. All of us had prayed and asked other people to be praying with us. We were in a tug-of-war.

Pastor Stowe, A special Christian friend of ours, reminded us on the phone, "Go with the peace." But Bill's "yes" on this brought us no peace. It was so difficult. Before leaving for work that day, he sat down in a chair and said, "I can't go through with it. I will have to back out today and call the specialists also." He felt in a very hard place.

After Bill left for work and I got Andrew to school, I decided to get dressed so I could meet Bill for lunch. It was fall in Arkansas, and I had the windows open. I could hear our little Dachshund, Tia, carrying on outside. I looked out the window and saw that she was all tangled up around a big tree. I went out to get her untangled, which was a big project. As I was getting her out of the mess, I heard the Holy Spirit speak to me. He said, "That is how you would be if you bought that dental office—tangled up!" It was a very divine appointment I had that day as I took care of our little dog. After much prayer, God had spoken clearly to me about the subject. At lunch, I told Bill about hearing the Lord's voice, and we discussed how much peace we had about our decision not to buy the dental practice. He was very tired from the big year we had and needed a rest. Because Bill was already helping at the dental office and because he had given his word to purchase it, he told the owner that he would be glad to continue running the practice for her until she could find a buyer. She hired him and paid him well to work there for the next seven weeks, which was a tremendous blessing for us.

A Test of Andrew's Health

The morning after Bill declined the purchase of the dental practice, we found ourselves in the emergency room at National Park Medical Center. Before we got up, we could hear Andrew laying on the couch in the living room where he was coughing. I knew something was wrong and went there to ask him. He said, "I can't breathe, and I hurt." I called my friend Deborah to find out where the nearest hospital was. We threw on our clothes, put on our flashing lights, and drove him quickly toward downtown about

7:25 a.m.. I was praying in the spirit for my son. Standing in the street was a policeman who was directing traffic for school children. He jumped in his car and gave us a police escort to the hospital!

That Thursday morning at the ER, they took a picture of Andrew's chest and found a spot on his lung. The doctor said it was a very unusual situation for a sixteen-year-old boy, but he hoped that the spot was caused by the pneumonia he had; they would hospitalize him and hope the spot would clear up with antibiotics. He was very sick.

Christian Ministries Academy rallied around Andrew, their new student, and Coach Stricker brought a van load of high school students to Andrew's hospital room. The huge card they had made for him was a great encouragement. They gathered around his bed, and Mark, a senior, led the group in a prayer for Andrew's healing. Teachers came and the church sent him flowers. We had only been part of our new church family for a month, and they were there for us!

By Saturday, Andrew was well enough to go home. Although he only had to curtail his normal activities of basketball practice, etc. for about two weeks, it took many months before the spot on his lung totally left. We would go back from time to time and see the pulmonologist and take a new X-ray. Eventually, after about eight months, the doctor dismissed him.

Dorm Struggles

In October, ORU gave their students a Fall Break, and Emily came home for a week. We enjoyed spending the vacation time together, resting, going to Company's Comin for cappuccino, and talking. She and her roommate had met before the semester began, but shortly thereafter, certain attitudes developed and had gotten worse. Emily had done all she knew to do except to move out. We prayed about the situation, and I traveled back to school with her at the end of the break and moved her to another room.

God is so faithful. Our daughter received a new roommate, Melody, who lived on the seventh floor. I could feel the peace in this new location, and the two girls discovered all they had in common as they bonded together. She and Melody, the daughter of missionaries, had both schooled at home, they both had a younger brother, and both were musical; Melody was a missions major and Emily was a pastoral ministries major, with an emphasis in evangelism. That same room on the seventh floor continued to be Emily's home for her four years at ORU.

Bill's Temporary Dental Position Ends

When the buyer was found for the dental practice in November 2000, Bill began a rest from his eventful year! He stayed at home where we continued to get settled in, organized our house, and tended to much business. We prepared for and held a garage sale in December, lightening our twenty-three-year load.

His time off from work allowed him time to spend with Andrew, carrying him to school and picking him up after school often. He used the time to teach Andrew some vital things. He told our son, "You must put yourself in a place (by your behavior) that I can bless you." We attended his basketball games and special activities.

Bill enjoyed having the free time to do some work at the church and to help James and Mandy, our new friends, who were building a house. We started exploring our beautiful new state. We felt so glad to have restaurants nearby, and we did not have to make a long drive to the next city for recreation or shopping.

One of the greatest blessings in our new home, besides our obvious school and church, were the friends we made. Bill and Lloyd would meet once a week somewhere for a Coke or coffee. I felt welcomed by several of the women. Andrew also made friends very quickly. He was always bringing in young people to eat with us or visit; we valued getting to know each one of them. Even though Emily lived away in Tulsa, she too developed some new relationships among the college group, who would include her in their activities when she was at home. Our new neighbors were pleasant, and the businesspeople welcomed us. It was a small town feel with the city benefits.

A month after Andrew started school at CMA, the principal and her staff decided to start a live Chapel Band and included Andrew as a lead guitarist. About the same time, he was invited to begin playing with the Youth Band, both of which were under Steven Sexton's leadership. This was such an exciting time for us. Dreams coming true!

Christian Ministries Academy helped us continue to encourage Andrew in growing his character! I began to see a change in my son's heart. I could see Andrew growing and maturing. He could be concerned about my well-being when he called me on the phone but focused on his next goal or accomplishment.

Our move to Arkansas was a win/win for all four of us. Our Louisiana home would have been eight hours from Emily. Our new home in the Village is a five-hour drive, and in those first two semesters during 2000/2001, she was able to come home nearly once a month, including holidays.

Our first Christmas in Arkansas was wonderful, and we enjoyed being only three and one/half hours from East Texas, where we went to be with our parents and siblings during the holidays.

Christian Ministries Church is a beautiful place to be at Christmas because it is obvious that we are truly celebrating the birthday of our Lord and Savior, Jesus Christ. The aroma of live trees filled our senses as they were placed in strategic places in the sanctuary. CMA Christmas Ministry, of which Andrew was a part, was second to none, as they took several weeks of school to rehearse for it and build the set. The women of our church had our own Christmas dinner together and program. I loved the CMA Elementary Children's Ministry at the Ranch Pavilion. Jesus

Christ is the only One who has a day that's set aside to honor His birthday around the world!

January 2001 arrived, and Emily returned to ORU, Andrew went back to CMA, and Bill and I were at home. He soon began to send out resumes and do some serious looking for a job. By the middle of March, he had about four job options.

Monarch Dental Associates has dental offices in twenty-six states, with four locations in Little Rock. The southwest location, about an hour from the Village, had an opening for a general dentist. Bill took the job on March 21, 2001, and began with a loyal and supportive staff, a hygienist, and a lab man. He continued to work there for over eleven years.

Bill left for work at 6:40 a.m. and Andrew's school day started at 8:25. I would drive Andrew to school and enjoyed visiting frequently with the other mothers who were bringing their children. Emily enjoyed her classes; I wrote to her frequently and we talked often on the phone. Andrew's schedule with school, basketball, homework, youth band ministry for Wednesday night services, and youth group kept us very active with our church and school. Bill thrived with his brothers in Christ in the Men's Sunday School Class and became the assistant teacher. I attended the Women's Sunday School Class, volunteered in the school, became part of the intercessors group, and wrote articles for the monthly church paper, "The Shofar."

Andrew had a solo part in Christian Ministries' annual Easter drama. After the service, we drove up the road to the Ranch where we were blessed to watch so many people be baptized in the cold lake, a real test that reminds us of Jesus' sacrifice for us. Lunch, fellowship, and an Easter egg hunt were other highlights of the day!

With summer fast approaching, Emily and Andrew made their plans for employment. Emily was interviewed and hired as a senior counselor at Brookhill Ranch Camp. To wear the red t-shirt that says "Brookhill Staff" was quite an honor. She was responsible for a cabin that would house twenty-two girls, ages nine to fourteen years old, every week. Emily reported for her counseling duties by 11:00 a.m. every Monday morning and the week of camp ended about 12:00 every Saturday, when the closing ceremonies were over and the campers had left with their parents. We would enjoy having her home that afternoon through Monday morning, enough time to eat some vegetables, take a nap, wash some clothes, and go back again. She felt blessed to be able to minister to so many young girls over that course of eight weeks.

Year Two

The middle of August 2001 found Emily back at ORU as a sophomore. She auditioned for and earned a position in the Chapel Choir, which sang at all the chapel services on campus, twice a week.

With the coming and going of Labor Day, Andrew began his senior year at CMA. Before the Fall Retreat, we visited with Andrew and told him he needed to step up to the plate and be a leader in the school. He and his friend, Casey, requested a special meeting with the founder, Hettie Lou Brooks, to discuss their ideas and strategies for the new year. She gave them her full encouragement and support on the day of the back-to-school retreat. Both young men announced to the students their plans to unite and have a truly Christian school for the next nine months.

Steven Sexton organized a Friday night outreach called The Source, which provided young people clean entertainment, fun, food, and fellowship after the local football games at the surrounding schools. He brought in visiting bands, but in my opinion, our own youth and college bands were the best, by far! Christian Ministries Youth Band members were Andrew, Susanna, Mary Ann, Chase, and Casey.

When my birthday rolled around September, 2001, the day went by, and it was time to say goodnight at our house. Andrew decided that he would sleep on the couch because he was so tired.

I knelt beside the couch to pray for him. He said, "I'm going to get you something for your birthday." In October, a month later, I picked Andrew up at school with the plan that he would take my van into town for servicing. He resisted the idea slightly and added that he had to meet some friends "at the top of the mountain." I agreed, and he let me off at the house and proceeded with his plans.

About two hours later he called to ask if I had enough supper to feed him and three friends. I told him to bring them on. When Casey, Melissa and Leah arrived with Andrew, he had a gift bag in his hand from Company's Comin. He hugged me and said, "Happy Birthday." I opened the bag to find a beautiful cup and saucer with the words "Mother O'Mine" inscribed on the side. Also enclosed was a book by Mary Engelbreit about motherhood. God was helping Andrew grow in his awareness of his family.

Call us old fashioned, but Bill and I have the philosophy on raising teenagers that when a parent equips his son or daughter with their own set of wheels too early, the parent gives up a lot of control over their youth and gives a freedom to them that they may not be ready for. Because of peer pressure, it was very difficult to "put off" buying an automobile for our children very early. They would keep reminding us that all their friends have something to drive that they call their own. We waited until the month Emily was graduating from high school to buy her car.

As soon as we moved to Arkansas, Andrew was ready to get his driver's license and began to inquire about when he was going to get his car or truck.

Many parents do the right thing at the wrong time, and children or teenagers who are not mature enough to handle the "blessing" go down the wrong road. God works in times and seasons, which must be a guide for successful parenting. God does not give us what we want, when we want it, because he knows how it will affect us. King David wrote in the Psalms, "God, don't make me poor, or I might become a thief; and don't make me too rich, or I might walk away from you." I believe that if Bill had bought Andrew's truck too soon, our son would have bypassed a very important step in surrendering his life to God.

October arrived, and Andrew was still waiting for his own set of wheels. I had carried him to school one morning that week, and he asked in a very concerning, anxious way, "When am I going to get a truck? Casey and I are the only students in our class who don't have one yet." I told him, "When God gets your heart, then he can give you your desires."

The annual Fall Festival at Christian Ministries Church is a main event. Some mothers get together and decorate the gym with scarecrows, bales of hay, a photo spot, and then all kinds of game booths for the kids. Adults, college students, youth, children, and babies dress up and come for an evening of fun. Andrew and Casey came in the house on October 31 with their special rented costumes. Andrew posed as a pink gorilla, and Casey was one of the seven dwarfs! Yes, they were very funny. Andrew won an award that night for the best costume.

The next day, November 1, he was getting ready after school to return the costume to a downtown store when he asked me if I had a box. "What size box do you need?" I asked. "One that will hold all these CD's," he replied. He had made the amazing decision to get rid of all his secular music, which was about forty CD's, including his Dave Matthews music! I had been praying that all that music would be gone from our house! I believed that at Andrew's age, it needed to be his decision and conviction, especially if it was going to last.

Within the next two days, he unloaded all forty CDs on a pawn shop, where he got pennies in comparison to the money he paid for them. Then he went to the store and bought Christian CDs to begin building up a new collection. What a victory God had won in his life, and what an answer to my prayers. I said, "Thank you, Lord."

Friday evening, November 2, Bill began the weekend at the Brookhill Men's Seminar. Andrew had made plans to go to Louisiana to visit, but I told him that we would hang out together and shop for him some clothes. As we started out that Saturday morning, we saw a small, black Toyota pickup on the side of Highway 7 with a "For Sale" sign on the front. We had to stop, check it out, and drive it. After showing it to his dad that evening, the decision was made to purchase the truck for Andrew. He realized that his obedience in getting rid of the secular CD's brought God's blessing and the desire of his heart! The blessing comes after obedience!

It is important to mention that after Andrew got rid of that secular music, his songwriting gift came to the forefront. Since that day in November, God has given him amazing songs, many of which we have copyrighted.

That same month of November 2001, Andrew, only 17 years old, came home from school one day telling me that because of his economics class at CMA, he was thinking about starting his own business. As mentioned earlier, Andrew had entrepreneurial experiences since third grade.

Andrew, the senior, and his younger friend, Andrew, came home from school one afternoon in November, got on our roof, removed the leaves, and cleaned out our gutters. Our son got an idea for roof and gutter cleaning. After running an ad in the *Village Voice,* his first phone call came. His new business, which he named BEASMITH, was started by him and his best friend, Casey. From that moment on, his customer base grew as he handed out business cards in different neighborhoods, and word of mouth caused our phone to ring. The truck God had blessed him with that month was essential to his work.

BEASMITH not only provided employment for Andrew and several friends for the next two summers, but it was an educational experience. He learned how to serve his customers, plan, and manage his time and money as he ran his own business, and worked through the day-to-day challenges and problem-solving experiences.

The new year, 2002, brought thoughts about Andrew's high school graduation and questions about what he would do afterward. Steven took Andrew, his office assistant for the year, for a Coke. He explained to him that all of the men who were influencing his life in a positive way had attended Applied Life Christian College. Our pastor, Tim Brooks, founded the small, discipleship college in 1985 to train young men and women to apply the Bible to daily living and to give them an "Arabian" experience, somewhat like that of Paul the Apostle. Andrew decided to apply to attend Applied Life Christian College.

Emily Met Her Future Husband

Meanwhile, Emily was a busy full-time student at ORU. One day in her Signs and Wonders Class, the teacher wanted all the students to hold hands and pray. A classmate named Jason Blais was beside Emily, and as they joined hands for prayer, she was reminded of her own father's hands. God gave her a word for Jason that day: "You will be a father to many people." He had a serious expression on his face and tried to get away very quickly. Later, when Emily saw him again, she asked him if that meant anything or had he ever heard that before. He said, "Yes, and that he wanted to be a pastor." Mr. Blais decided that he wanted to get to know our daughter better, and their friendship began.

As that spring semester continued, Emily was feeling called to participate in ORU'S Summer Missions Program. She would be part of a team that met weekly to prepare for ministry in May and June to parts of Mexico.

Her semester ended, and after some training, Emily left for Mexico believing God to do miracles as they traveled to several locations. She was moved by the love and faith of the people but found God to speak to her in simple ways. Previously, she had envisioned herself traveling to the nations to minister. Upon her return, she realized that she wanted marriage and a family and to evangelize through the local church. Her arrival home in June required a much-needed rest from school and ministry. She spent the rest of the summer relaxing, planning for the fall semester, and visiting on the phone with Jason. He was spending his summer working and living at home in Florida.

Andrew Graduates from Christian Ministries Academy

Meanwhile, Christian Ministries Academy wrapped up their school year, and held their graduation exercises in May 2002. Andrew Beasley was among the twelve students who received diplomas that night. Each student gave a speech, and we were blessed as our son shared his testimony of how he grew spiritually at CMA! Andrew was supported on his graduation by both sets of his grandparents, his cousin, Kris, his church family, his Uncle David and Aunt Sharmaine, and Matthew, his friend from Louisiana.

We celebrated the following day at our home with a catered barbeque dinner in Andrew's honor. Bill gave a "Father's Blessing" over Andrew before our meal. Members of his senior class, along with chaperones from the school, traveled to St. Augustine, Florida for the following week where they enjoyed vacationing at two condos near the beach.

After Graduation Day, Matthew talked with us about his desire to move to Hot Springs and finish high school at Christian Ministries Academy the following school year. We agreed to pray with him about the matter.

Summer 2002

Andrew and Casey returned from their senior trip to work BEASMITH, where they served customers in the Village and surrounding area cleaning gutters and doing lawns and landscaping for the summer. Chase joined the crew, making it a threesome; after several weeks, Casey was offered a job at Brookhill Camp. After a hot and busy morning outside, the guys would come to my kitchen hoping for some sweet, iced tea and home cooking. Andrew and Chase continued their teamwork, with Andrew making enough money to pay his daddy back for the two mowers and equipment he had bought in the spring to begin the business.

In June of 2002, we had Vacation Bible School at Christian Ministries. I volunteered to help and wanted my nephews, Matthew, Joel, and Stephen to attend VBS. They came from Texas to spend the week with us. Each evening I would prepare supper early and we would go off to our Church. Andrew and the Youth Band were a blessing as they provided the music each night. The arts and crafts were fun, and at the end of the week, Joel and Stephen both received special awards. Even though Matthew was too old to attend the classes, he had fun with other youth and helped where he could. Vacation Bible School is a lot of hard work, but the seeds that are planted in young lives are eternal. What price can be put on the salvation of the young souls we won to the Lord during that week?

In July 2002, the first annual Christian Ministries Women's Conference was held at our church under the direction of JaDean Stricker. It was a wonderful time of hearing our own sisters in Christ speak a message from the Lord or to give their personal testimonies. The fellowship was sweet, and it was a time of refreshing just for us.

When the conference ended on Saturday morning, Andrew went to the church to practice some youth band music. As he sat there on the stage, he wrote the following song, his story about how his life was changed at Christian Ministries Church!

"The Oath"
Song written by Andrew T. Beasley

On these altar steps I found the Lord
In this house I felt his holy hands

Surrounded by these people I knew his love
I walked these floors as a stair to his throne
This is the beginning of my oath unto you
This is the beginning of my oath unto you.

Chorus:
I'll praise him, with the actions of my life
I'll praise him, with the echoes of my voice
I'll praise him, with the shadows of my life
I'll praise him, so that he will be praised.

On these lands I learned how to serve
On this stage I learned how to lead
Through these people's lives I've seen God
This is the beginning of my oath unto you
This is the beginning of my oath unto you.

Questions Asked
Where to go
What to Say

Why do I believe But I do.

About August 4, Bill carried Andrew to the airport in Little Rock. His destination—Summit Ministries, Colorado Springs, Colorado. It was during the next two weeks that Andrew would continue developing a Biblical worldview and receive the heart of an evangelist. Emily and I had been the evangelists in the family until Andrew returned home that hot month in 2002. He had witnessing on his mind, from customers during the day to those he met in town at night. From the hot tub to the bookstore, he was striking up evangelism conversations with the people he met!

On Jason's way back to ORU that August, he came by to see Emily and visit with us for the weekend. We showed him around and had some good conversations. Emily and Jason caravanned back to ORU for the fall semester.

I prayed about whether Matthew should live with us and go to school at CMA, and God showed me that we were to welcome Matthew like a son into our home! He came to live with us on August 30, 2002, two years and a day after our move to Hot Springs Village. He began his senior year at Christian Ministries Academy the following week. We celebrated his move to Arkansas at our house drinking sparkling grape juice with his mother, Angela, and sister, Chelsea, and our friends, Chase and Casey. We had fun together playing board games in our dining room. We were excited. Our new adventure of mentoring was beginning; God was "enlarging our territory!"

"And the things that thou hast heard of me among many witnesses, the same commit thou to faithful men, who shall be able to teach others also" (II Timothy 2:2).

In Louisiana, God had given us love and compassion for young people. Now God had brought another "son" to be trained up at Christian Ministries Academy. Matthew had not only been part of the youth group at our former church, but he was a musician with Andrew on the worship team and spent numerous days and nights at our home. In a previous chapter, I shared about how he was miraculously healed at an Eastman Curtis Youth Convention!

The same week that Matthew drove Brookhill Road to begin as a senior at CMA, Andrew started Applied Life Christian College. It would be in those experiences that God would continue to conform our son into His image. Matthew was a blessing at CMA in numerous ways. He almost immediately took his place in the chapel and youth bands. He became Steve's office assistant, and Steve began to mentor him to be a leader. The basketball coaches put him to work announcing the home games.

God Transplants More Louisiana Friends to Arkansas!

In January of 2002, we visited with Pat and Karen and their children, Claire, Catherine, and Chas, as they had come up from Louisiana to visit Christian Ministries Church. Nearly every weekend for about eight months our friends made the four-hour drive from Lake Providence to Hot Springs, as they too, contemplated making a major move for their family.

In September we also rejoiced over our new Village neighbors! God also transplanted this special family and provided just the house Karen had prayed for, which was only three minutes from ours! She asked God for a four-bedroom house, on a flat lot, where her children could enjoy a basketball goal.

Karen and Pat's move to CMC has been a win/win for the whole family as God has provided jobs, new friends, a place for the entire family to use their amazing gifts in the Body of Christ, and an environment of faith where they have all grown in the Lord.

Time passed, and more friends from Louisiana joined us in our community of believers. Michelle and Jamie and their sweet daughter, Kayla, came and then Matthew's mother, Angela lived nearby.

A New Nephew

In October 2002, David and Sharmaine had their first child, a little boy whom they named Dominick Victor Moore, after both of his grandfathers. I drove my parents to David's home in Olathe, Kansas so that we could see and welcome our precious new family member and celebrate together. Dominick, a handsome young man, has become a great follower of Jesus!

Bill and I endeavored to treat Matthew like a son. Although he was very busy and on the go, we used our time around the table to talk about our day together. We did our best to encourage him and to pray for him.

Matthew graduated with honors from Christian Ministries Academy in May 2003. He also received several special awards presented by the school. We were proud of Matthew and thankful to have a part in his life. He was supported by his family from Louisiana and his new church family, who had also come to love him.

Summer 2003

Because he had summer work as a lifeguard, Matthew requested to live with us through June, July, and August. Andrew moved home after completing his first year of college. He and Matthew had some free time to visit and play some video games. Toward the end of the summer, we received the good news that Joshua, another of our Louisiana youth group, was coming to CMA as well to finish his junior and senior year. Also a worship leader, he was a blessing in the chapel band and school while he was receiving a Christian education and a diploma in 2005!

Another Miracle Scholarship!

Our prayers for Matthew's education were answered! The end of August, he received an important call from Paul Kern, Dean of Applied Life Christian College. Three businessmen from Kansas City, who had attended Men's Seminars at

Brookhill Ranch called and said they wanted to sponsor one ALCC student with tuition, books, and grocery money for their two full years of school! Matthew was the recipient of the miracle educational funds, and he did not even know his sponsors!

Four College Students

Emily began her senior year at Oral Roberts University in August 2003. With the responsibility of writing her senior paper and thoughts of marriage to her best friend, Jason Blais, she started her fall semester with a full plate. Jason had just completed his undergraduate work on his Theology Degree. He was beginning courses toward his Master of Divinity Degree while he also began his first year as a teacher's assistant at ORU. He and Emily would both receive their Bachelor of Arts Degree in Commencement Exercises together the following May 2004.

Andrew and Matthew moved from our house to the dorm at Applied Life Christian College for the fall semester. Andrew, a second-year student and Matthew in his first year, served together as guitarists leading the college chapel band. Both guys had both become mentors to some younger students at CMA. They both worked in the youth group with Steven. As part of their Christian Service, Andrew and Matthew were privileged at that time to serve as the voice on The Shine, the KALR 91.5 FM Friday night youth radio show.

During the 2003-2004 school year, we enjoyed having Karen and Pat's kids, Claire, Catherine, and Chas come to our house for drum and guitar lessons from Andrew. What a precious gift are our children, and how great it is to watch them grow up in Christ, and develop their gifts and talents to use for His glory! When a child/youth follows Jesus, He is the "keeper of their hearts." They have a personal relationship with Christ, and He is keeping them from temptation. There is no greater investment a parent can make than in taking time and paying the price in the right season to lead our children to the Lord, and then to see His character being formed in them. There are countless blessings that come to us from knowing Jesus at an early age and having the Holy Spirit lead even in the smallest details of our lives.

Christmas Vacation and Serious Conversations

It was December 2003, and I anticipated having Emily and Andrew both at home with us to celebrate Christmas. God has a way of preparing us for what lies ahead, and He led me to do a twenty-four hour fast the week they came home. I wanted to talk with Emily about some things. Andrew was playing music, and we went to his concert together. Toward the end, Andrew called Emily up to sing with him, and I could feel the wonderful presence of the Lord when they were singing.

We had a great Christmas together as a family. It always feels good to this Mom to get my kids back home again.

It was during the Christmas holidays that Emily told me that she and Jason were planning to visit the Eastern Orthodox Church the next semester. I did not understand and wondered why! Her answer was, "Jason and I want to honor Jesus."

Before our daughter returned to ORU for the Spring Semester, Bill talked to Emily about The Orthodox Church. He reminded her that we had raised her in a church that supports the five-fold ministry and how we felt about her and Jason considering a liturgical church.

Andrew's First Mission Trip

During Spring Break in March of 2004, Andrew went on his first mission trip to Honduras. In his testimony to our church on his return, he focused on the main missionary who works there. Alvin Anderson has such a passion and love for the people he serves that they follow him and call him "Poppy." In many young lives, Alvin has taken the place of the father they have never known! Andrew shared, "As I watched those people run after Alvin, I began to think, how many people are chasing after us? We need to live the life of Christ that people are drawn to follow us or get in touch with us or ask us a question, just like they were drawn to Jesus!"

Emily and Jason Are Engaged

Emily used her Spring Break week to zero in on finishing her senior paper. She and Jason came to see us for the weekend. We went to our church that Sunday morning and to the altar to pray together and take communion. Emily and Jason did not take communion with us.

This was the beginning of their Orthodox Church journey because The Orthodox Christians believe in closed communion in their own church.

After our Sunday dinner at home, while still seated around the table, Jason and Emily presented us with a well-prepared budget. He said they wanted to be married at the end of the year.

After talking about their budget and wedding plans, Bill brought up the subject of The Orthodox Church. He said that we didn't understand their decision to go from being in a Protestant Family and ORU students to a Liturgical Church. But that is what they decided to do. Emily called me the next week to say that they wanted to join The Orthodox Church and be married there in Tulsa in the summer.

May 1, 2004: Two College Graduations

It had come to our attention the previous fall that both Emily's and Andrew's graduations were scheduled to be held on the same day in two different states! What? We couldn't attend both their graduations! Since we had no control over the scheduled events, we decided to count our blessings that they were graduating and go with the flow, even though it was difficult. I was sad not to be able to attend Andrew's graduation, and Bill was sad not to be able to attend Emily and Jason's graduation!

Our daughter, who had received the Oral Roberts University Miracle Scholarship, was receiving her Bachelor of Arts Degree in Pastoral Christian Ministries, with an emphasis in Evangelism. Her fiancée, Jason, was the ORU Theology Student of the Year for 2004 and was receiving his Bachelor of Arts Degree in Old Testament Literature. The theology department held its hooding ceremony the afternoon before graduation, so Bill drove to Tulsa to be with our daughter and future son-in-law at their departmental ceremony. Jason's honor as Student of the Year awarded him the privilege of speaking. My parents traveled from Texas and joined them too.

Andrew's Baccalaureate from Applied Life Christian College was the night before graduation. I was there, with tears in my eyes, to see him wearing his cap and gown and ministering worship with the college band for the last time. Each ALCC teacher exhorted the class members. Applied Life gets its name because students are taught a Biblical worldview and how to apply God's word to every area of life. They are taught how to defend their faith because we live in a world where many teachers who are atheists and agnostics stand behind the podium of countless university classrooms across this nation. They seek to intimidate young students who have come from Christian homes, but who have not been taught apologetics! Applied Life (now Leadership Academy) teaches students how to live the Christian life everyday as employees, husbands, wives, and leaders. Students get "intern" experience in Christian Ministries Church.

Two College Graduations on the Same Day!

Bright and early the next morning, I was on the road to Tulsa for Emily and Jason's 1:00 commencement ceremonies at the Mabee Center on the campus of ORU. It was a very rainy day and a bad time to drive anywhere. Glad to arrive, I found a seat way up high. When the graduates all marched in, I looked down on more than 900 students and hoped I could figure out which two were mine! Emily and Jason, both with big smiles on their faces, waved at me as they walked in together in cap and gown. The graduation was a grand ceremony, and I enjoyed the praise and worship and the beautiful colors. Emily and Jason both graduated magna cum laude, and I was especially proud of each of them as they walked across the stage to receive their degree. Afterward we met Jason's parents, Michael and Colleen, and sister, Angie, and took group pictures together outside.

Celebrating with Three Graduates

Pennie and Tom brought Bill's parents to Andrew's Graduation. That evening after Bill and Andrew were finished with ALCC graduation exercises, they traveled to Tulsa to meet up with us to celebrate with our three graduates! We all met at a local restaurant for dinner. We took pictures, ate, visited, and gave gifts to the three honorees and the engaged couple, Emily and Jason. Bill and Michael Blais both gave speeches in honor of their grown kids who earned their degrees.

Andrew Answers Call of Worship Pastor

The following week after graduation, we were back on the road to Oklahoma to move Andrew to live in Enid. He was taking his place as the new worship pastor at Faith Center Fellowship Church in Meno, a small town near Enid. We felt good about Andrew's first church assignment, although we missed him, and he was seven hours from our home.

We were able to attend church at Faith Center on several occasions. I felt so joyful and pleased that Andrew was following the Lord in leading worship, and he was anointed for the assignment!

Our Children Get Married Emily and Jason Blais

Emily and Jason took summer jobs and proceeded to make wedding plans. As I prayed, God gave me peace, and showed me our part in their wedding. We had to release Emily to do what she felt called to do. I made several trips to Tulsa to help them plan the wedding they wanted. They joined the Antiochian Orthodox Christian Church in July and married there in a beautiful ceremony in August 2004. Emily was the most peaceful and radiant bride I have ever seen. During their ceremony, as I stood on the front row, I heard the Holy Spirit say to me, "I will make a place for them."

Afterward, we honored the bride and groom with a lovely reception at The Marriott Hotel. The host of family and friends who traveled great distances were there to celebrate with us, Emily and Jason, and their large wedding party, who all enjoyed good food, fellowship, and pictures.

After their honeymoon cruise, they visited us in Arkansas and then made their way to Florida, where they lived, worked, and served in The Orthodox Church. They both worked a variety of jobs at first to pay the bills. As they pursued getting their teaching certificates, God provided ready-made teaching positions for both of them in a middle school! Jason taught social studies and Emily taught language arts. He was awarded "Middle School Social Studies Teacher of the Year" at the conclusion of 2006. His students appreciated the way he "put his heart" into his lectures by wearing costumes of the characters they learned about in the textbook!

Andrew Married Ali

Andrew met Ali in the Fall of 2002, when they both began college at Applied Life Christian College. As she and Andrew were classmates for two years, they studied and led the chapel band together. They continued a long-distance relationship after graduation.

Andrew proposed and gave Ali an engagement ring on Christmas Eve, 2004. They were married in a beautiful outdoor ceremony on May 15, 2005, at White Oak Plantation, in Baton Rouge, before God and many wonderful relatives and friends. They made their first home in Enid, where Andrew was already working as a worship leader. The newlyweds worked together in the church.

Finishing

One of the truths that we received from our pastors at Christian Ministries is the importance of "finishing." The Apostle Paul said, "I have fought a good fight, I have finished my course, I have kept the faith..."(II Timothy 4:7).

Matthew received his associate degree from Applied Life Christian College on April 30, 2005. He was invited back to complete the four-year program. He married his wife, Rachel in 2011, and they have one son.

I love weddings and new babies. Both are some of God's greatest gifts to his people! God brings a man and a woman together to love and marry. Then God blesses them with children! It's a joy to see young people we have encouraged to grow into outstanding and productive adults and have their families.

CHAPTER 13

MORE CHRISTIAN GUIDANCE AND EXPERIENCE

"Beloved, I wish above all things that thou mayest prosper and be in health, even as thy soul prospereth." (III John 2).

"I beseech you therefore, brethren, by the mercies of God, that ye present your bodies a living sacrifice, holy, acceptable unto God, which is your reasonable service." (Romans 12:1).

In his book *Growing Strong in The Seasons of Life (1994),* one of my favorite authors, Charles Swindoll, gives us an important reminder: "Next to having a good conscience, health is to be valued most. But it isn't! Of all the good and perfect gifts God grants us, it is the least recognized. Mistreated and misunderstood, it exists without encouragement and serves us without reward" (p. 493).

I wholeheartedly agree with Pastor Swindoll. I have come to recognize and take seriously my responsibility to have and maintain my good health. It is not the doctor's job to keep me healthy; it is mine. It is part of being a "Doer" of the Word.

God says that "our body is the Temple of the Holy Spirit." I want to take care of the place where He dwells.

I can take care of my body by eating healthy food and getting proper exercise. Eating healthy requires planning. Wise planning gives us success because we will have in our pantry, fridge and freezer what we need.

Exercise is a real discipline for me. I have lost the same ten pounds over and over again. Bill encouraged me to walk for exercise. After observing others who lost their weight quickly because they walked, I started doing that too. The sunshine on our faces and the fresh air makes us feel and think better.

*   *   *

The Older Women Teach the Younger Women (Titus 2)

> *"Or don't you know that your body is the temple of the Holy Spirit, who lives in you and was given to you by God? You do not belong to yourself, for God bought you with a high price. So, you must honor God with your body." (I Corinthians 6:19).*

I believe that Mary, the mother of Jesus, had been trained by her parents and her synagogue to know and obey God. If not, she would have probably resisted Gabriel's message from God when he suddenly appeared to her and said, (Luke 1:28-38)

> *"Greetings, favored woman! The Lord is with you! Don't be frightened, Mary," the angel told her, "For God has decided to bless you! You will become pregnant and have a son, and you are to name him Jesus. He will be very great and will be called the Son of the Highest. And the*

Lord God will give him the throne of his ancestor David. And he will reign over Israel forever; his Kingdom will never end!"

Mary said, "But how can I have a baby? I am a virgin." The angel replied, "The Holy Spirit will come upon you, and the power of the Highest will overshadow you. So, the baby born to you will be holy, and he will be called the Son of God. What's more, your relative Elizabeth has become pregnant in her old age! People used to say she was barren, but she's already in her sixth month. For nothing is impossible with God."

Mary responded, "I am the Lord's servant, and I am willing to accept whatever he wants. May everything you have said come true."

I believe Mary knew the law. She knew what could happen to a young woman who was pregnant out of wedlock in her culture. But she did not submit to the fear of man but trusted in God. As the Lord's servant, it was not "her body," it was the temple of The Holy Spirit! And she was looking for The Messiah! It had been prophesied in The Old Testament that Jesus would come to save His people! Mary had been trained in the things of God!

Ways Our Culture Influences Our Health

1. Growing up, I ate most meals at home. Mother cooked at our house every day, unless we were going shopping or on a vacation. Other mothers did also. Today, working people and the fast pace of families push many to grab fast food and "be done with it." I understand that because cooking requires time and planning. But, fruits and vegetables are in limited supply at most fast-food establishments, and starches and sugary drinks are in abundance in the diet of many young and old Americans. We are paying for it!

2. We live in a culture that says that babies are inconvenient, expensive, and not part of the equation for success. Proverbs 127:3-5 in the Passion Translation Bible says:

> Children are God's love-gift; they are heaven's generous reward.

> Children born to a young couple will one day rise to protect and provide for their parents.

> Happy will be the couple who has many of them.

> A household full of children will not bring shame on your name but victory when you face your enemies, for your offspring will have influence and honor

> To prevail on your behalf!

> Why do we allow ourselves to be cheated out of "a gift from God?"

What Your Doctor May Not Tell You About Menopause (1996), The Breakthrough Book on Natural Progesterone by John R. Lee, M.D. with Virginia Hopkins, is a book that I have used as a reference. Don't let the title deceive you. It is a handbook for women of all ages because our bodies are in a process and each of us has different time clocks. I'm including these important facts to help us guide our young daughters.

One important point here from Dr. Lee, a retired medical doctor of thirty years, is:,

The biggest threat to hormone balance in young women is doctors who insist on giving them birth control pills. There is a mountain of evidence showing that birth control pills cause numerous and serious health problems, including depression, headaches, nausea, fluid retention, high cholesterol, high triglyceride levels, liver disease, urinary tract infections, all the estrogen dominance symptoms, all the side effects caused by the progestins, and most dangerous of all, blood clots leading to pulmonary embolisms (blood clots in the lungs) and strokes. These dangers to individual women are swept under the carpet for the "higher good" of reducing the population, but you can bet that a drug that dangerous would never be given to men on such a wide scale.

I strongly urge parents to educate their daughters about the delicacy of hormonal balance and discourage the use of hormonal contraceptives of any kind. (p. 309)

Since the 60's, doctors have been prescribing birth control pills for young women. I was one of those, and my doctor said, "You have a textbook case of side effects from using birth control pills. Go off them."

3. Culture says to enjoy your sexual pleasures with whoever and whenever!

But God tells us in the Old Testament and the New Testament that sex outside of marriage is sin. Fornication, sex outside of marriage, adultery, and being married but having sex with someone else is sin in the sight of God. These sins displease God, cause pain, and destroy relationships and marriages.

God doesn't owe us an explanation of why he set these principles in motion, but we must remember that He is our creator, and He knows what is good and bad for us. God will often grace us with scientific truth to underline something for us. So, I share with you the findings of an expert.

In his article from the 2015 Christian Counseling Today, Vol. 21 No 1 "Sex and Media in Today's Culture; Why the Real Problem Isn't What You Think", Joshua Straub, Ph. D, says,

"The more sexual partners one has, the greater the potential emotional ramifications. 'Hooking up' literally inhibits the brain's ability to connect in long-term relationships." Further researchers describe how we become addicted to one another through a process of sexual imprinting.

The problem is these hormones are value neutral...they cannot tell the difference between a one-night stand and lifelong soul mate. Connectedness and bonding, at a certain level, will form no matter the nature of the sexual relationship. When the connection is quickly replaced by another sexual relationship, it often causes damage to the brain's natural bonding system." (Dr. Straub also states on Page 27 of the same article)" The emotional and relational consequences are eye-opening: "Sexually active boys and girls are three times more likely to be depressed than their virgin counterparts. Sexually active girls are three-times, and boys seven times, more likely to commit suicide. Sexually active boys and girls are more likely to get divorced."

4. This is about keeping a healthy temple. If we live sexually pure, we can avoid sexual diseases or STDs. Some of these are treatable and some are not. Culture does not warn you about these things. They say, "Live and let live." They don't post billboards with pictures of weeping women and men who are experiencing the pain of their sins!

    A few years ago, I soberly listened to a true story about a young woman who had followed the cultures guidelines on free sex. Later, she was in love with and about to marry her Prince Charming; she was ready to spend her life with him and have his children. But there is a problem! She must tell him that she has an STD that made her sterile, and she can't have his children!

Natural Supplements, Healthy Diet, and Exercise Provide Restoration

In September 2003 I began treatment by a doctor of naturopath, who started me on a rigorous schedule of natural supplements, which included digestive enzymes. Three months later, I experienced one of the best Christmases. I felt better physically, had lost some weight, and could sleep through the night. Bill and I decided not to overspend. Emily and Andrew were both at home from college for several weeks. I had so much peace; it was truly a gift from God. Most Christmas seasons in the past would find me stressed out and exhausted. I planned to do less preparation and enjoy the celebration. It was the Christmas that I began to learn that "less is more."

Cooking Healthy

We all know that what we bring into our house from the grocery store and what we cook are very important. If I don't bring it into the house, I won't be tempted to eat it. I try to cook more fresh or frozen vegetables. I cook them in some olive oil by roasting them in the oven rather than boiling them to death and losing all the nutrients. Processed foods are not as healthy for us as meals I cook from scratch.

I became weary of "feeling bad" and worked to change that. It is not easy, but my reward is good health and an even better marriage and family. We will have the energy to play with our children and grandchildren! Our church will prosper from our good health because we will have more energy to work for God's Kingdom, more money and time.

Nutritious food for your growing children is especially important. They need lots of fruits and vegetables. Sometimes children will begin to like raw vegetables the best—carrots, broccoli, celery, apples, oranges, and grapes are such great snacks.

We have learned that after their first birthday, children don't need to drink a lot of milk. Too much milk is not good for their kidneys. I prefer almond milk.

Also, I don't want to be a young widow. Do you ever think about what you are cooking for your spouse? Will your cooking make him/her healthy or sick? How many heart attacks and strokes could be prevented by just watching what we swallow? I know that what I feed my husband can prolong his life. If I feed him fast, processed, fatty, or sugary foods, he won't feel good. You may say, "My husband or wife is young." Over a period of years/decades, you and your spouse could physically pay for what you are eating now.

Fasting

The Bible talks about fasting. Through the years God has called me to several fasts from food to PRAY and intercede for a person, a specific need(s) or to get an answer. Fasting is what God's people did throughout the scriptures when they were repentant of their sins, honoring God, obeying God, or seeking His face about a matter. It still works today in the same amazing way.

Fasting is definitely a way to present our body as a living sacrifice unto the Lord. We are denying what our flesh wants or craves to accomplish something bigger and eternal—to focus on God. Some fasts have been easy, but some have been very difficult for me. However, Spirit led fasts and obedience always reap fruit. Most of the time when I have fasted in obedience to the Lord, it was after the fast ended that I heard the voice of the Lord, received direction or the answer to my prayers!

Fasting is also a way to cleanse the body of harmful toxins. It lets your digestive system rest from all the work. I have learned, and it's still very hard for me to do, that our body needs twelve hours between our dinner and our breakfast! That means that we are not eating anything for twelve hours—a lot happens in that time in our digestive system.

A wonderful reward for being a son or daughter of God is seeking God's heart about a matter, reading His word, and hearing The Holy Spirit supply the answer. John 15:14 says, "You are my friends if you do what I command." My relationship with Jesus Christ and his guidance through The Holy Spirit, are my greatest and most precious treasures!

Healthy Living Summary

If you are healthy, be thankful and work to maintain that gift from God. In this day of transplants, we must remember that some things can't be replaced. God holds us responsible for keeping His temple healthy and holy. Don't put anything in it or on it that God would not want in His house! Clothe yourself the way you would if Jesus was sitting beside you or across the table from you. If you have any health problems, I encourage you to look at what you can do naturally and practically to walk in divine health. God wants this for you. If you will "Ask, Seek, and Knock," His wisdom just for your needs will be opened before you. He has your answers; you will see your situation in a new way and be filled with hope! "My God shall supply all your needs, according to his riches in glory, through Christ Jesus" (Philippians 4:19).

SUBMISSION

"Submitting yourselves one to another in the fear of God.
Wives, submit yourselves unto your own husbands, as
unto the Lord. For the husband is the head of the
wife, even as Christ is the head of the church:
and he is the savior of the body.
Therefore, as the church is subject unto Christ,
so let the wives be to their own husbands in everything.

Husbands, love your wives, even as Christ also loved the church, and
gave himself for it;
That he might sanctify and cleanse it with the washing of water by the word,
That he might present it to himself a glorious church, not having spot, or wrinkle, or any such thing; but that it should be holy and without blemish.
So, ought men to love their wives as their own bodies.
He that loveth his wife loveth himself."
(Ephesians 5:21-28).

The year that Andrew started Bible college and Emily began her junior year at ORU, was a very difficult year for me. I was suffering with some health issues and needed some answers.

The Holy Spirit impressed on me to buy and read Stormie Omartian's book *The Power of a Praying Wife*. It was a discipline and an act of obedience as I read and prayed the prayers at the end of each chapter.

Usually, when we want God to change someone else, He begins by changing us first. Stormie was truly anointed to write from her experiences as a wife and how God transformed her as she prayed for her husband.

Bill and I reached a point where about every one to two months, something would happen to set off a disagreement or misunderstanding between us. In our first twenty years of marriage, we seldom had a disagreement. I recognized that as Bill grew spiritually, he has taken his place more decisively as the head of our home. While I was doing some soul searching after our disagreements, I was also seeking answers to my health problems.

One day after pondering why conflict resulted from our conversation, something became very clear to me. "I'm going to have to submit to doing some things Bill has asked of me if we are going to get through this together." I had always thought of myself as a submissive wife, but God began to show me that I was very strong-willed. I became willing, after suffering through conflict, to really listen to Bill and act on what he said.

I recommend that every woman should read James Dobson's book *Raising Boys to Be Men*. The chapter entitled "Men Are Wimps" will help anyone understand what feminism has done to men, women, boys, and girls in this nation and why so many families have been torn apart. The devil does not want strong men of God to come forth.

Our enemy has used the television and movie industry and our educational system as a platform to perpetuate lies about men. Through these avenues, men are put down and women and children are taught to disrespect and act disdainfully toward men. They say, "Don't let a man tell you what to do." This wrong belief system is hurting/destroying men and families in our culture; the agenda is to weaken the family and then our America!

When Andrew had gone on the mission trip to Honduras, their assignment during that week was to build a feeding center where 200 children come during the week to be fed oatmeal and hear about Jesus. As I listened to my son share about his work there, I thought about the feminists. How many women could have done the manual labor required to put the four walls on the unlevel mountainside, lift, and place the twenty-foot-high beams necessary to put a roof on that building? Then after putting in a ten-hour day in the sun, twenty feet in the air, or lifting large rocks to landscape the area, how many women could lead a worship service or street ministry? I don't want to do a man's job! Let our men be men so we can be women!

"A few good men"—Uncle Sam wasn't the first to look for a few good men! God has always been looking for men who will step up and say "Yes" to serve Him. It is not easy to submit to our husband, but our submission is needed for him to be the leader of our home! When we submit to our husband, we are submitting to God!

Remember that two heads usually create a monster. During a lifetime, decisions for the family will need to be made that the husband and wife may not be able to agree on. Hopefully, the couple can talk it through and come up with an agreeable decision. But, when a couple has different opinions on a matter, and if the marriage is to stand strong, someone must make the final decision. That is one reason that God made the man the CEO of the family.

Submission does not mean being abused! When a man loves his wife as Christ loves the church, his wife will want to submit to him. If we will give our husbands the honored place they deserve, we will be honored by them. It's a two-way street.

If your husband is abusing you or your children, you should leave him. Don't stay in an abusive relationship!

We stood before the altar with the spouse of our dreams and agreed to love them in sickness and in health, until death do us part; we made a commitment to God and to our spouse in the presence of witnesses. God calls it a sacred covenant! God takes Covenants very seriously! He never said that it would be easy! Feelings follow actions! Love is not a feeling; it is an action. Love is an act of my will and remaining committed to my husband.

Satan will attack your marriage. I have experienced this kind of warfare. Prayer is the key! Words don't solve this problem! More words can create more strife! Pray it through. Get alone by yourself, pray for yourself, pray for your mate, and ask God to help you choose your words carefully and solve your problems together. Ask Him to help both of you to be able to communicate lovingly and honestly. You may need to step back or step away from the conversation—space and time help. God will help you. Read the book of Ephesians; Ephesians 6 tells us how to "put on the full armor of God." Satan hates marriage because God has designed it and ordained it.

Read I Corinthians 13 for an understanding of the real meaning of love. I have this scripture framed and on our wall. It can be very convicting, and God has used it to show me when I'm not showing love. Our children will model what they see us doing and saying. We must live the life before them if they are to have successful marriages and families.

You should build up your husband for your children. Maybe your husband has an area of weakness that really bothers you, but he is an excellent provider. Brag on his strong points to your son and daughter by saying, "Your dad is a hard worker and good provider and you're going to be a hard worker too!" Or say this: "Your dad is a hard worker, and you should give him a hug, and thank him for working hard to provide for you." Dad's should also build up their wife for their children. "Your mother worked all day and came home and cooked our dinner or spent all evening helping you with your homework. You need to show her your love and appreciation." Or "Your mother took her whole day off to take you shopping for clothes, and you need to appreciate her." This is how you teach them to be thankful, loving, kind and unselfish.

A woman wants to feel loved and cherished, not put down or talked to harshly. A man needs to feel respected. God created marriage, and he will help you with any struggle or issue that comes into your life! Look to him first. He is the author of LOVE!

Suffering

The first kind of suffering is physical, and all of us have experienced this at one time or another. We know that when we are sick and/or don't feel well that our outlook and attitude are affected. We must guard against our flesh ruling and Satan's attack when we are going through a time of sickness and weakness. A Christian's two enemies are our flesh and the devil, not people!

The second kind of suffering is that of the spirit. When my spirit aches either because of grief, a burden for someone who needs prayer, a time of affliction, or an attack from Satan, I am experiencing a kind of suffering.

The way we deal with the enemy and his tactics is according to God's word, "Submit yourselves therefore to God, resist the enemy, and he will flee from you" (James 4:7). There are three parts to this verse:

Part 1: "Submit yourselves to God...": You cannot do what you want and resist the enemy. We must submit ourselves first to God; in other words, agree with Him. Many times, we want relief or an answer from the Lord, but we are not willing to submit to him and do it His way.

Part 2: Here you need to "resist the devil"; if we keep entertaining the temptation or the fear or the vain imagination that the enemy has planted in our minds, then he will continue to hang around; but, when we resist him (after we have submitted our will to God's) the next step will happen.

Part 3: In this step, "Satan will flee."

Christian Suffering involves walking through the tests that the Lord allows to come into our lives and doing our best to have a good attitude about them. The Bible is full of stories about people who were tested and their attitudes during the test. My favorite hero of the faith was Joseph. He was tested and mistreated for years and years but kept right on trusting God and obeying Him. We must know that Satan hates us and wants to thwart God's plans and purposes for our individual lives, our marriage, and our children.

There have been many times in my life when I was in a spiritual trial and just wanted to be done with it! Because as a young girl, I was taught the power of prayer and praying through, I was able to endure some intense and severe times of testing. As an elementary student, I can remember sitting in church and hearing my pastor, Brother Elrod, saying, "Just hang on to the horns of the altar" (I Kings 1:49). That means that when you are going through a difficult personal struggle, you just continue or remain in an attitude of prayer, never giving up until the breakthrough comes. It may be a release in your spirit, peace of mind or heart, or just a direct answer to a need you or your family member has. Ask another believer to pray with you and for you too. The point is: The way you don't give up is to hang on to the Lord in prayer, just like you would a life raft!

As you are continuing in prayer, stand on the promises of God because they are our sword, our weapon against Satan. Look for the scriptures that apply to your situation. Write them on a 3 x 5 card or in your phone, memorize it, and refer to it in your next battle.

Last, but certainly not least, worship the Lord. Several years ago, I was in a spiritual storm; I began to realize that God wants us to worship him during the storm because He is with us, and we know we can trust Him. Pastor Tim Brooks taught us, "He is with us in the boat going to the other side," so we can trust Him to say, "peace be still." The enemy cannot stand where there is true praise! Praise pushes back the enemy; it is a mighty weapon! How hard can it be to sing when you are in a trial? Begin to thank God for your salvation and many blessings. I believe that God created music not only for our pleasure and His pleasure, but with the power to accomplish great victories for His Kingdom.

The Bible says in Matthew 10:38, "And he that taketh not his cross and followeth after me, is not worthy of me. He that findeth his life shall lose it: and he that loses his life for my sake shall find it." Romans 8:17-18 says, "And since we are his children, we are his heirs. In fact, together with Christ we are heirs of God's glory. But if we are to share his glory, we must also share his suffering. Yet what we suffer now is nothing compared to the glory he will reveal to us later." One can clearly see that suffering is not only part of living in this fallen world but is something that every Christian will experience.

When I was a girl, Daddy told me, "There may come a time in your life when you have to lay your head down on the chopping block and give your life for Jesus!" That was not easy to hear! Numerous disciples (Hebrews 12) died for the sake of Christ. Many Christians have been torn limb from limb by hungry lions in Rome's arenas because some mean king hated Christians. The word says, "For the joy set before him, Jesus endured the cross." He saw me, and he saw you and the millions of others who God wanted. The scripture says, "The Lord...is not willing that any should perish but that all should come to repentance."(IIPeter 3:9).

As Christians, we must "endure hardship as a good soldier of Jesus Christ." "For our light affliction, which is but for a moment, worketh for us a far more exceeding and eternal weight of glory. While we look not at the things which are seen, but at the things which are not seen: for the things which are seen are temporal: but the things which are not seen are eternal" (II Corinthians 4:17). In the words of Pastor Paul Kern, "Refuse to let an offense or any dumb demon knock you off course."

We must have a strong resolve or determination to run this race to win the prize of eternal life. One of my favorite verses is Isaiah 50:7, "For the Lord God will help me; therefore, shall I not be confounded; therefore, have I set my face like a flint, and I know that I shall not be ashamed." Don't ever give up and quit. The goal of our life should be to cross the finish line, which is heaven, and hear Our Father say, "Well done, good and faithful servant. Enter into the joys of the Lord."

LAUGHTER

"A merry heart doeth good like a medicine: but a broken spirit dries up the bones."(Proverbs 17:22).

Do you laugh? Do you laugh with your family? Several years ago, after we moved to Arkansas, we received a "card-like" advertisement in the mail from a dental supplier. When the card is opened there is the sound of a crowd applauding. Bill had the idea of opening that card every time one of us accomplished something or God blessed us in some special way. We kept it in view where we could reach for it at random and bring an applause to the room when we wanted to celebrate! This almost always brought a smile, laughter, and a good feeling.

The Bible is full of times of celebrations. Laughter is a gift God has given us to bring health to our minds and bodies and joy into our lives. If you are not laughing regularly, there is a lack in your life. Look for ways to make yourself and your family members laugh. Better yet, ask God to bring a spirit of laughter into your life and home, and he will do it because He has done it for us.

I'll never forget when Andrew and I first started homeschooling. He was always clowning around. Serious Mom was all about reading, writing and arithmetic! As my friend Molly would say, "I was wound very tight!" I shared this earlier, but it bears repeating— One day as I was exasperated with Andrew and scolded him, he replied to me, "Mom, I'm just trying to make you laugh!" Boy, that really spoke to me! I felt convicted!

Costumes

The end of December of 2003, I was planning for New Year's Eve, gathering up groceries and thinking about how we would celebrate and welcome 2004. Andrew was gone with Tom and Danette and youth in their big bus to The International House of Prayer in Kansas City. It would just be Bill, Emily and me at home for the evening. I went into Walgreens and saw some blue and red top hats with "Happy New Year" written on the front in glitter. Also available were glittery crowns. I bought the two top hats and two crowns and brought them home. Around midnight, the three of us celebrated with food and wore our hat and crowns. Bill posed for a picture in his hat, and Emily and I truly got our belly laughs! He looked like a new version of the old poster "Uncle Sam wants you!"

Laughter is so important that I thought it would be special to enclose some humorous family stories—true personal experiences that showed our sense of humor or caused our family to laugh together through the years.

Story #1: The Angels were Here

It was a cold winter school day in East Texas in 1972, and Mother had gotten an early morning call to substitute. We hurried out the door to take David to stay with Mrs. Green and so as not to be late for school. When we arrived back home at the end of the day, Mother discovered the electric heating pad that was left on, lying on one of the twin beds. She was shocked and thankful that there was no fire from it. She said, "I'm sure glad the angels were watching over us." My five-year-old little sister, Mary Evelyn, said, "I wish while they were here that they made the bed!"

Story #2: David and the Skunk

One afternoon at home in Naples when my younger brother, David, was about ten, he had gotten his first BB gun and was so proud of it. While Mother was helping

Mary Evelyn with homework at the kitchen table, David took his gun and headed off into the woods behind their house to shoot a squirrel. He had only been gone a few minutes when he appeared wild eyed at the back door—a horrible stench preceding him—screaming "Mama! I got too close to a skunk, and he sprayed me—right in my eyes!! But I prayed, and I'm OK."

In Mother's opinion, he looked anything but OK. Mother was not OK. She was worried about David's eyes.

"Flush them with plenty of water," advised the nurse. Then she asked, "do you know how to eliminate the odor?"

Since Mother had no idea, the nurse instructed her to bathe David in tomato juice and follow with soap and water. She got him into the bathtub and doused him thoroughly with the juice before he took his bath. She hung his stinky clothes on a tree for several days until she had the nerve to put them in the washer.

Mother said this incident was scary because she was worried about David's eyes, but it is so funny in retrospect.

Story #3: Laughing at the Devil

One afternoon after finishing our homeschooling lessons, I was at my wits end! I went to my bathroom and cried and cried.

Then I went outside behind our house and started making myself laugh, by a sheer act of my will, at the devil. It went something like" Ha, ha, ha, ha, ha..." very loudly. I really felt like anything but laughter.

It was early fall or late spring, and our windows were open. After a little bit, Andrew came out and said, "Mama, what are you doing?" "Laughing at the devil," I said. "OK..." Then after a while longer, Emily came out and said, "Mama, what are you doing?"

"I'm laughing at the devil."

"OK.," she said.

I cared about achieving a victory that day! One lady had told me about homeschooling. "The only way you can fail is to quit." That is what the devil wants, to get us to quit our marriage, quit our children, quit our job, quit our church, quit our school, quit our tithing, quit our ministry, quit voting, quit forgiving, and quit loving! When you laugh at the devil and refuse to quit, you are winning the victory, regardless of how you feel!

Our emotions are not always accurate. If we live life based on how we feel, we will be weak, spineless Christians and accomplish little that will remain. Live by the truth of God's Word and prayer and you can rise above any circumstance. Laughter is a mighty tool in our arsenal!

What one thing gives you joy? For me, it has always been seeing a newborn baby or a small child. There's something good that happens in my heart when I see a newborn baby. A baby is such a miracle from God. How can anyone doubt God's greatness? God makes His home in People; He is looking for hearts who will welcome Him!

"Moore" Joy From a Newborn Baby!

Our Moore family received a beautiful gift from God in April 2006, when Hannah was born to my brother, David, and his wife, Sharmaine. Big brother, Dominick, was so proud of little sister too. Hannah is my parents' seventh grandchild and second granddaughter. She is our beautiful, blond niece who loves Jesus!

CHAPTER 14

OUR GRANDCHILDREN

"But the love of the Lord remains forever with those who fear him. His salvation extends to the children's children of those who are faithful to his covenant, of those who obey his commandments!" (Psalm 103:17).

In 2006 Bill turned fifty-three, and we purchased our home in Hot Springs Village from our wonderful landlords, Norm and Donna. The four of us enjoyed visiting over a good lunch of Mexican food. It had already been an eventful day, and the two of us were back at home relaxing on the patio when the phone rang. It was Andrew and Ali calling to say that we were going to be grandparents! They were expecting their first child in February 2007! We were so excited.

At the time of their announcement, they were living in Nashville, Tennessee. As their due date approached, they decided they would like to relocate near Ali's parents. On Thanksgiving Day 2006, they moved to Denham Springs, Louisiana. Oh, how much I had enjoyed Andrew; this would be little Andrew, the second!

As Ali's due date approached, the doctor said if she didn't deliver by February 5, they would induce. Lots of prayers went up that she would go into labor by herself. About 4:15 a.m., on a Saturday morning in February 2007, the phone beside my bed rang, and it was Andrew. He said, "Mom, we're going to the hospital." The first words out of my mouth were, "I'm getting my prayers answered." We had already planned to leave for Baton Rouge that day to spend time with them before the baby's birth. We were on the road by 7:00 a.m.

Drew weighed in at 9 1/2 pounds and was nearly 22 inches long. I called Andrew about 10:18 a.m. and could hear our new grandson crying in the background. We were so excited. Ali's Mom, Sherry, called me on the cell phone and said, "Elizabeth, you're going to think you have another little Andrew all over again." And she was right!

We arrived at Women's Hospital in Baton Rouge to see baby Drew and his proud parents. All of us grandparents took lots of pictures and rejoiced over this new little life God has sent us to love and teach. Drew has lots of family members—parents, grandparents, great-grandparents, one great-great-grandmother, aunts and uncles, and friends who love him very much. The next day, we had a Super Bowl party right there in the hospital room, with good food and fellowship. It was celebration time! We love this grandparent adventure! Proverbs 17:6 says, "Children's children are the crown of old men..."

The next month, Drew's aunt Emily came from Florida to our house to see him for the first time! Emily began to think she would like to have a baby and carried her enthusiasm back home to tell Jason all about their first nephew.

Several weeks before Father's Day 2007, our phone rang again. It was Emily and she wanted us to put the speaker phone on. She and Jason gave us the happy news that they were expecting their first child in February 2008! We were so very excited!

We were blessed to see our first grandchild nearly once a month for his first year. In July, Andrew came to Arkansas to work in the insurance business and brought his family. We had fun taking

Drew to the beach and pushing him in his stroller around our neighborhood. That became Bill's routine after work every day.

From July 31-August 6, I visited Jason and Emily in their townhouse in Florida. They had just moved, and Emily being four months pregnant, tired easily and needed a visit from Mom, which I was happy to provide. I did some cooking, we went to the beach, only about ten minutes from their house, and just enjoyed talking in person. Before I left for home, we got to purchase her first maternity clothes.

When Drew was eight months old, he came to Arkansas with his mother, his other grandmother, and his great-grandmother from Louisiana. While they attended the Women's Seminar at Brookhill Ranch, Bill and I got to keep Drew. It's hard to describe how much pleasure we felt at having him with us at our house. It's like the fun you had with your children with chocolate cake, vanilla ice cream and hot fudge on top! It is a very "SWEET" time in our lives. I bought Drew his first mylar balloon, and when he laughed out loud about it, I got a great laugh enjoying it with him. It was amazing how much fun and entertainment $1 could buy!

The weekend after Christmas 2007, which was Drew's first, we traveled to Denham Springs to see our family. We were there to celebrate Christmas with them and to attend Drew's baby dedication at Healing Place Church. It was a beautiful ceremony. What a privilege to be part of dedicating a second generation of our offspring to the Lord! We believe that Drew will be a great man of God like his dad.

Second Valentine Arrives in Florida

Emily and Jason stayed very busy as they taught at middle school every day, worked in their church, and prepared for their new little girl. They kept us updated on her pregnancy progress, her showers, nursery selections, etc. As we approached her due date, we prayed about when to go, knowing I wanted to be there for Abigail's birth.

On Drew's first birthday, I was in an airplane traveling to Florida for the birth of our second grandchild! Emily, Jason and I had a great visit together. We went out to eat, ran short errands, took walks, enjoyed Jason's special cappuccinos, watched movies, visited Emily's friends, and waited.

Finally, Emily had her last doctor's visit, which was a week after her due date. I had told Emily, "The Hebrew women had their babies quickly and you can too!" (See Exodus 1:19). The doctor said if you don't come back on your own, we will induce. We prayed that Emily would not have to be induced and that she would have a quick labor and delivery.

That evening, labor began before midnight and found us arriving at the hospital about 3:00 a.m. We had a great nurse and doctor who, along with Jason, coached Emily well. I was privileged to be there for the birth of Abigail at 7:04 a.m. on a great February morning in 2008. She weighed a healthy eight pounds and six ounces and was twenty inches long! She had a head full of coal black hair, just like her daddy and her granddaddy. The doctor and nurse attending Emily told her that she held a new mother record for labor time and delivery! She quickly told them that we had prayed for that and that she gave the Lord the glory for it.

We brought our second little Valentine home from the hospital on Valentine's Day 2008! How blessed and rich we felt to have two precious little lives to love and enjoy and teach about Jesus. Emily and Jason and Abigail began to make the adjustment that all new parents must make. Jason changed diapers, cooked, cleaned, vacuumed, shampooed carpet, and taught sixth to eighth graders every day at the middle school.

The day after we brought Abigail home, Bill flew in to be with us and to hold our first granddaughter. He enjoyed visiting with Jason and Emily and taking long walks in their beautiful, shaded neighborhood. The day before he went home, we just had to see the

Atlantic Ocean and take a walk on the beach. God truly answered our prayers about when to go to Florida, a good price on our tickets, a very quick labor and delivery for our precious daughter and a healthy granddaughter!

September Sunshine: Our Third Grandchild

After being with Emily and family for more than two weeks, I arrived back home, and Bill and I got settled into our routine. It was hard to say goodbye to the new mother and baby Abigail, but Emily and Jason felt ready to brave it on their own! March came with its spring flowers, and I went to Texas to help Mother celebrate her birthday. Easter followed quickly, coming very early that year at the very end of March!

In April, Andrew and Ali gave us the big news—they were expecting a second child in the fall! We began making plans that I would go keep Drew while they were having the baby. The months passed very quickly. I went to Baton Rouge before the end of September, and Andrew and Ali left early one morning for the hospital. The labor went very fast, and Jackson weighed seven pounds, four ounces and was twenty inches long.

Drew and I arrived at the hospital shortly after Jackson was born, and Drew just stared at the crying baby as the nurses got him all dressed. When Ali was moved to her own room, Drew had missed his mommy so much that he had to get up in the bed beside her. I placed baby Jackson in Ali's arms for a picture, but Drew cried when we took him away. He wanted to hold his new baby brother. Sleeping at home without Mommy and Daddy stretched Drew very much, but he and Gran and Granddaddy had fun together and celebrated bringing Jackson and his mommy home in a short time.

Jackson Grant Beasley was a happy baby full of smiles and adventure. I took him from his crib, and he started clapping!

Gathering Our Growing Family Under One Roof for Christmas

Christmas 2008 would not only be the celebration of our Savior's birth, but it would be a celebration of having all our children at home together for the first time since they married. Abigail and Jackson had been born that year. Emily, Jason and Abigail arrived in Little Rock by plane from Tuckahoe, New York, where Jason was a seminary student at St. Vladimir's Orthodox Theological Seminary. We were excited to see them!

David, and family, en route after spending Christmas in Naples with our parents, met us at our house in Hot Springs Village. It was a special reunion, to say the least. David's children, Dominick and Hannah, loved Abigail, and we had fun visiting around the table at dinner. The next morning David and Sharmaine left for their home in Missouri. Emily and I made it to Company's Comin for cappuccino and shopping, and then on to get our nails done.

My mother had planned a family reunion, so we left the next morning to drive over to East Texas to see our extended family. We went first to see Bill's parents, who were so excited to see Abigail and hold her for the first time! Bill's sisters, their families and Aunt Rowene and Uncle C were there too. Abigail was not shy in meeting her relatives. We took lots of pictures and enjoyed being together.

After our visit in Omaha, we drove to Mother's where all her family had gathered. Uncle Bob and Aunt Liz were there from San Antonio. Mother's sister, Linda and her husband, Danny, and their family; and, Don and his wife, Sheila, were all there from the Dallas Metroplex. My sister, Mary Evelyn and her sons, Joel and Stephen, came. Daddy hadn't seen Emily in a while, and he anticipated meeting his new great-granddaughter, Abigail. There was joy, a great feast, much conversation, and many pictures.

We spent the night with my parents. The next morning, we enjoyed the delicious breakfast Mother lovingly prepared for us. Afterward, there was a fun visit on the screened-in porch, talking and watching Abigail open her Christmas and birthday gift–a talking bear that reads nursery rhymes from "Nana" and Granddaddy. Late in the morning we left to go back to Arkansas.

Andrew and his family dropped by for a visit in Naples on their way to our house from their home in Baton Rouge. It was also Jackson's first visit to see his Texas relatives as well! He was only three months old! Everyone loved seeing him and big brother Drew!

The Bill Beasley Family at Our Home Together

It was very exciting when Andrew, Ali, Drew, and Jackson drove up in our driveway on January 2! We all went out to greet and hug them. Jason and Drew had never met in person, so they got to know each other. Andrew, Ali, Drew, and Jackson had never seen Abigail, so they got to enjoy her. Emily, Jason and Abigail had never held Jackson. It was a moment in time when we felt so much joy at having our whole family together!

The first evening after dinner while still at the table, Andrew said it would be a good night for the four of them—Andrew, Ali, Jason and Emily— to get out together. We agreed to keep the three babies and off they went. Wow! You forget how busy you can be with one baby. Abigail slept. Jack slept but was somewhat restless. Drew slept in Bill's arms, but when he woke up, he wanted his parents. A little love and firm assurance from Gran calmed him down soon.

The weekend continued with lots of good visits, pictures, and good food. Sunday morning it was by a small miracle that all of us made it to our church together with three babies! Afterward we had time for a family picture, which was a priority of mine. We ordered pizza for lunch and had a great time in our living room by the Christmas tree opening our presents.

We all needed that first reunion! When Tuesday morning, January 6, 2009, rolled around, it was out the door to the airport with Emily, Jason and Abigail. It was hugs and goodbyes to Andrew,

Ali, Drew and Jackson as they headed home. We felt very, very blessed to have all nine of us together in our home for the first time.

Loving Our Lives as Grandparents

I have stirred up my creativity to be a long-distance grandmother. Little children are usually happy with anything you send them—the simple pleasures. My young grandkids all liked books, so God put several neat books in my path for them. Most of them fit easily in a padded mailer. They all like certain snacks. Sometimes I found an outfit, a special shirt or pajamas, or a little money, and they all fit in a padded mailer or envelope. Ten years ago, I was praying about how I could influence my young grandchildren for the Lord. I signed up to support the Christian Broadcasting Network's animated Series called "Superbook". It is so well done telling Bible stories in a cutting edge way. I would get three copies in the mail—keep one to use with my Sunday School class and send the other two to our grandkids across the miles. They loved Superbook! Children across the world come to know Jesus as their Savior and lead their families to Christ! Their lives are changed by Jesus!

Grandchild #4 on the Way

The winter months of 2009 flew quickly by, and before Easter, our phone rang, and it was Andrew. The news was another grandbaby on the way! Their nest was getting very full—three babies in three years. "Children are a gift from the Lord; ...(Psalm 127:3-5).

We were very excited about grandchild #4. I told Andrew and Ali that I would come again and help them if they would like.

My First Trip to New York—A Birthday Present September 2009

Emily called at the end of August and said, "Dad, I think Mom should come to New York to visit us for her birthday." Bill agreed, and I had to say yes and pack my bag. That was a gift. I was the one who usually planned these things and made the reservations.

On September 5, I was in an airplane on my way to Newark, New Jersey. The airport was about forty-five minutes from Emily and Jason's apartment in Tuckahoe. I was so excited to see them as it had been four months. Abigail smiled at me from her car seat in the back and seemed to remember me. We made the long drive through traffic, arriving home that Saturday night about two hours later.

The next morning, we were up early to dress and make the hour drive from their house to their assigned church in Danbury, Connecticut. The church was very beautiful, and Jason helped serve. They had coffee hour afterward, and since we were all dressed up, we had to pose for a picture in our green outfits. On the way home, we got some tacos to go, and Abigail took a nap.

Arriving back to their apartment after church, little Abigail found the Dora backpack I had brought her, and she loved it! She pulled it all around and said "backpack." A little later Jason came into the room with his backpack on and stooped down to hug Abigail goodbye as he was going to study. When she touched his shoulder and felt that backpack, she said, "Backpack." She wanted her backpack. So, we took a picture of Daddy and Daughter both wearing their backpacks. Abigail and I went to the seminary playground where we enjoyed the slide and the swing and met the other children and their mothers.

Emily and Jason soon began preparing my birthday dinner for that Sunday evening. Jason marinated and grilled a delicious pork loin. Emily made green beans, potatoes, and walnut brownies with ice cream. It was so delightful to be together to celebrate!

Monday morning, we left at 8:50 a.m. to catch a train for my first trip to New York City, and I was excited. We arrived at Grand Central Station and what a huge place it is with beautiful architecture. We stepped out onto the street and began walking.

It was not as crowded that day because it was a holiday—Labor Day. Our first stop was the seven story Toys R Us, the biggest toy store in the nation. Abigail immediately spotted a large pink ball she wanted. Then she found a keyboard, which was a great idea for Christmas. We went into the full-size Barbie house. Abigail and Gran both enjoyed the toy store.

Bryant Park was the destination to eat our picnic lunch. From there it was to Macy's, the world's largest store. Wow! Because we had to be back at the seminary by 4:30, our time in Macy's was limited. After seeing the parades my whole life, it was fun to visit the Macy's store. A quick stop into Starbucks, and we were on our way back to Grand Central Station for the ride home.

The next day was Tuesday, and my birthday! Abigail had a doctor's appointment, so that was our first destination. Afterward, we had a very eventful time at a nearby tearoom! The problem was that the tearoom did not have a highchair. We tried to make-do with one of their regular chairs, but we were upset when Abigail fell out of her chair two times!!! She was crying and hurt so Emily carried her out so as not to disturb others who were having tea. Then after being placed in her stroller to sit, she bumped her head on the corner of the table! I decided it was my turn to carry her out. Just outside the door was a planter of flowers, so I distracted her by picking one and suggesting she take it to Mommy. We will never forget our tearoom birthday celebration near Sleepy Hollow, New York!

My last day in Tuckahoe with Emily and family was a stay-at-home day. Emily made us some pancakes for a late breakfast, and we enjoyed spending time together. For a late lunch, she made some tuna salad. Then it was time for a walk in the neighborhood to the library, a cute little house with the whole downstairs for children's books. Upon our arrival at the library, we took some pictures and I read *Clifford the Big Red Dog* to Abigail.

The highlight of the afternoon happened on our walk home to the apartment. We heard some music and Emily said, "There's the ice cream truck." We looked all around and listened closely to purchase the cold refreshing treat. Boy, did it cool our tongues and thrill us on a warm day as we walked home in the charming neighborhood!

The next morning at 2:45 a.m. the alarm went off. That was way too early! I had to catch a plane out of Newark at 6:00 a.m. On my return back to Little Rock, I called Bill to pick me up at the airport when he took his lunch break from work.

Fourth Grandchild Makes Early Surprise September Arrival

I secured my luggage, sat down at a table nearby and when I opened my phone to call Bill, I was shocked! There it was, a text message from Andrew: "Pray, Ali is in early labor at the hospital." I immediately began to pray fervently because the baby was not due until December! By the time Bill picked me up later that morning, Andrew had told me they wanted me to come to Baton Rouge to stay for two weeks. The doctors at Women's Hospital said, "There's a 50% chance that this baby will be born within the next week. There's a 100% chance that she will make it in this hospital!"

Bill and I were glad to be reunited, and I took a little nap while he finished seeing patients for the day. I called Karen, a friend from church, formerly from Louisiana, and asked if anyone in her family was traveling to Baton Rouge the next day. Her daughter, Whitney, was driving down to New Orleans! Perfect!

I arrived at my house with enough evening left to wash some clothes and repack my suitcase. The next morning, Whitney and I enjoyed visiting during our eight-hour trip. I was glad to see Andrew, who met us at the mall, and took me to get Drew and Jackson.

Much prayer went up daily for Ali and baby Avery that God would keep her until time to be born. After a week and two days, Ali delivered tiny little Avery, who weighed 2.156 pounds and was

15 inches long. She was immediately taken to NICU where she received such good care. Ali and Andrew went daily to the hospital to see her for the next two months.

Jackson turned one year old a few days after Avery was born. We were there to celebrate his first birthday party with him, and it was so much fun to watch and hold our handsome and sweet one-year-old grandson!

Much prayer went up for our second little granddaughter. Before they could bring her home the first week of November, her parents had to take a CPR class. The baby came home with a heart monitor, as well. We felt very blessed for the progress Avery had made. She is truly a miracle—beautiful, very intelligent, very conversational, very loving, and respectful.

Drew's favorite toys were Thomas the Train and Friends. Two days after Avery arrived home, Drew, not quite three years old, was holding her with the help of his Mommy. He looked at her and said, "Hey baby sister, I'm Drew, the train man!"

I was with Avery on her first Valentine's Day. She weighed eleven pounds and was beautiful—the picture of health in her red and white dress. We praise God from whom all blessings flow. I spent about a month and a half with Andrew, Ali and children between September 11, 2009, and Valentine's Day, 2010. It was a privilege for me to be with my growing family! I enjoyed watching Jack just look at Avery as he was still studying this smaller little person who was sharing his house and his Mommy and Daddy! Jackson and Avery have a special bond with each other and have always enjoyed being the same age together for several days every year in September!

After three months and three babies under three, I proposed a little vacation time to Andrew and Ali. I would take Drew and Jackson home with me and take care of them for at least a week. The tired and busy parents agreed, and I was on the road on Valentine's Day with Drew and Jackson riding happily, first to Texas to see their great-grandparents and then on to our home the next day to see their Granddaddy. Drew had a huge tub full of Thomas the Train toys that would cover our living room floor, and I loved it!

As I was driving down the road that Valentine's Day, my phone rang. Emily was calling to tell me that she just found out that she and Jason were pregnant with their second child, due in October! I was so excited. Grandchild number five was on the way!

Birth of Fifth Grandchild

The months flew by and we were planning for me to be in New York for the birth of Luke, due before the end of October 2010. But he was not here. I arrived in New York before Luke made his appearance. Abigail loved Dora the Explorer, so that was her costume for Halloween. I got to go with Abigail through the Seminary neighborhood where the students and teachers were giving the children candy!

Emily said she would rather I stay with Abigail and let Jason go with her to the hospital. Abigail and Gran had fun together. Luke made his debut in November! He is named after Luke the Evangelist, his grandfather, and great-grandfather. Bill flew in to see his fifth grandchild, and we had a grand celebration with special treats from a nearby bakery and takeout from a great l restaurant.

I pray "that all my children and grandchildren will be taught of the Lord, and great shall be their peace."(Isaiah 54:13).

My Favorite Things Our Grandkids Have Said to Us Through the Years

DREW: Drew, Jackson and Avery had spent a week with us. Their dad came to visit and went into the movie store. I sat in the car with the kids and asked them, "So, what is your favorite thing we did together this week?" There was silence for a few. Then Drew, the oldest, said, "You, Gran. We had fun with you." My heart promptly melted!

ABIGAIL: I love the vintage card game FLINCH. One time upon beating me at my favorite game, Abigail said, "I love myself!"

When Abigail was three, she was watching a show called "Word World." She heard them say, "Words hold the world together." Abigail promptly talked back to the TV and said, "No, God holds the world together. Letters hold words together!"

JACKSON: When Jackson was four, he got an ear infection, and I was visiting them in Baton Rouge. Their other grandparents were about to take them to the beach, but they didn't know that Jackson had just been diagnosed with an ear infection. So, I asked his parents if I could bring him home with me, and we had ten fun days together. After our visit, Jackson told me on the phone, "Gran, I love you with my whole heart." My heart melted again!

AVERY: In 2012, I went to see Andrew and the kids in Baton Rouge. He and Ali were separated, and she brought the kids over to us at Andrew's third floor apartment. Avery was crying when she was walking up the stairs. I was standing at the door to meet them. I picked my three-year-old granddaughter up and she said, "I happy now!" My heart melted again!

LUKE: Every summer for several years we tried to get the grandkids to spend the week at our house. We have four acres and the armadillos were invading us. So, Bill told Luke, "Tonight, when it gets dark, we're going armadillo hunting." Luke was so excited. Bill got his 22 and put his bullet in his pocket. Sometimes they just got in the truck and shined the headlights around as they looked for the little, fat pests. Sometimes, they wore a headlight and walked around outside. Luke absolutely loved doing this.

I gave Luke and Abigail $10 to spend on something they wanted. That week we went to a local Gift Shop. When we walked in the door, there upon the top of the refrigerated Coke box was a stuffed toy armadillo holding a can of Pringles! Luke spied it immediately, and I got it down for him to look at. He said that was what he wanted to get with his $10. Abigail and I both told him to "think about it for a bit." So, he did. He asked, "Do the Pringles come with it?" They said no. So, with a little help from Gran, Luke got the stuffed animal armadillo and the Pringles he was holding!

We got home that day before Bill got home from the dental office. By this time, Luke had become a pretty good reader, and he loved to learn about insects and animals. When Bill got home and sat down in the kitchen chair, Luke had a surprise for him! He said, "Did you know that armadillo literally means 'Armored little thing?'" His Papa said, "I did not." I was videotaping him, so I said, "What were you thinking when you bought that, Luke?" Luke said, "I wanted to bring him here to show Papa and to take him home to remember Papa—And to have him for a stuffed animal....I thought the Pringles came with it, but it didn't, so Gran got it for me, and I pretended to open the can and let him (the armadillo) eat some of them." Luke named his new stuffed friend, Digger!

We have enjoyed the annual cousin/grandchildren reunion we have done two years in a row. Making memories together and passing on our knowledge and faith to our grandchildren are very important to us.

Grandparents have been influential for several generations in both our families. Bill and I are carrying on this legacy with our sweet grandchildren.

"If becoming a grandmother was only a matter of choice, I should advise every one of you straight away to become one. There is no fun for old people like it!"
-Hannah Whitehall Smith

CHAPTER 15

THE GIFT GOES ON

"The Lord is my strength and song, and he has become my salvation: he is my God, and I will prepare for him a habitation; my father's God, and I will exalt him." (Exodus 15:2).

"God is good, all the time!" is a song written by Dean McIntyre, recorded by Don Moen in 1988, and sung on Sunday morning in churches across America! We sing about how great our God is. Regardless of the weather (rain or shine, night or day), our physical condition (healthy or sick), or our emotional health –(happy or sad), our God never changes. Psalm 100:5 tells us "For the Lord is good. His unfailing love continues forever, and his faithfulness continues to each generation."

To personally know the living God, we must begin by placing our faith in His Only Begotten Son, Jesus Christ. He alone is the atonement for all our sins. We cannot do enough good things to earn our way to heaven. We must go only by the way of the cross, by trusting that Jesus took our sins, and we are forgiven! Too many people only know "about" God. The book of Romans declares that "God has planted eternity in our hearts." He speaks to us through creation, as well. Each of us has been created with the desire to know our Creator. He has made us in His Image. One of my favorite writers, Max Lucado, in his book, The Great House of God (Page 40), describes my God:

Nature is God's workshop. The sky is his resume. The universe is his calling card. You want to know who God is? See what he has done. You want to know his power? Take a Look at His creation. Curious about his strength? Pay a visit to His home address:

1 Billion Starry Sky Avenue.

He is untainted by the atmosphere of sin, unbridled by the timeline of history, unhindered by the weariness of the body.

What controls you doesn't control Him. What troubles you doesn't trouble Him. What fatigues you doesn't fatigue Him. Is an eagle disturbed by traffic? No, he rises above it. Is the whale perturbed by a hurricane? Of course not, he plunges beneath it. Is the lion flustered by the mouse standing directly in his way? No, he steps over it.

How much more is God able to soar above, plunge beneath, and step over the troubles of the earth?

*   *   *

My dad enjoyed his retirement years until a stroke in 1999 left him disabled. He missed a lot of church too until he got some hyperbaric treatments. His pastor and family of believers there in Naples decided they were missing him at church and purchased a recliner for him! There he would be, every Sunday, with Mother's help, and that of several church members who would meet them at the car.

Mother stayed very active her whole life. When I was growing up, she was a full-time homemaker. When my siblings were in school, their church, Life Tabernacle Assembly of God, started a Christian school. David and Mary Evelyn were students there, and Mother was one of the teachers. Later, she got a position as the

Reading Teacher at Paul H. Pewitt School, our alma mater. She taught there for twelve years and retired in 2003. By that time, Daddy was disabled at home, and she took good care of him. God truly provided for them when Mother retired.

I admired Mother for the way she used her singing talent her whole life. Sometimes people get busy as adults and their voice and instrument get pushed aside for what seems like a greater priority. Mother loved to sing about Jesus and his greatness! In 2009, she made her second recording, a CD that she called "The Anchor Holds." It was a musical tribute to the Lord for seeing them through the difficult years that Daddy was disabled.

One day as I returned home after a visit with my parents, it came to me how they served each other through the years. When Daddy was the sole breadwinner, Mother kept the home running, took care of her children, and always had a good dinner cooked for him at the end of day. When Mother was teaching school full-time and Daddy was healthy and retired, he did the same for her. That allowed her to come in and prop up her feet after her workday.

After Daddy became disabled, she would prepare his meals, help him from his chair to his bed, take him to all his doctor visits, which were many, and all the other duties that go with caring for a handicapped man. I do not know of a more joyful servant in her home than my mother. If that is not enough, she home schooled two of her grandsons for the majority of one year. She also hosted women's fellowship meetings at their home, planned meals, and cooked with her church family for many who were sick or bereaved. And she did that even with a disabled husband to care for! Proverbs 31 says, "Her children will rise up and call her blessed."

A Favorite Grandchild Story

Emily and Jason moved to New York in 2008 to attend seminary when Abigail was six months old! They lived in married housing on the campus of St. Vladimir Orthodox Seminary for three years. Abigail was allowed a limited time in front of the TV, but they read her lots of books, and she loves books! You may remember the show "Dora, the Explorer"; Dora was the cute little girl, but Swiper the Fox was the villain who was lurking around the corner looking to steal something!

It was Super Bowl Sunday, and the Seminary hosted the Super Bowl Game for the students and their families. The two teams in the playoffs that day were the Green Bay Packers and the Pittsburgh Steelers. Three-year-old Abigail was there, and the game was on. Suddenly, she asked her parents, "Do the Steelers give back what they take?" Emily and Jason were so shocked at her question. Finally, Jason said, "No, it's not that kind of stealing." Out of the mouth of children ! Don't underestimate what your child or grandchild can learn and understand and remember!

Saying Goodbye to My Great Dad

In the fall of 2010, we noticed that Daddy was growing weaker. His pastor, Reverend Bryan Peck, was also a hospice chaplain. We decided after talking together to put Daddy in hospice so he and Mother would have the help and support they needed at home.

On Easter of 2011, I hugged Daddy, told him how much he meant to me and said goodbye. I honestly thought I would not get to talk to him again on this side of heaven. But I went back home in May to lend my support. That evening, he aspirated, and they could not give him anything else by mouth.

Two days later, as I went in to check on him, he was looking up and all around. His tired blue eyes looked bright, and his face was lit up as if he was seeing something very pleasing and exciting to him. We believe he was beholding the angels! It was the most alert we had seen him in days, and he had not been talking to us.

One night as Daddy was sleeping, we thought it was his last. Mother, Mary Evelyn, Matthew, Joel, Stephen and I sat around his bed sharing memories about Daddy. We laughed, and we cried together. Matthew shared about how "Grandaddy" had taught him to work by having him pick up some sticks in the yard and some spankings he got for disobeying. Daddy slept right through all our tears and laughter.

But our father lived through the night and was with us the next day. David, Sharmaine, Dominick, and Hannah got home on Thursday; they also got to see him behold the angels too! It was sweet! His face lit up and his blue eyes were dancing!

Daddy went home to be with Jesus on May 16, 2011. We were with him when he took his last breath and crossed over into Heaven. His Church family, Restoration Family Church, formerly Life Tabernacle Assembly of God, along with our family members and neighbors, brought in lots of food and supplies for us.

We honored my war-hero daddy and champion of the faith with a beautiful celebration of life service in his church, where he had served as Elder, Door Keeper, and a teacher of goodness for over forty years. Andrew played his guitar and sang "I Can Only Imagine." Five people stood and shared a personal memory about Daddy. Reverend Bryan Peck and Reverend Don Couch did the service, sharing great personal memories about Vic Moore. Our Korean War veteran and recipient of The Purple Heart was honored at the Vissering Family Cemetery with a Military Honor Guard. As is the custom, the folded American flag was presented to Mother. The Church Family provided all of us a wonderful lunch and place to visit afterward in the fellowship hall.

Although she missed Daddy, Mother was able to enjoy her life. She treasured every memory and continued to live in their home where Daddy was born in 1928 and where we grew up. She said, "I keep my mind active with reading and studying and interacting with family and friends." She would tell me on the phone, "Last night after church, I went to Mary's house; we had coffee and played dominoes until 11:30."

Mother continued to sing on her church praise team and sing solos too. Her favorite thing to do was to teach her adult Sunday School Class. Of course, she also enjoyed spending time with her children, grandchildren, great-grandchildren, brothers, sisters and friends.

Mother was a great cook! I think that cooking was her love language because she took on so many tasks and gatherings that required her to plan, cook and clean up. One of her signature desserts was her buttermilk pies. She started making them to take to friends, neighbors, family, or to the schoolteachers she had worked with. Everyone loved to get her pie because it was delicious. She also made the best dressing, fudge, cookies, chicken spaghetti, meatloaf, and peas and cornbread. She loved her family and she also found joy in cooking a big breakfast for her guests. Several of us teased her that we loved coming to her "Bed and Breakfast." Mother and I enjoyed our cup of coffee and warm conversation as we sat on her screened-in porch early in the morning!

We had some fun times and made some great memories together. She came home with me after Daddy's funeral and stayed a week or two. We savored eating out and shopping together. I helped her find new clothes and shoes. I took her for her first pedicure and she loved it. After taking such good care of Daddy at home for twelve years, Mother was able to enjoy the freedom that comes with retirement, and she deserved it!

Jason Graduated From Seminary

Just five days after Daddy went to heaven, Jason graduated with his Master of Divinity Degree in New York. What an accomplishment after much hard work and many sacrifices! Serving the Lord requires sacrifice.

Still waiting on their church assignment, Emily and Jason moved their furniture into a pod and came to our house in Arkansas and lived with us for five months. Abigail was three and Luke was seven months, and we made so many great memories together. One of the highlights was having Abigail participate in our Christian Ministries Kid's Choir that I directed. I loved hearing her sing, "Dare to be a Daniel." I am proud of all those choir members; several of them are worship leaders now.

A highlight for our family of eleven was making a trip to Baton Rouge to visit Andrew's family in the latter part of August. We went to a nearby water park, enjoyed some good food and just had fun being together.

Bill's Mother in Heaven

That Sunday evening after the fun at the waterpark, Bill received the call from his sister, Kay, that his mother had died in East Texas.

The next morning, Bill and I said our goodbyes and traveled up to Naples/Omaha to be with his dad and family. We had a visitation, and then a beautiful graveside service at Concord Cemetery. Emily, Jason, Abigail and Luke joined us there. Bill spoke about his beautiful Mother, the life she lived and the important things she had taught him. We enjoyed a delicious lunch afterward at Mary Kay's home, provided by First Baptist Church.

Character Counts

There are many things about my grown children that I am proud of. Character has been one of the most important attributes I worked to foster in them growing up. Usually, when one is pressed with difficult circumstances, what's on the inside will surface. I have observed both Emily and Andrew as they handled tough situations with wisdom. I was especially moved by the love and sacrifices Andrew has shown when he was presented with life as a single dad; he has done heroics!

Tragedy Strikes Our Family

On Saturday, August 1, 2015, I called Mother to check on her. She answered with a ring in her voice and in her usual jovial morning mood! She was excited to tell me about hosting her seventeen church ladies the night before.

Later in the afternoon, about 5:30 p.m., we got the phone call that Mother had been in a tragic car wreck. She was airlifted to Tyler, Texas, where she was a patient in the Trauma ICU! Very, very sadly, four people died that day in the car wreck.

My mother never opened her eyes to talk to us again, and she died the following Friday, August 7, 2015. This was a lot to take in. This was a lot to process. Saturday morning, Mother was full of life, and Saturday afternoon they were giving her blood to keep her alive! The nurse told us that we were blessed that she even made it up from the ambulance to the Trauma ICU; many don't. We sat with Mother, hoping and praying she would wake up and talk to us. She never did. She did not want to be on life support. Heaven, the destination of every Christian, the place my mother had read about, sung about and taught about her whole life is now a reality for her—her eternal Home.

Brother Bryan, Mother's pastor, was there to comfort, pray, and counsel us through a most difficult time. We celebrated Mother's beautiful life in a special church service on August 11, 2015 at her home church, Restoration Family Worship Center. The church was packed. Mother had served the Lord faithfully there for over fifty years! She had served her community as a teacher, friend, and soloist. She had served her family and extended family with love her whole life! During her funeral, Brother Bryan said they had given Mother a nickname at the church, "Hurricane Wanda," because when she had a vision for ministry, she wanted it done and got everybody involved to do it. That brought us a chuckle; we knew that our mother was a get-er-done kind of Kingdom Woman!

Finding a New Normal

Life had changed for our family in just a day—in just a week! Daddy had been gone four years, and now Mother was in Heaven too. The old home was empty of the one we loved and who loved us. She would never greet us in the driveway upon our arrival! She would never cook us that Christmas fudge or turkey and dressing. The home fires would not be burning upon our arrival. We would have to light the fires ourselves! We would have to fry our own bacon and perk our own coffee. She would not be there to answer our phone call or pray for us, to laugh at our jokes or to tell us hers—she would not be there to share our lives. We would have to process our sudden grief and losses, develop a new normal of seeing each other; we would have to live without our mother, who was the loving "Queen Bee" of our family.

The Bible talks about our prayers, that they are not wasted, but continually rise before God in the throne-room. Mother prayed daily for her family. There were several needs we were praying about before she passed, and some prayers were answered not long after she went to Heaven. My sister-in-law, Sharmaine, had been looking for a job and found one. My sister, Mary Evelyn, got a better job. There are numerous other answers to prayers. Mother prayed for her children, grandchildren, and great-grandchildren. She and Daddy would be so proud of the accomplishments of each of their descendants!

A Memorial Service to Honor Thomas E. Beasley

Bill's wonderful Dad went to be with the Lord ten months later in June 2016. We had his service at Concord Baptist Church. Bill gave a beautiful message about his godly Dad; he was a man of integrity, a leader in his field in the steel industry, influential and generous with love and devotion to his whole family. He was a man who loved people! A wonderful father-in-law, grandfather and great-grandfather too, he is missed.

One thing that made us happy was that Emily and Andrew were able to fly in from their homes in other states to be with us for their grandfather's service. Bill and I realize that we were so blessed to have some of the best parents—and for so long! We would not be who we are today without the love and time our parents invested in us. We think of them often, miss them, and look forward to our reunion with them one day in Heaven.

Life Without Our Parents

Bill and I were both busy working and taking care of estate business. It took awhile to sell Mother's house. My parents had lived for fifty years in the same house. My grandparents, Hattie and Cluren Moore, had bought the house in 1927. There was so much sentiment in the older Victorian home. Brother Elrod had started the First Assembly of God Church in the very room that Daddy was born in. Daddy became an elder in the First Assembly of God Church years later. Me and my siblings, Mary and David, grew up there. Upon finding a buyer for the house, we realized in 2018 that it had been in our Moore Family for 90 years! What a treasure! If those walls could talk, they would tell us many family stories!

Now for Some Joy!

April 2018, I found myself on a plane to San Diego, California because Andrew and Valerie were engaged. I was invited to be a guest at their lovely wedding shower in Del Mar. It was the most beautiful one I've ever attended, and my new daughter-to-be was "Over the moon" excited! I was excited! I met Valerie's dad, Craig, her mom, Sherry, and her sisters, Michelle and Vanessa. Some quality time with Andrew, Drew, Jackson and Avery was a perk! It was a very fun, fulfilling trip for me.

Two months later, June 9, Bill and I were both in an airplane headed to beautiful San Diego, LA Jolla, to welcome Valerie into our family. Emily met us there, spent time with Andrew and his friends, and her nephews and niece and had part in the wedding.

Valerie and Andrew had such a beautiful wedding at the Birch Aquarium. We had a spectacular view of the Pacific! The ocean danced and the air was electric as we watched the beautiful couple be united in marriage—Valerie, radiant in her white dress, Andrew, handsome in his black tuxedo, his young sons, Drew and Jackson, looking like models, and eight-year-old Avery, the perfect flower girl, blushing as she watched her dad kiss his bride! It was "The best day ever!"

The reception included a delicious buffet dinner and entertainment. We felt so joyful as we celebrated our beautiful daughter-in-law and saw our son so happy. Valerie is a wonderful blessing to our family.

While the newlyweds flew off on their honeymoon, we had some good times with our grandkids. We got to explore La Jolla; the beach is my happy place!

Summing It Up!

I'm so thankful for my parents who trained me when I was a little girl in their home. Now as a wife, mother and grandmother, I'm enjoying our family—the dynasty the Lord has helped me and Bill to continue building! I am blessed to have a faithful and godly husband. I have watched him grow spiritually into a man who understands the power of grace and extends it to others, but one who takes a stand for what is right and speaks the truth when people need to hear it. He is a man of prayer, one who has compassion for people, a diligent student of God's Word, and one who can teach it too. I have experienced with him his joy at professional victories and vicariously shared his struggles, disappointments, and difficulties.

Bill gives me unconditional love and support, and I do the same for him. He is a great provider and his generosity is amazing.

Of the forty-five years we have been married, we worked forty-two years as a team to achieve his success in providing gentle dental care to hundreds of patients in Louisiana and Arkansas. I am thankful to say that we have experienced more happy times than sad.

Bill and I worked as a partnership "with a vision" to parent Emily and Andrew in the faith and to see them get a Christian education. As a father to Emily and Andrew, Bill has a proven track record of providing, protecting, listening, counseling, guiding, and encouraging our kids until they could stand on their own two feet and pay their own bills, and they do that well. I also enjoy seeing Bill interacting with our five grandchildren because his joy increases when he spends time with them.

I love to encourage married people younger than us! Hang in there when times are hard, and don't quit or leave because you can't take it anymore; be faithful, and when you're our age you will be so glad you did. If you need help with communication or conflict management, seek out a good Christian counselor. Ask God to help you to be a loving, enduring spouse. You can't do it in your own strength! Having a lifetime marriage partner takes a lot of help from God, His grace, hard work, patience, prayer and wisdom. Staying together pays big dividends.

Mentoring Moms and teaching children is my passion. I have written this book not only to honor my parents for training me and to share how I have taught my children to follow Christ, but to help you, Mom and Dad, in your parenting roles to overcome and succeed as a parent in this difficult culture. It is my hope and prayer that from this book you take much inspiration and encouragement. Then, as you apply the lessons I've shared, you will achieve success at building your own "Dynasty of Faith."

We are proud of our adult children and grandchildren who are serving the Lord in their respective families, churches and communities. Emily is a school counselor and former middle school language arts teacher. Her husband, Jason, is not only an

Orthodox priest, but a gifted teacher. They work well together, are dedicated parents, and have accomplished quite a lot in their more than eighteen years of marriage and as a clergy family. Abigail, their daughter, is a gifted student, winning writer, winning debater, and sings and plays two instruments. Their son, Luke, enjoys science, learning about insects, reading and learning to play the keyboard. Andrew is a wise and successful leader in his family at home and in his business. He and his wife, Valerie, work hard with their jobs, parenting and supporting their church. Their children, Drew, Jackson and Avery are high achievers. Drew is a 6 '2 " tall offensive-defensive lineman for his high school football team and takes accelerated classes planning for college. Jackson loves the sport of free-style climbing at his local gym and is an honor roll student in his Christian school. Avery loves writing and acting and is an honor roll student too. She is following her Dad as she learns to play the guitar.

We believe our family members will do great things to leave their mark on this world and advance God's Kingdom. I'm excited and optimistic about the future and generations to come. The e principles and promises of God to us from His Word, The Holy Bible, and our relationship with our Lord Jesus, will go on and guide our family forever!

"FIND US FAITHFUL"

Words and Music by Jon Mohr
Hebrews 12:1,2
We're pilgrims on the journey of the narrow road
And those who've gone before us line the way
Cheering on the faithful
Encouraging the weary
Their lives a stirring testament
To God's sustaining grace

Surrounded by so great a cloud of witnesses
Let us run the race not only for the prize
But as those who've gone before us
Let us leave to those behind us
A heritage of faithfulness
Passed on through godly lives

(CHORUS)
Oh, may all who come behind us find us faithful
May the fire of our devotion light their way
May the footprints that we leave
Lead them to believe
And the lives we live inspire them to obey
Oh, may all who come behind us find us faithful

After all our hopes and dreams
Have come and gone
And our children sift through
All we've left behind
May the clues that they uncover
And the memories they discover
Become the light that leads them
To the road we each must find

AUTHOR BIO PAGE

Elizabeth Moore Beasley lives in Arkansas with Bill, her husband of forty-five years. She successfully completed Shannon Ethridge's 12-Month B.L.A.S.T.(Building Leaders, Authors, Speakers, Teachers) Program. She enjoys mentoring young mothers in her community and ministering in her local church through music and hospitality. Traveling to make memories with her children and grandchildren brings her joy. Elizabeth's hobbies include reading, photography, piano and singing with kids. She believes little seeds planted into hearts will grow and bear good fruit!